Fodor's

BERLIN

D1466978

WELCOME TO BERLIN

Überhip, energetic Berlin has grabbed the world's attention with its exuberant urban life and vibrant arts scene. Gone are the days of drab Cold War Germany and a city divided by the Wall. In this cosmopolitan and affordable capital, neighborhoods like Mitte, Friedrichshain, Prenzlauer Berg, and Kreuzberg bustle with restaurants, cafés, and nightlife. Museums and sights such as the Pergamon on Museum Island, the Brandenburg Gate, and the Jewish Museum provide a window into Berlin's rich history. Today the stitched-together heart of Germany beats fast.

TOP REASONS TO GO

★ **Affordability:** High culture and low prices—the city is "poor but sexy," said the mayor.

★ **Nightlife:** Art installations, festivals, and parties vie to keep you up all night.

★ **Art:** Museums and galleries hold treasures both ancient and utterly contemporary.

★ **Shopping:** High-end design boutiques and secondhand shops make a stimulating mix.

★ **History:** Cobblestone markers are evidence of the Wall that once divided the city.

★ **Palaces:** Berlin's Schloss Charlottenburg, Potsdam's Schloss Sanssouci, and more.

10

TOP EXPERIENCES

Berlin offers terrific experiences that should be on every traveler's list. Here are Fodor's top picks for a memorable trip.

1 The Reichstag

Take a tour of the seat of Germany's Parliament to see where 20th-century world history was shaped and, especially, to check out the striking Norman Foster–designed glass cupola. The views of Berlin from here are spectacular. *(Ch. 2)*

2 Spree River

The Spree is one of the city's finest natural features. Clubs and cafés line its banks, and you can relax in a beach chair by the water in the summer months. *(Ch. 1)*

3 Street Art

Berlin is famous for edgy street art, with thousands of pieces in areas including Mitte, Friedrichshain, and Prenzlauer Berg. The East Side Gallery has some great examples. *(Ch. 1)*

4 Berlin Wall

The Wall fell in 1989 but is still an essential part of the city. The museum at Checkpoint Charlie has incredible stories about those who escaped through, under, and over it. *(Ch. 2)*

5 Beer Gardens

Many beer gardens are open all day when the weather's fine. In Germany, a *weisswurst*, a pretzel, and a wheat beer are considered an excellent breakfast. *(Ch. 6)*

6 Holocaust Memorial

The Memorial to the Murdered Jews of Europe is made up of 2,711 concrete slabs of different heights. Some visitors point out the memorial's resemblance to a cemetery. *(Ch. 2)*

7 Museumsinsel

Five state museums on "Museum Island" showcase architectural monuments and art treasures. The Pergamonmuseum, with its artifacts from the ancient world, is a standout. *(Ch. 2)*

8 Curry 36

Sausage with curried ketchup—it's a Berlin street food must. Stands around the city, like the renowned Curry 36, entice customers from morning till well past midnight. *(Ch. 3)*

9 DDR Museum

Experience a taste of life in Soviet East Germany at this interactive museum. Exhibits include a Trabi car you can "drive" and an apartment with a wiretapped phone. *(Ch. 2)*

10 Brandenburg Gate

Restored to Prussian glory after being partially destroyed, the Brandenburg Gate is one of Berlin's major landmarks. You can't miss it at the head of Unter den Linden. *(Ch. 2)*

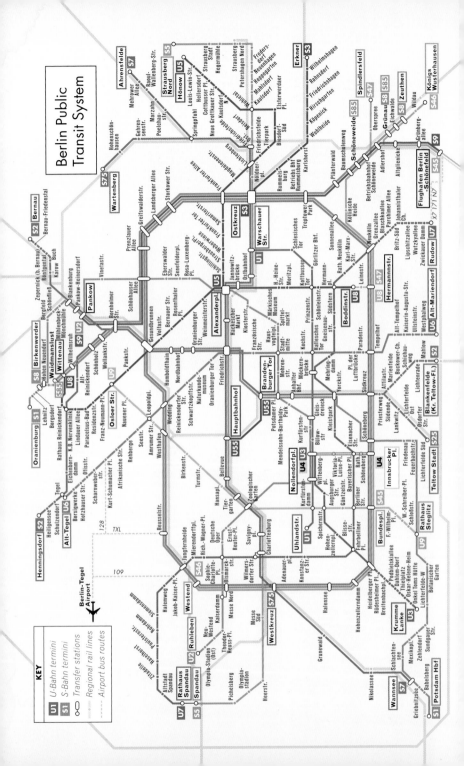

Berlin Public
Transit System

CONTENTS

ABOUT
THIS GUIDE

Fodor's Recommendations

Everything in this guide is worth doing—we don't cover what isn't—but exceptional sights, hotels, and restaurants are recognized with additional accolades. Fodor's Choice★ indicates our top recommendations; and **Best Bets** call attention to notable hotels and restaurants in various categories. Care to nominate a new place? Visit Fodors.com/contact-us.

Trip Costs

We list prices wherever possible to help you budget well. Hotel and restaurant price categories from **$** to **$$$$** are noted alongside each recommendation. For hotels, we include the lowest cost of a standard double room in high season. For restaurants, we cite the average price of a main course at dinner or, if dinner isn't served, at lunch. For attractions, we always list adult admission fees; discounts are usually available for children, students, and senior citizens.

Hotels

Our local writers vet every hotel to recommend the best overnights in each price category, from budget to expensive. Unless otherwise specified, you can expect private bath, phone, and TV in your room. For expanded hotel reviews, facilities, and deals visit Fodors.com.

Restaurants

Unless we state otherwise, restaurants are open for lunch and dinner daily. We mention dress code only when there's a specific requirement and reservations only when they're essential or not accepted. To make restaurant reservations, visit Fodors.com.

Credit Cards

The hotels and restaurants in this guide typically accept credit cards. If not, we'll say so.

Top Picks
★ Fodor's Choice

Listings
✉ Address
✉ Branch address
☎ Telephone
📠 Fax
⊕ Website
✉ E-mail
🎟 Admission fee
☉ Open/closed times
Ⓜ Subway
✣ Directions or Map coordinates

Hotels & Restaurants
🏨 Hotel
🛏 Number of rooms
🍽 Meal plans
✕ Restaurant
🍴 Reservations
👔 Dress code
▭ No credit cards
⑤ Price

Other
⇨ See also
☞ Take note
🏌 Golf facilities

EXPERIENCE
BERLIN

BERLIN TODAY

"Berlin is poor but sexy," the city's flamboyant mayor Klaus Wowereit once declared, and the apt description became the German capital's de facto motto. Thanks to cheap rent and government-subsidized cultural venues, this artistically rich city is also one of Europe's most affordable metropolises. And it's not only the struggling artists who have taken notice. Recently, European tech entrepreneurs have begun setting up shop in the formerly communist eastern part of the city, invigorating the nascent tech sector and helping undo the lingering economic effects of Reunification. The German capital is poised to grow more prosperous (and expensive), but for now, the edgy, fashionable metropolis remains a great European bargain for visitors.

Abundant Art

Forcible division, it turns out, had its advantages. For decades East and West Berlin were locked in an artistic arms race, trying to outdo one another with cultural bragging rights. As a result present-day Berlin boasts nearly 200 museums, three opera houses, and five world-class orchestras, not to mention some 450-odd galleries and countless alternative performance spaces. The city's bohemian vibe continues to attract a stream of creative types from all over the world, feeding the city's theater troupes and dance companies. The German capital's artistic offerings are as diverse as the city's denizens, ranging from the stupendous collections of classical art on the Museum Island to street art; world-class opera performances in the neoclassical State Opera House and bawdy cabarets on coaster-size stages; celebrated contemporary canons at the Hamburger Bahnhof and street art on just about every corner.

Invisible Wall

2014 marks the 25th anniversary of the fall of the Berlin Wall. Save for a few segments preserved as historic monuments, much of the reviled Wall has been demolished. Yet the differences between the two Germanys persist. According to a survey by *Bild*, the largest national daily paper, three-quarters of the population believe East and West Germans have different mentalities; only one in three West Germans would entertain the idea of marrying someone from the East. According to a 2013 report by the Halle Institute for Economic Research, Easterners regard West Germans as arrogant and materialistic, while West Germans think of their

WHAT WE'RE TALKING ABOUT

Back in 1991, politicians agreed to build a gleaming new airport befitting the capital of reunified Germany. Twenty-some years later, the Berlin Brandenburg International Airport has yet to see a single plane take off or land. Whatever happened to the famous German punctuality? The new hub was supposed to open in 2010 to bring together all the air traffic, which is divided between the two Cold War–era airports. Reportedly more than 66,000 construction problems have led to multiple delays as the costs ballooned to €4.3 billion, twice the budget, and mounting. Meanwhile, the engineers still haven't figured out how to turn off the lights! The airport is slated to open in 2015—for now.

Speaking of airports, the historic Tempelhof Airport where the Allied forces foiled

Eastern countrymen as whiny. Perhaps it is fitting that, because of the two different street light systems in Berlin (gas in the East, electric in the West), the division is visible even from space.

Too Cool for School?

Already at the height of the Weimar decadence in the 1920s, when Marlene Dietrich performed in packed gay bars in Schöneberg, Berlin was notorious for its unrestrained hedonism. Today, the German capital's nightlife has again reached mythical status, thanks to its acclaimed electronic music scene and a young population. Berlin's legendary clubs, which may operate out of a decommissioned power plant or an abandoned department store, incubated some of the world's top DJs like Paul van Dyk, Ellen Allien, and Paul Kalkbrenner. With the absence of VIP areas or ostentatious cliques, people of all ages, backgrounds, and sexual orientations lose their inhibitions in these temples of electronic music well into the morning. Berlin, after all, prides itself for being the only European city without a mandated closing time for bars and clubs.

It's not just the nightlife that reflects the city's live-and-let-live vibe. Neighborhoods like Neukölln, Prenzlauer Berg, and Friedrichshain have emerged as hubs for international artists and young dreamers flocking to Berlin in search of inspiration (and cheap places to stay). This diversity, combined with the city's decidedly down-to-earth working class roots, creates an atmosphere that is at once cool yet unpretentious. Every coin has two sides, of course. Some locals are tired of Berlin's reputation as a playground for slackers; others worry about the rising cost of living.

Economy

In the past few years, unemployment has gone down, and thanks to an emerging computer tech scene, rent is going up faster than you can say "stock options." Gentrifying or developing, whichever way you look at it, Berlin is fast changing.

the Soviet blockade, recently opened as a park where roller bladers, kite surfers, and bicyclists speed down the runways once used by the Raisin Bombers.

Berlin's slacker street cred is in danger as tech entrepreneurs flock to Berlin in search of young talents and low operating costs. The recent proliferation of start-ups has earned the city the moniker "Silicon Allee," or Silicon Alley, with giants like Google opening offices alongside homegrown upstarts like Soundcloud. But some fear that, like any hyped trends, the recent development of the start-up scene is a bubble waiting to burst. Only time will tell if Berlin can rival its Californian counterpart.

WHAT'S WHERE

1 Mitte. Mitte is, figuratively and literally, Berlin's "center."

2 Tiergarten. Once a royal hunting estate, Tiergarten, or "animal garden," is Berlin's largest park.

3 Potsdamer Platz. The site of the world's first automatic traffic lights was reduced to ashes during WWII and left abandoned during the Cold War. Today, the glittery skyscrapers symbolize Germany's renaissance.

4 Friedrichshain. Neobaroque landmarks and socialist architecture compete for attention in the former East, where cheap rent, offbeat bars, edgy clubs, and beautiful parks attract students and creative types from around the world.

5 Kreuzberg. Tenement blocks and anarchist squats have given way to sidewalk cafés and handsome canalside apartments, but the remaining artists, punks, and Turkish immigrants continue to make this one of the most dynamic areas in Berlin.

6 Schöneberg. Historically Berlin's gay neighborhood, Schöneberg is yet another up-and-coming hip neighborhood.

7 Neukölln. From bleak to chic, Neukölln's abandoned storefronts have turned into art galleries, fashion shops, bakeries, and wine bars.

8 Treptow. Up-and-coming Treptoww, with its park and canal-side location, is poised to become the next trendy Berlin neighborhood.

9 Prenzlauer Berg. Once a working-class neighborhood, Prenzlauer Berg is now one of the city's most gentrified—and international—areas.

10 Wedding. A working-class neighborhood perennially touted to be up-and-coming, this western district has everything from underground bunkers to an underground art gallery serving reindeer burgers.

11 Charlottenburg. This elegant West Berlin neighborhood is home to the bustling high-street commerce of Ku'Damm and elegant coffeehouses of Savigny Platz.

12 Friedenau, Grunewald, Zehlendorf, Wannsee and Oranienburg. Outside Berlin proper are forests, lakes, and stately villas in Grunewald and Zehlendorf, and the Sachsenhausen Concentration Camp in Oranienburg.

13 Potsdam. A short trip from Berlin, the former center of the Enlightenment continues to draw learned visitors to its splendid Sanssouci Palace.

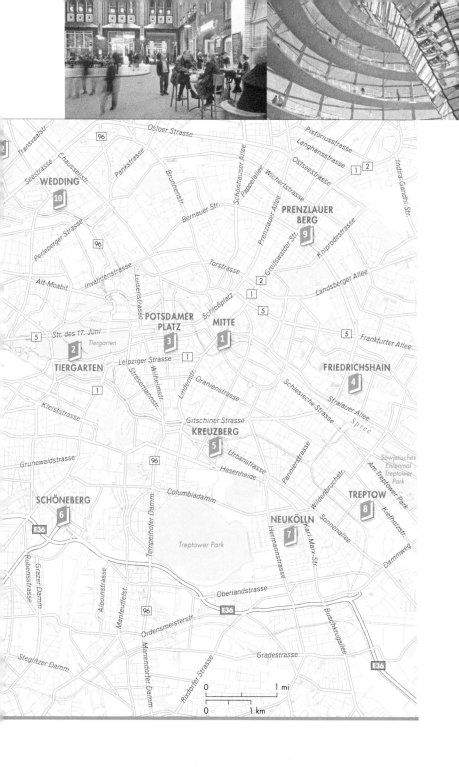

BERLIN PLANNER

When to Go

Berlin tends to be gray and cold; it can be warm and beautiful in summer but there's no guarantee, so it's best to always pack a jacket.

The best time to visit is from May to early September, though late July and early August can get hot—in which case, everyone heads to one of the city's many lakes.

In summer, daylight lingers well past 9 pm in this northern city, giving plenty of time for happy denizens to picnic in parks, swim in lakes, and cycle about town. Many open-air events are staged in summer, when the exceedingly green city is at its most beautiful.

October and November can be overcast and rainy, though the city occasionally sees crisp blue autumn skies.

If you want to get a real feel for Berlin, come during the long winter months, when a host of indoor cultural events combat perpetually gray skies and you can experience the prized feeling *Gemütlichkeit* (coziness), but bring a heavy winter coat to combat the sleet, icy rain, strong winds, and freezing temperatures.

Getting Here and Around

Air Travel: Major airlines continue to serve western Berlin's Tegel Airport (TXL), which is just 6 km (4 miles) from the city center, while suburban Schönefeld Airport (SXF) is used mostly by charter and low-cost airlines. The Willy Brandt Berlin-Brandenburg International Airport, which has been built next to Schönefeld, will eventually open and replace them both.

Bicycle Travel: Designated bike lanes and relatively flat topography make Berlin a pleasure to explore on two wheels. The same traffic laws apply to bicyclists as motorists, and police have been known to give out tickets.

Public Transit: Berlin has an integrated network of subway (U-bahn), suburban (S-bahn) train lines, buses, ferries, and trams (almost exclusively in eastern Berlin) divided into three zones. Zone A covers central Berlin, B includes the suburbs, and C extends into Brandenburg. Most visitor destinations are in the broad reach of the fare zones A and B, which can be covered with a €2.60 ticket (valid for two hours). The €1.50 Kurzstrecke tickets are used for trips up to three train and subway stops. A day ticket costs €6.70 in zones AB and €7.20 for ABC. The **Berlin WelcomeCard** (see Discounts and Deals) includes unlimited public travel. Make sure to validate your ticket in the small yellow or red box on the platform—ticket inspectors may ask to see your ticket. Being caught without a ticket will get you a €40 fine.

Berlin's transit authority BVG (⊕ *www.bvg.de*) has up-to-date information and a "Journey Planner" function in English. The free "Fahrinfo Mobil" app can also help plan your journey. Note that ticket agents and machines only take cash.

Taxi Travel: Berlin's taxis are efficient and numerous. The base rate is €3.20, after which prices vary according to a complex tariff system. Figure on paying around €8 to €10 for a ride the length of the Ku'damm. You can flag a taxi on the street, go to a taxi stand, or order one by phone. U-bahn employees will call a taxi for passengers after 8 pm.

For more Transportation information, including best ways to get into the city from the airport, see the Travel Smart chapter.

Language

Though German is the official language, English is widely spoken. It's not uncommon to meet expats who have lived in Berlin for years who barely speak German.

Hours

Businesses stay open longer hours in Berlin than in most other German cities. Most large shopping establishments are open from 10 am to 8 pm from Monday through Saturday. Most shops close on Sunday. Restaurants tend to stay open through the weekend and close on Monday or Tuesday. Many museums are closed on Monday.

Discounts and Deals

The **Berlin WelcomeCard** (sold by EurAid, BVG offices, the tourist office, and some hotels) entitles one adult and three children under the age of 14 to either two or three days of unlimited travel in the ABC zones for €20.50 or €27.50, respectively, and includes admission and tour discounts detailed in a booklet. A three-day ticket, including admission to all the Museum Island collections, costs €40.50, but it only pays off if you plan on visiting a lot of museums.

Many of the 17 Staatliche Museen zu Berlin (state museums of Berlin) offer several ticket options (children up to 18 are welcomed free of charge). A single ticket ranges from €4 to €8. A three-day pass (*Museum Pass Berlin*) to 60 museums, including all state museums, costs €24.

Money

Most Germans still make most of—if not all—their purchases the old-fashioned way: with cash. The use of credit cards in Germany is among the lowest in Europe. That said, you should be able to pay your hotel bill, train tickets, or car rental with a credit card. But if you're picking up a snack at a bakery, a little souvenir, or having a cup of coffee, you'll need cash. The same goes for buying tickets on public transportation or paying for a taxi.

Smoking

Repeated attempts at banning smoking in public spaces have failed in Berlin. In theory, pubs smaller than 75 square meters are allowed to designate themselves as "smoking bars"—in practice, most clubs and bars get smoky as the night wears on. Some restaurants have smoking sections.

Etiquette

When addressing someone always use the formal *Sie* until you are begged by them to switch to the informal *du*. When in doubt, shake hands; both as a greeting and at parting.

It's polite to ask if someone speaks English (*Sprechen Sie Englisch?*) before addressing them in English.

Dress

Berliners dress down. Go to the opera, and you'll see music lovers in everything and anything between ball gowns and tattered bike shorts. Even the most famous clubs have no dress codes. Eccentricity and personal style is celebrated, but an ostentatious display of wealth is frowned upon.

BEST FESTIVALS

48 Stunden Neukölln

For two days in June, the working-class neighborhood of Neukölln, now home to boutiques and hipster hangouts, celebrates the district's diversity and artsyness. An old brewery may host a concert, or an avant-garde opera performance may take over an art nouveau swimming pool; some venues are as intimate as someone's living room. From a modest block party in 1999, the homespun festival has evolved into a major cultural happening that the city's creative class looks forward to every year (⊕ *www.48-stunden-neukoelln.de*).

Berlinale: International Film Festival

February is synonymous with international cinema in Berlin. Unlike the other red carpet festivals around the world, all the showings in this 10-day celebration are open to the public, making Berlinale (⊕ *www.berlinale.de*) the largest public movie festival in the world. Queue up for premieres of films from around the world, or just party with an estimated 20,000 film professionals who brave the cold Berlin winter yearly.

Christmas Markets

Berlin is home to more than 60 Christmas markets, from the traditional kitsch fest to hipster flea markets full of handmade goodies. Most are open from late November to the end of December. At Trend-Mafia (⊕ *www.trendmafia.de*), Berlin's designers emerge from their workshops to show their one-of-a-kind products every weekend in December. The Gendarmenmarkt Christmas Market is a classic cuckoo-clocks-and-wursts affair, with the opulent architecture providing the most Teutonic ambience.

Gay Pride

Originally a political rally commemorating the 1969 Stonewall riots, this flamboyant parade has become one of the city's most popular street parties. The annual June celebration draws crowds from around the world, and culminates in a large open-air dance party at the Victory Column (⊕ *www.csd-berlin.de*).

International Berlin Beer Festival

One August weekend each year, the socialist style "workers' paradise" apartments of Karl-Marx-Allee provide the backdrop for Berlin's largest suds-theme party. Visitors sample 2,000 types of beer from around the world, including ales handcrafted by independent German brewers (⊕ *www.bierfestival-berlin.de*).

Karneval der Kulturen

A celebration of Berlin's diversity, this multicultural street festival takes over bohemian Kreuzberg every Pentecost weekend (usually in May or June). From traditional ethnic arts to cutting-edge contemporary dance, the festival is a microcosm of present day Berlin culture. The weekend peaks with a parade of musicians, dancers, and other performers showing off their skills to an enthusiastic crowd (⊕ *www.karneval-berlin.de*).

Long Night of Museums

Taking place in spring and fall, the Long Night of Museums (⊕ *www.lange-nacht-der-museen.de*) is exactly what the name suggests: Almost 100 museums open their doors to the public from 6 pm to 2 am with exhibitions, guided tours, and special programs. Browsing classical art at late night while a DJ spins ambient music is a quintessential Berlin experience. Long Night of Operas and Theaters, a similar concept with performing arts, is slated to be revived in 2014 after a hiatus.

1

BEST TOURS

There's so much to see and do in Berlin; sometimes it makes sense to a take a tour and leave the itinerary to someone else. These are some of our favorites.

Walking and Bike Tours

In addition to daily city highlight tours, companies have themed tours such as Third Reich Berlin, Potsdam, and pub crawls. **Berlin Walks** (☎ *030/301–9194* ⊕ *www.berlinwalks.com*) offers a Monday "Jewish Life" tour, a Potsdam tour on Thursday and Sunday, and visits to the Sachsenhausen concentration camp. **Insider Tours** (☎ *030/692–3149* ⊕ *www. insidertour.com*) has a "Cold War" Berlin tour about the Soviet era and a bike tour as well as a Cruise'n'Walk tour, a combination of boating and walking. Brit Terry Brewer's firsthand accounts of divided and reunified Berlin are a highlight of the all-day "Brewer's Best of Berlin" (☎ *0177/ 388–1537* ⊕ *www.brewersberlintours. com*) tour. Tours cost €15. **Fat Tire Bike Tours** (☎ *030/2404–7991* ⊕ *www. fattirebiketours.com*) rides through Berlin daily early March–November and has a Berlin Wall tour. The 4½-hour city tour costs €24, bike rental included. For a truly memorable experience, check out **Berliner Unterwelten** (☎ *030/499-1517* ⊕ *www. berliner-unterwelten.de*), which translates as "Berlin Underworlds." The company offers access to several of Berlin's best-preserved underground WWII bunkers that are normally closed to the public.

Boat Tours

Tours of central Berlin's Spree and the canals give you up-close views of sights such as Museum Island, Charlottenburg Palace, the Reichstag, and the Berliner Dom. Tours usually depart twice a day. Drinks, snacks, and *wurst* are available during the narrated trips. **Reederei Riedel** (☎ *030/6796-1470* ⊕ *www.reederei-riedel. de*) offers several different trips around Berlin. Prices range from €11.50 to €20 depending on theme and distance.

Stern und Kreisschiffahrt (☎ *030/536– 3600* ⊕ *www.sternundkreis.de*) offer tours of the Havel Lakes (which include Tegeler See and Wannsee). The trip begins at the Wannsee, where you can sail on a Mississippi-style boat, and cruise 28 km (17 miles) through the lakes and past forests. Tours can last from one to seven hours, and cost between €10.50 and €20.

Bus Tours

Four companies—**Berliner Bären Stadt-rundfahrten** (☎ *030/3519–5270* ⊕ *www. bbsberlin.de*), **Berolina Berlin-Service** (☎ *030/8856–8030* ⊕ *www.berolina-berlin.com*), **Bus Verkehr Berlin** (☎ *030/ 683–8910* ⊕ *www.bvb.net*), and **BEX Sightseeing** (☎ *030/880–4190* ⊕ *www. bex.de*)—jointly offer city tours on yellow, double-decker City Circle buses, which run every 15 or 30 minutes, depending on the season. The full circuit takes two hours, with a recorded narration on headphones. For €20 you can jump on and off at between 13 and 20 stops depending on the company. The bus driver sells tickets. Most companies have tours to Potsdam. The **Stadtrundfahrt-büro Berlin** (☎ *030/261–2001* ⊕ *www. stadtrundfahrtbuero-berlin.de*) has 2¼-hour (€15) or 2¾-hour tours (€20) at 10:15, 10:45, 11, 11:30, 1 pm, and 1:30 pm, 2 pm, 3:30 pm, and 4 pm. A guide narrates in both German and English. The bus departs from Tauentzienstrasse 16, at the corner of Marbuger Strasse.

BEERS OF GERMANY

Beer, or "liquid bread" as it was described by medieval monks who wanted to avoid God's anger, is not just a vital element of German cuisine, but of German culture. The stats say Germans are second only to the Czechs when it comes to per capita beer consumption, though the Germans have been losing their thirst recently—from a peak of 145 liters (38.3 gallons) per head in 1980, each German now only manages 102 liters (26.9 gallons) every year. And yet the range of beers has never been wider.

In Berlin, Pils is the most common variety of beers that you'll find. Some of the famous brands you'll see are Berliner Kindl, Schultheiss, and Berliner Pilsner. They're all worth trying. Don't hesitate to explore Germany with other varieties of beer, though.

Reinheitsgebot (Purity Law)

There are precisely 1,327 breweries in Germany, offering more than 5,000 types of beer. Thanks to Germany's legendary "Beer Purity Law," or *Reinheitsgebot,* which allows only three ingredients (water, malt, and hops), they are pretty much all terrific. The water used in German beer also has to meet certain standards—a recent discussion about introducing fracking in certain parts of Germany was roundly criticized by the German Beer Association because the water in the area would become too dirty to be made into beer.

Germany's Major Beer Varieties

PILS

One effect of the Beer Purity Law was that Germany became dominated by one kind of beer: *Pils.* Invented in Bohemia (now the Czech Republic) in 1842, and aided by Bavarian refrigeration techniques, Pils was the first beer to be chilled and stored thus allowing bottom fermentation, better clarity, and a longer shelf-life. Today, the majority of German beers are brewed in the Pils, or Pilsner, style. German Pils tends to have a drier, bitterer taste than what you might be used to, but a trip to Germany is hardly complete without the grand tour along these lines: Augustiner in Bavaria, Bitburger in the Rhineland, Flensburger in the North.

HELLES

Hell is German for "light," but when it comes to beer, that refers to the color rather than the alcohol content. *Helles* is a crisp and clear Bavarian pale lager with between 4.5% and 6% alcohol. It was developed in the mid-19th century by a German brewer named Gabriel Sedlmayr, who adopted and adapted some British techniques to create the new beer for his famous Spaten Brewery in Bavaria. Another brewer, Josef Groll, used the same methods to produce one of the first German Pils, Pilsner Urquell. Spaten is still one the best brands for a good Helles, as are Löwenbräu, Weihenstephaner, and Hacker-Pschorr—all classic Bavarian beers.

DUNKELBIER

At the other end of the beer rainbow from Helles is dark beer, or *Dunkelbier.* The dark, reddish color is a consequence of the darker malt that is used in the brewing. Despite what you might think due to the stronger, maltier taste, Dunkelbier actually contains no more alcohol than Helles. Dunkelbier was common in rural Bavaria in the early 19th century. All the major Bavarian breweries produce a Dunkelbier to complement their Helles.

BOCK

Dunkelbier should not be confused with *Bock,* which also has a dark color and a malty taste but is a little stronger. It was first created in the middle ages in the northern German town of Einbeck, before it was later adopted by the Bavarian breweries, which had come to regard themselves as the natural home of German beer. In fact, the name Bock comes from the Bavarian interpretation of the word "Einbeck." Bock often has a sweeter flavor, and is traditionally drunk on public holidays. There are also subcategories, like *Eisbock* and *Doppelbock,* which have been refined to make an even stronger beverage.

KÖLSCH

If you're looking for lighter refreshment, then *Kölsch* is ideal. The traditional beer of Cologne, Kölsch is a mild, carbonated beer that goes down easily. It is usually served in a small, straight glass, called a *Stange,* which is much easier to wrangle than the immense Bavarian *Mass* (liter) glasses. If you're part of a big party, you're likely to get Kölsch served in a *Kranz,* or wreath—a circular wooden rack that holds up to 18 *Stangen.* Kölsch is very specific to Cologne and its immediate environs, so there's little point in asking for it anywhere else. Consequently, the major Kölsch brands are all relatively small; they include Reissdorf, Gaffel, and Früh.

HEFEWEIZEN

Also known as *Weissbier* or *Weizenbier,* *Hefeweizen* is essentially wheat beer, and it was originally brewed in southern Bavaria. It has a very distinctive taste and cloudy color. It's much stronger than standard Pils or Helles, with an alcohol content of more than 8%. On the other hand, that content is slightly compensated for by the fact that wheat beer can be very filling. For a twist, try the clear variety called *Kristallweizen,* which tastes crisper, and is often served with half a slice of lemon. Hefeweizen is available throughout Germany, and the major Bavarian breweries all brew it as part of their range.

WINES OF GERMANY

Germany produces some of the finest white wines in the world. Although more and more quality red wine is being produced, the majority of German wines are white due to the northern continental climate. Nearly all wine production in Germany takes place by the River Rhine in the southwest. As a result, a single trip to this lovely and relatively compact wine region can give you a good overview of German wines.

German Wines: Then and Now

A BRIEF HISTORY

The Romans first introduced viticulture to the southernmost area of what is present-day Germany about 2,000 years ago. By the time of Charlemagne, wine making centered on monasteries. A 19th-century grape blight necessitated a complete reconstitution of German grape stock, grafted with pest-resistant American vines, and formed the basis for today's German wines. With cold winters, a relatively northern climate, and less sun than other wine regions, the Germans have developed a reputation for technical and innovative panache. The result has traditionally been top-quality sweet Rieslings, though Germany has been making excellent dry and off-dry white wines and Rieslings in the past 30 years.

TODAY'S WINE SCENE

For years, German wines were known by their lowest common denominator, the cheap, sweet wine that was exported en masse to the United States, England, and other markets. However, more recently there has been a push to introduce the world to the best of German wines. Exports to the United States, Germany's largest export market, have grown steadily, followed by England, The Netherlands, Sweden, and Russia. Eighty-three

percent of its exports are white wines. The export of *Liebfraumilch*, the sugary, low-quality stuff that gave German wine a bad name, has been steadily declining, and now 66% of exports are so-called *Qualitätswein*, or quality wines. Only 15% of exports are destined to be wine-in-a-box. This is a more accurate representation of German wine as it exists in Germany.

Germany's Dominant Varietals

WHITES

Müller-Thurgau: Created in the 1880s, this grape is a cross between a Riesling and a Madeleine Royale. Ripening early, it's prone to rot and, as the grape used in most Liebfraumilch, has a less than golden reputation.

Riesling: The most widely planted (and widely famous) of German grapes, the Riesling ripens late. A hardy grape, it's ideal for late-harvest wines. High levels of acidity help wines age well. When young, grapes have a crisp, floral character.

Silvaner: This grape is dying out in most places, with the exception of Franconia, where it is traditionally grown. With low acidity and neutral fruit, it can be crossed with other grapes to produce sweet wines like Kerner, Grauburgunder (pinot gris), Weissburgunder (pinot blanc), Bacchus, and others.

REDS

Dornfelder: A relatively young varietal. Dornfelder produces wines with a deep color, which distinguishes them from other German reds, which tend to be pale, light, and off-dry.

Spätburgunder (pinot noir): This grape is responsible for Germany's full-bodied, fruity wines, and is grown in more southerly vineyards.

Terminology

German wine is a complex topic, even though the wine region is relatively small. Wines are ranked according to the ripeness of the grapes when picked, and instead of harvesting a vineyard all at once, German vineyards are harvested up to five times. The finest wines result from the latest harvests of the season, due to increased sugar content. Under the category of "table wine" fall *Deutscher Tafelwein* (German table wine) and *Landwein* (like the French Vin de Pays). Quality wines are ranked according to when they are harvested. *Kabinett* wines are delicate, light, and fruity. *Spätlese* ("late-harvest" wine) has more-concentrated flavors, sweetness, and body. *Auslese* wines are made from extra-ripe grapes, and are even richer, even sweeter, and even riper. *Beerenauslese* are rare and expensive, made from grapes whose flavor and acid has been enhanced by noble rot. *Eiswein* ("ice" wine) is made of grapes that have been left on the vine to freeze and may be harvested as late as January. They produce a sugary syrup that creates an intense, fruity wine. Finally, *Trockenbeerenauslese* ("dry ice" wine) is made in tiny amounts using grapes that have frozen and shriveled into raisins. These can rank amongst the world's most expensive wines. Other terms to keep in mind include *Trocken* (dry) and *Halbtrocken* (half-dry, or "off-dry").

Wine Regions

Mosel: The Mosel's steep, mineral-rich hillsides produce excellent Rieslings. With flowery rather than fruity top-quality wines, the Mosel is a must-stop for any wine lover. The terraced hillsides rising up along the banks of the River Mosel are as pleasing to the eye as the light-bodied Rieslings are to the palate.

Nahe: Agreeable and uncomplicated: this describes the wines made from Müller-Thurgau and Silvaner grapes of the Nahe region. The earth here is rich not just in grapes, but also in semiprecious stones and minerals, and you might just detect a hint of pineapple in your wine's bouquet.

Rheinhessen: The largest wine-making region of Germany, Rheinhessen's once grand reputation was tarnished in the mid-20th century, when large, substandard vineyards were cultivated and low-quality wine produced. Nonetheless, there's plenty of the very good stuff to be found, still. Stick to the red sandy slopes over the river for the most full-bodied of Germany's Rieslings.

Rheingau: The dark, slaty soil of the Rheingau is particularly suited to the German Riesling, which is the major wine produced in this lovely hill country along the River Rhine. Spicy wines come from the hillsides, while the valley yields wines with body, richness, and concentration.

Pfalz: The second-largest wine region in Germany, the Pfalz stretches north from the French border. Mild winters and warm summers make for some of Germany's best pinot noirs and most opulent Rieslings. Wine is served here in a special dimpled glass called the *Dubbeglas*.

Baden: Farther to the south, Baden's warmer climate helps produce ripe, full-bodied wines that may not be well known but certainly taste delicious. The best ones, both red and white, come from Kaiserstuhl-Tuniberg, between Freiburg and the Rhine. But be forewarned: The best things in life do tend to cost a little extra.

BERLIN WALL WALK

The East German government, in an attempt to keep their beleaguered citizens from fleeing, built the Berlin wall practically overnight in 1961. On November 9, 1989, it was torn down, signaling the dawning of a new era. Most of the wall has been demolished but you can still walk the trail where it used to stand and visualize the 12-foot-tall border that once divided the city.

Follow the Cobblestones

These days, it's hard to believe that Potsdamer Platz used to be a no-man's-land. But in front of the gleaming skyscrapers, next to the S-bahn station, a tiny stretch of the Berlin Wall stands as a reminder of the place's history. And just over on Erna-Berger-Strasse is the last of the hundreds of watchtowers that stood along the wall.

When the wall fell, Berliners couldn't wait to get rid of it and souvenir hunters came out in droves with hammers and chisels to take pieces away. You can still follow the rows of cobblestones on the ground that mark where the wall used to stand, though. The path illuminates the effects the Wall had on the city: it cut through streets, neighborhoods, and even through buildings, which were then abandoned.

Go East

Walk south along Stresemanstrasse from Potsdamer Platz, and then head east along Niederkirchnerstrasse two blocks to Checkpoint Gallery, a border crossing that foreign nationals used to cross between the American and Soviet zones. Niederkirchnerstrasse turns into Zimmerstrasse. Continue east along that to the modest column engraved "He only wanted freedom," in German, at Zimmerstrasse 15, commemorating Peter Fechter, an 18-year-old who was shot and killed while trying to escape to the West. Follow Zimmerstrasse and turn left on Axel-Springer-Strasse, then right, onto Kommandantenstrasse. Keep walking past Sebastian and Waldemar streets and you'll reach Engelbecken Pond. This is a good place to rest.

Peace in the Shadow of the Wall

Keep walking along Bethaniendamm and you'll come to a colorful ramshackle wooden structure. This is where a Turkish immigrant named Osman Kalin planted vegetables in the shadow of the Wall, in West Berlin in a small area that had been strewn with garbage. Little did he know that this piece of land actually belonged to East Berlin but the Wall had missed it. His family still grows onions and cabbages on the plot. Even the most bizarre circumstances were normal in Cold War Berlin—and some of these oddities have survived the change of times.

Plus Ça Change . . .

Cross the Spree River at the Schilling Bridge and turn right to walk parallel to the river. Fast-forward on Holzmarkt and Mühlen streets to the famous East Side Gallery, where artists from all over the world decorated the remaining 4,000-some-foot Wall with colorful paintings. A section was demolished to construct a riverside condo. The future of this iconic piece of the Wall remains unclear.

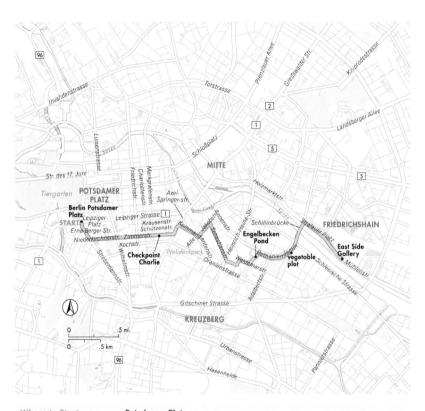

Where to Start:	Potsdamer Platz
Distance:	4 miles
Timing:	Half a day
Highlights:	The former border crossing of Checkpoint Charlie and the East Side Gallery
Best Time to Go:	During the day
Worst Time to Go:	Avoid the winter, or bundle up
Best Place to Stop for a Rest:	Engelbecken Pond

BERLIN ITINERARIES

One Day in Berlin

If you only have one day in Berlin, start the morning at the city's most iconic symbol, the **Reichstag**. March through the **Brandenburg Gate**, and stroll down the tree-lined boulevard Unter der Linden while marveling at its Prussian glory.

Head south to visit the **Topographie des Terrors**, which marks where the Gestapo headquarters used to be, and experience the moving silence in the maze of the Holocaust memorial, the **Denkmal für die Ermordeten Juden Europas**. Stop by **Potsdamer Platz**, which embodies the city's renaissance: Once a no-go zone between East and West Berlins, the square now teems with glittering towers of optimism. Hop on the double-decker public bus 200, which travels down Unter der Linden to the colossal **Berliner Dom** cathedral. You can then devote the entire afternoon to the stupendous collections of the **Museuminsel**. The beautifully restored Neues Museum and the majestic Pergamon are standouts, as is the excellently curated Deutsches Historisches Museum (German History Museum)—and its delightful Café im Zeughaus is a perfect place for a mid-afternoon pick-me-up.

Later, you can wander **Scheunenviertel** for window-shopping and dinner, perhaps at one of the neighborhood's German restaurants like Altes Europa, Hackescher Hof, or Weinbar Rutz. Finish the evening at the unpretentious **Clärchens Ballhaus**, a century-old dance hall that attracts everyone from cool twentysomethings to dressed-up senior citizens.

Three Days in Berlin

Follow the one-day itinerary above, then spend the second day exploring the young side of Berlin, in Kreuzberg. It's a good time to rent a bicycle. Browse the street's secondhand clothing and indy boutiques and have lunch at **Martkthalle IX**, home to all bevy of delicious local vendors, then head south to **Tempelhofer Park**, the historic airfield-turned-popular park. These days you can share the runways, which the American bombers used during the Berlin Airlift, with windsurfers and skateboarders.

Exit the park to Neukölln, a working-class neighborhood that has emerged as an epicenter of hipsterism. For lunch, there are many Middle Eastern eateries as well as the popular Italian restaurant **Lavanderia Vecchia** *(see full review in Where to Eat)*.

Continue east and cross the Spree over the redbrick **Oberbaum Bridge**, which served as a border crossing between East and West Berlin. On the other side of the river is Friedrichshain and the famous **East Side Gallery**, where international artists covered the remnant of the Berlin Wall with colorful murals. Also in Friedrichshain, you can see the magnitude of socialist urban planning along **Karl-Marx-Allee**, a wide boulevard lined with the so-called workers' paradise apartments. Afterward, sample the food and nightlife offerings of youthful Simon Dach and Boxhagner streets.

Go west on Day 3 and spend the day in Charlottenburg. Spend the morning at **Schloss Charlottenburg**, the largest palace in Berlin with rococo flourishes and an impeccably manicured garden. Take Bus 109 to the **Käthe Kollwitz Museum** on Fasanenstrasse, featuring works by Berlin's best known sculptor. Next door, the café in the **Literaturhaus**, set in a 19th-century villa, is a perfect place for a leisurely lunch.

Visit the **Kaiser Wilhelm Memorial Church**, a reminder of the devastations of WWII. Scour antiques on Bleibtreustrasse, or pop into big-name shops on Kurfürstendamm, one of the most famous avenues in Berlin. The top floor of the **Kaufhaus des Westerns** (KaDeWe to the locals) department store is popular for its selection of gourmet food.

Take Bus 29 and get off on Potsdamer Strasse. Berlin's galleries are notorious for playing musical chairs, and this unassuming street has emerged in the past five years as the epicenter of Berlin's contemporary art scene. If you're short on time, however, beeline to the established museum of **Gemäldegalerie**, West Berlin's collection of classical European paintings including Caravaggio and Rembrandt. Round off the evening with a classical concert at the world-famous Philharmonie nearby.

Five Days in Berlin

With five days in Berlin you'll have time to get out of the city and head to **Potsdam** on the fourth day. The former residence of the Prussian kings, Potsdam is a quick regional train or S-bahn ride away. Start the day at **Sansoucci Palace**, the Teutonic answer to Versailles. The summer home of Frederick the Great, this Unesco World Heritage site is crisscrossed with gorgeously landscaped trails. You can try to plan your rambles with the free map from the tourist office, but you'll inevitably get lost—and that's the beauty of it. Put on your most comfortable shoes and lose yourself in the Prussian splendor.

On your final day, check out the up-and-coming district of Wedding, a multicultural working-class neighborhood once squeezed on two sides by the Berlin Wall. Walk around and then join a guided tour of the **Berlin Unterwelten**, which includes an underground WWII bunker filled with artifacts from the war.

Afterward, hop on the S-bahn and head to Schönhauserallee to experience Prenzlauer Berg, arguably the most sought-after neighborhood in Berlin. Have lunch in the neighborhood, perhaps at Fleisherei, or saunter to Kastanienallee, dubbed Casting Alley for its fashion-conscious denizens who strut up and down the street: perfect for people-watching. On weekends, a flea market pops up along the remnants of the Berlin Wall at the Mauerpark. Later, head to Prater, Berlin's oldest beer garden, for a pint or two.

BERLIN WITH KIDS

For all its trendy reputation, Berlin is actually quite a kid-friendly city. With abundant open space, family-friendly cafés, and fun educational attractions, the German capital is an ideal place for a family holiday.

Animals Everywhere!

Berlin is home to the oldest in Germany: the 1844-built Berlin Zoological Garden, in the Tiergarten. It receives 3 million visitors a year, making it the most visited zoo in Europe. More than 1,570 species including pandas, orangutans, and other cuddly creatures call this central piece of greenery home. Next door is an adorably old-fashioned aquarium.

If the kids are into underwater creatures, you'll want to head to **Sea Life Berlin**, the urban aquarium near Alexanderplatz, where moray eels and sharks reside are on view. The highlight, however, is in the Aquadom, next door in the Radisson Blu Hotel, where the elevator travels through a 52-foot tropical fish tank (included with the admission to Sea Life).

Fun Learning

At the **DDR Museum**, history comes alive with hands-on exhibits, like exploring a typical East German apartment or climbing into a Trabi automobile for a simulated ride. Kids and adults both get a kick out of the experience, and the museum is conveniently located in Mitte, right across from the Berliner Dom.

Another great museum that keeps the kids entertainted is the **Deutsches Technikmuseum.** What used to be a train depot in Kreuzberg has become an expansive museum that displays the impressive evolution of modern transportation, from steamer trains to aircraft.

The **Labyrinth Kindermuseum** is a hands-on fun factory for children between 3 and 12, especially during the Saturday crafts classes. It's been known to engross the parents as much as the kids, and even to entice some grown-ups without children in tow.

Burning Off Energy

Berlin has plenty of room to run around. There are several excellent urban oases of greenery, including the vast, central **Tiergarten**, right in Mitte. Those in the know, though, head to the relatively new **Tempelhofen Park**, which was converted from the old Tempelhof Airport into a fabulous outdoor area where families, bike, picnic, and fly kites.

EXPLORING
BERLIN

Updated
by Sally
McGrane and
Giulia Pines

Since the fall of the Iron Curtain, no other city in Europe has seen more change than Berlin, the German capital. The two Berlins that had been physically separated for almost 30 years have become one, and the reunited city has become a cutting-edge destination for architecture, culture, entertainment, nightlife, and shopping. After successfully uniting its own East and West, Berlin now plays a pivotal role in the European Union. But even as the capital thinks and moves forward, history is always tugging at its sleeve. Between the wealth of neoclassical and 21st-century buildings there are constant reminders, both subtle and stark, of the events of the 20th century.

Berlin is quite young by European standards, beginning as two separate entities in 1237 on two islands in the Spree River: Cölln and Berlin. By the 1300s, Berlin was prospering, thanks to its location at the intersection of important trade routes, and rose to power as the seat of the Hohenzollern dynasty. The Great Elector Friedrich Wilhelm, in the nearly 50 years of his reign (1640–88), touched off a cultural renaissance. Later, Frederick the Great (1712–86) made Berlin and Potsdam glorious centers of his enlightened yet autocratic Prussian monarchy.

In 1871, Prussia, ruled by the "Iron Chancellor" Count Otto von Bismarck, unified the many independent German states into the German Empire. Berlin maintained its status as capital for the duration of that Second Reich (1871–1918), through the post–World War I Weimar Republic (1919–33), and also through Hitler's so-called Third Reich (1933–45). The city's golden years were the Roaring '20s, when Berlin evolved as the energetic center for the era's cultural avant-garde. World-famous writers, painters, and artists met here while the impoverished bulk of its 4 million inhabitants lived in heavily overpopulated quarters. This "dance on the volcano," as those years of political and economic upheaval have been called, came to a grisly and bloody end after January 1933, when Adolf Hitler became chancellor. The Nazis made Berlin their capital but ultimately failed to remake the city into a monument to their power, as they had planned. By World War II's end, 70% of the city lay in ruins, with more rubble than in all other German cities combined.

Along with the division of Germany after World War II, Berlin was partitioned into American, British, and French zones in the West and a Soviet zone in the East. The three western-occupied zones became West Berlin, while the Soviets, who controlled not only Berlin's eastern zone but also all of the east German land surrounding it tried to blockade

West Berlin out of existence. (They failed thanks to the yearlong Berlin Airlift [1948–49], during which American airplanes known in German as "raisin bombers," dropped supplies until the blockade lifted.) In 1949 the Soviet Union established East Berlin as the capital of its new satellite state, the German Democratic Republic (GDR). The division of the city was cruelly finalized in concrete in August 1961, when the GDR erected the Berlin Wall, the only border fortification in history built to keep people from leaving rather than to protect them.

For nearly 30 years, the two Berlins served as competing visions of the new world order: Capitalist on one side, Communist on the other. West Berlin, an island of democracy in the Eastern bloc, was surrounded by guards and checkpoints. Nonetheless, thanks in part to being heavily subsidized by Western powers, the city became a haven for artists and freethinkers. Today, with the Wall long relegated to history (most of it was recycled as street gravel), visitors can appreciate the whole city and the anything-goes atmosphere that still pervades.

MITTE

After the fall of the wall, Mitte, which had been in East Germany, became the geographic center of Berlin, once again. The area has several minidistricts, each of which has its own distinctive history and flair. Alexanderplatz, home of the TV Tower, was the center of East Berlin. With its communist architecture, you can still get a feel for the GDR aesthetic here. The Nikolaiviertel nearby, was part of the medieval heart of Berlin. Left largely intact by the war, it was destroyed for ideological reasons, then rebuilt decades later by the Communist regime. The Scheunenviertel, part of the Spandauer Vorstadt, was home to many of the city's Jewish citizens. Today, the narrow streets that saw so much tragedy house art galleries and upscale shops. Treasures once split between East and West Berlin museums are reunited on Museuminsel, the stunning Museum Island, a UNESCO World Heritage Site. Bordering Tiergarten and the government district is the meticulously restored Brandenburger Tor (Brandenburg Gate), the unofficial symbol of the city, and the Memorial to the Murdered Jews of Europe, whose design and scope engendered many debates.

The historic boulevard Unter den Linden proudly rolls out Prussian architecture and world-class museums. Its major cross street is Friedrichstrasse, which was revitalized in the mid-1990s with car showrooms (including Bentley, Bugatti, and Volkswagen) and upscale malls.

The hip part of Mitte, the historic core of Berlin, is best experienced in the narrow streets and courtyard mazes of the Scheunenviertel (Barn Quarter), part of the larger Spandauer Vorstadt (the old Jewish neighborhood), and the area around Oranienburger Strasse. There are upscale shops, tony bars, and increasingly excellent restaurants, as well as successful art galleries. During the second half of the 17th century, artisans, small-businessmen, and Jews moved into this area at the encouragement of the Great Elector, who sought to improve his financial situation through their skills. As industrialization intensified, the quarter became poorer, and in the 1880s many East European Jews escaping pogroms settled here. Today, Mitte's Scheunenviertel is quite popular with tourists.

TIMING

You must reserve a spot on a tour in advance in order to visit the Reichstag, but don't let that stop you: the new rules have done a lot to dissipate the lines that used to snake around the building. The Hamburger Bahnhof, Museum für Gegenwart–Berlin is just down the street from Hauptbahnhof. A quick ride on Berlin's newest—and with only three stops, shortest—underground line, the U55, will get you there from the Brandenburg Gate or the Reichstag.

To speed your way down Unter den Linden, there are three bus lines that make stops between Wilhelmstrasse and Alexanderplatz and are sort of unofficial tourist buses. Note that a few state museums in this area are closed Monday.

TOP ATTRACTIONS

Bebelplatz. After he became ruler in 1740, Frederick the Great personally planned the buildings surrounding this square (which has a huge parking garage cleverly hidden beneath the pavement). The area received the nickname "*Forum Fridericianum,*" or Frederick's Forum. On May 10, 1933, Joseph Goebbels, the Nazi minister for propaganda and "public enlightenment," organized one of the nationwide book-burnings here. The books, thrown on a pyre by Nazi officials and students, included works by Jews, pacifists, and Communists. In the center of Bebelplatz, a modern and subtle memorial (built underground but viewable through a window in the cobblestone) marks where 20,000 books went up in flames. The **Staatsoper Unter den Linden** (State Opera) is on the east side of the square. **St. Hedwigskathedrale** is on the south side. The **Humboldt-Universität** is to the west.

Berliner Dom (*Berlin Cathedral*). A church has stood here since 1536, but this enormous version dates from 1905, making it the largest 20th-century Protestant church in Germany. The royal Hohenzollerns worshipped here until 1918, when Kaiser Wilhelm II abdicated and left Berlin for Holland. The massive dome wasn't restored from World War II damage until 1982; the interior was completed in 1993. The climb to the dome's outer balcony is made easier by a wide stairwell, plenty of landings with historic photos and models, and even a couple of chairs. The 94 sarcophagi of Prussian royals in the crypt are significant, but to less-trained eyes can seem uniformly dull. Sunday services include communion. ⊠ *Am Lustgarten 1, Mitte* ☎ *030/2026–9136* ⊕ *www.berlinerdom.de* 🖼 *€8 with audio guide, €5 without* ☉ *Mon.–Sat. 9–8, Sun. noon–8* Ⓜ *Hackescher Markt (S-bahn).*

FAMILY **Berliner Fernsehturm** (*TV Tower*). Finding Alexanderplatz is no problem: just head toward the 1,207-foot-high tower piercing the sky. Built in 1969 as a signal to the west (clearly visible over the Wall, no less) that the East German economy was thriving, it is deliberately higher than both western Berlin's broadcasting tower and the Eiffel Tower in Paris. You can get the best view of Berlin from within the tower's disco ball–like observation level; on a clear day you can see for 40 km (25 mi). One floor above, the city's highest restaurant rotates for your

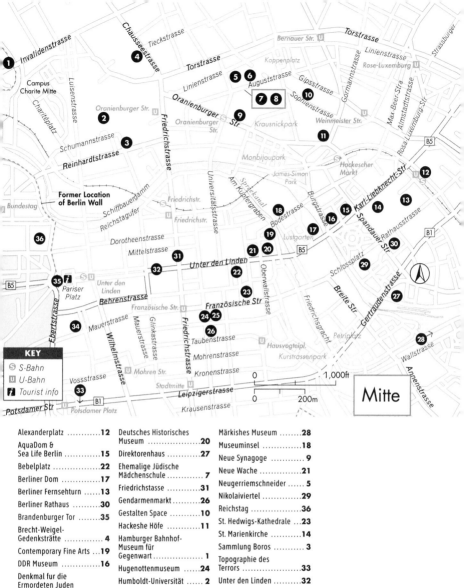

panoramic pleasure. ■TIP→ During the summer season, order VIP tickets online to avoid a long wait. ⊠ *Panoramastr. 1a, Mitte* ☎ *030/247–5750* ✉ *info@tv-turm.de* ⊕ *www.tv-turm.de* ⊡ *€12.50* ⊗ *Nov.–Feb., daily 10 am–midnight; Mar.–Oct., daily 9 am–midnight; last admission ½ hr before closing* Ⓜ *Alexanderplatz (U-bahn and S-bahn).*

Fodor'sChoice ★ **Brandenburger Tor** (*Brandenburg Gate*). Once the pride of Prussian Berlin and the city's premier landmark, the Brandenburger Tor was left in a desolate no-man's-land when the Wall was built. Since the Wall's dismantling, the sandstone gateway has become the scene of the city's Unification Day and New Year's Eve parties. This is the sole remaining gate of 14 built by Carl Langhans in 1788–91, designed as a triumphal arch for King Frederick Wilhelm II. Its virile classical style pays tribute to Athens's Acropolis. The quadriga, a chariot drawn by four horses and driven by the Goddess of Victory, was added in 1794. Troops paraded through the gate after successful campaigns—the last time in 1945, when victorious Red Army troops took Berlin. The upper part of the gate, together with its chariot and Goddess of Victory, was destroyed in the war. In 1957 the original molds were discovered in West Berlin, and a new quadriga was cast in copper and presented as a gift to the people of East Berlin. A tourist-information center is in the south part of the gate.

The gate faces one of Europe's most famous historic squares, **Pariser Platz,** with bank headquarters, the ultramodern French embassy, and the offices of the federal parliament. On the southern side, Berlin's sleek Academy of Arts, integrating the ruins of its historic predecessor, and the DZ Bank, designed by star architect Frank Gehry, stand next to the new American embassy, rebuilt on its prewar location and reopened on July 4, 2008. The legendary Hotel Adlon (now the Adlon Kempinski) looks on from its historic home at the southeast edge of the square. ⊠ *Pariser Pl., Mitte* Ⓜ *Unter den Linden (S-bahn).*

Contemporary Fine Arts. From its perch on Am Kupfergraben, Contemporary Fine Arts (CFA) Berlin has a perfect view of Museum Island and its hoard of daily visitors. Those looking for a different kind of Berlin art scene will find it in this elegant gallery. Housed in a David Chipperfield–constructed, ultramodern building, it stands out from its Prussian surroundings. CFA has been a fixture in Berlin since the early 1990s, showing Berlin-based artists like Jonathan Meese and Anselm Reyle, and big-timers like Juegen Teller and Julian Schnabel. ⊠ *Am Kupfergraben 10, Mitte* ☎ *030/288–7870* ⊕ *www.cfa-berlin.com/* ⊗ *Tues.–Sat. 10–6* Ⓜ *Hackescher Markt (S-bahn).*

Fodor'sChoice ★ **DDR Museum.** Half museum, half theme park, the DDR Museum is an interactive and highly entertaining exhibit about life during socialism. It's difficult to say just how much the museum benefits from its prime location beside the Spree, right across from the Berliner Dom, but it's always packed, filled with tourists, families, and student groups trying to get a hands-on feel for what the East German experience was really like. Exhibitions include a re-creation of an East German kitchen, all mustard yellows and bilious greens; a simulated drive in a Trabi, the only car the average East German was allowed to own; and a walk inside a very narrow, very claustrophobic interrogation cell. For an added glimpse into the life of an "Ossi" (an "easterner"), stop at the DDR Restaurat Domklause, where traditional East German dishes provide sustenance with a side of history. ⊠ *Karl-Liebknecht-Str. 1, at the Spree, opposite the Berliner Dom, Mitte* ☎ *030/8471–2373* ⊕ *www.ddr-museum.de* 🖭 *€6* ⊙ *Open Sun.-Fri. 10-8, Sat. 10-10.* Ⓜ *Alexanderplatz (U-bahn and S-bahn), Hackescher Markt (S-bahn)*

> **WORD OF MOUTH**
>
> "Quite possibly one of our top museum experiences of the holiday, the hour or so spent at the DDR Museum. More than just exhibits of 'Ostalgia,' the museum offered real, and sometimes interactive glimpses into life behind the wall. We all came away more informed, and humbled."
>
> —fourfortravel

Fodor's Choice **Denkmal für die Ermordeten Juden Europas** (*Memorial to the Murdered*
★ *Jews of Europe*). An expansive and unusual memorial dedicated to the 6 million Jews who were killed in the Holocaust, the monument was designed by American architect Peter Eisenman. The stunning place of remembrance consists of a grid of more than 2,700 concrete stelae, planted into undulating ground. The abstract memorial can be entered from all sides and offers no prescribed path. ■TIP➔ **An information center that goes into specifics about the Holocaust lies underground at the southeast corner.** ⊠ *Cora-Berliner-Str. 1, Mitte* ☎ *030/2639–4336* ⊕ *www.stiftung-denkmal.de* 🖭 *Free* ⊙ *Daily 24 hrs; information center: Oct.–Mar., Tues.–Sun. 10–7; Apr.–Sept., Tues.–Sun. 10–8 (last admission 45 min. before closing)* Ⓜ *Unter den Linden (S-bahn).*

Deutsches Historisches Museum (*German History Museum*). The museum is composed of two buildings. The magnificent pink, baroque Prussian arsenal (Zeughaus) was constructed between 1695 and 1730, and is the oldest building on Unter den Linden. It also houses a theater, the Zeughaus Kino, which regularly presents a variety of films, both German and international, historic and modern. The new permanent exhibits, reopened after much debate in mid-2006, offer a modern and fascinating view of German history since the early Middle Ages. Behind the arsenal, the granite-and-glass Pei-Bau building by I. M. Pei holds often stunning and politically controversial changing exhibits, such as 2010's unprecedented blockbuster "Hitler und die Deutschen" ("Hitler and the Germans"), which explored the methods of propaganda used by Hitler and the Nazis to gain power, and 2013's "Zerstörte Vielfalt" or "destroyed diversity," which documents the multi-faceted societal, ethnic, and political ruination of Berlin in the years leading up to WWII. The museum's Café im Zeughaus is a great place to stop and restore your energy. ⊠ *Unter den Linden 2, Mitte* ☎ *030/203–040* ⊕ *www.dhm. de* 🖭 *€8* ⊙ *Daily 10–6.*

Direktorenhaus. Just as much a draw for its architecture and history as for the quirky, off-kilter art shows and events that take place here, Direktorenhaus is a relative newcomer to the Berlin art scene. This Spree-side building was once part of the State Mint. The large, Berlin-heavy roster of artists includes Olaf Hajek, Daniel Becker, and Lauren Coleman. ■TIP→ **The gallery has no public hours, and viewings are by appointment. One-hour tours run on weekends and can be booked online.** ✉ *Am Krögel 2, Mitte* ☎ *030/4849–1929* ⊕ *www.direktorenhaus.com* ⌚ *€7* Ⓜ *Alexanderplatz (S-bahn and U-bahn) and Klosterstrasse (U-bahn).*

Fodor's Choice
★

Ehemalige Jüdische Mädchenschule. This boxy brick building in central Berlin, which formerly served as a Jewish girls' school and then a military hospital during WWII, sat neglected until recently. Now it is one of the city's newest star attractions: a renovated multiplex with art galleries, restaurants, and a bar. The former gymnasium is now the restaurant Pauly Saal; upstairs, three art galleries share space with the newly relocated Kennedys museum. Berlin's now-thriving Jewish community still owns the building and leases it out to the current management. Both Jewish and non-Jewish visitors will rejoice at the inclusion of Mogg & Melzer, a deli dedicated to Jewish delicacies like matzo ball soup, pastrami, and shakshuka. ✉ *Auguststr. 11–13, Mitte* ⊕ *www.maedchenschule.org/* ⊘ *Varies according to business* Ⓜ *Oranienburger Strasse (S-bahn).*

Friedrichstrasse. The once-bustling street of cafés and theaters of prewar Berlin has risen from the rubble of war and Communist neglect to reclaim the crowds with shopping emporiums. Heading south from the Friedrichstrasse train station, you'll pass hotels and various stores (including the sprawling, comprehensive bookstore **Dussmann** and its large but cozy new English-language bookshop around the corner). After crossing Unter den Linden, you'll come upon the Berlin outpost of the Parisian department store **Galeries Lafayette** on your left. North of the train station you will see the rejuvenated heart of the entertainment center of Berlin's Roaring Twenties, including the somewhat kitschy **Friedrichstadt Palast** and the meticulously restored **Admiralspalast,** the rebirth of a glittering jazz age entertainment temple, with several stages, a club and a restaurant.

Gendarmenmarkt. This is without a doubt the most elegant square in former East Berlin. Anchored by the beautifully reconstructed 1818 **Konzerthaus** and the **Deutscher Dom** and **Französischer Dom** (German and French cathedrals) and lined with some of the city's best restaurants, it also hosts one of Berlin's classiest annual Christmas markets.

Hugenottenmuseum. Inside the Französischer Dom (French Cathedral), built by Kaiser Friedrich II for the Protestant Huguenots who fled France and settled in Berlin, is the Hugenottenmuseum, with exhibits charting their history and art. The Huguenots were expelled from France at the end of the 17th century by King Louis XIV. Their energy and commercial expertise contributed much to Berlin. ✉ *Französischer Dom, Gendarmenmarkt 5, Mitte* ☎ *030/229–1760* ⌚ *€2* ⊘ *Tues.–Sun. noon–5.*

Gestalten Space. This courtyard space serves as art gallery and bookshop for the lauded Berlin-based publishing company of the same name, whose books focus on design, illustration, art, architecture, and photography. Recent exhibitions have featured the whimsical and colorful works of Sarah Illenberger and Olaf Hajek, and nearly 100-year-old photographs of the Russian empire by Sergei Mikhailovich Prokudin-Gorskii. ⊠ *Sophienstr. 21, in Sophien-Gips-Höfe, Mitte* ☎ *030/2021–5821* ⊕ *www.gestalten.com* ⊗ *Wed.-Mon. noon–7* Ⓜ *Weinmeisterstrasse (U-bahn) or Hackescher Markt (S-bahn).*

Hackesche Höfe (*Hacke Courtyards*). Built in 1905–07, this series of eight connected courtyards is the finest example of art nouveau industrial architecture in Berlin. Most buildings are covered with glazed white tiles, and additional Moorish mosaic designs decorate the main courtyard off Rosenthaler Strasse. Shops (including one dedicated to Berlin's beloved street-crossing signal, the "Ampelmann"), restaurants, the variety theater Chamäleon Varieté, and a movie theater populate the spaces once occupied by ballrooms, a poets' society, and a Jewish girls' club. ⊠ *Rosenthaler Str. 40–41, and Sophienstr. 6, Mitte* ☎ *030/2809–8010* ⊕ *www.hackesche-hoefe.com* Ⓜ *Hackescher Markt (S-bahn).*

KW Institute for Contemporary Art. This gallery cum museum got its start in the 1990s, when a group of art fans and aficionados led by Klaus Biesenbach came upon a practically collapsing former margarine factory and decided it would be a great place for their project. Since then, KW (which stands for 'Kunst Werke' or 'art works') has been presenting exhibitions, site-specific works, and various events in the three-floor space (there's also an enclosed courtyard with a café). ⊠ *Auguststr. 69, Mitte* ☎ *030/243–4590* ⊕ *www.kw-berlin.de* ⊠ *€6* ⊗ *Wed., Fri.–Mon. noon–7, Thurs. noon–9* Ⓜ *Oranienburger Strasse (S-bahn) and Oranienburger Tor (U-bahn).*

Fodor'sChoice ★ Museumsinsel (*Museum Island*). On the site of one of Berlin's two original settlements, this unique complex of five state museums, a UNESCO World Heritage Site, is an absolute must.

The **Alte Nationalgalerie** (Old National Gallery, entrance on Bodestrasse) houses an outstanding collection of 18th-, 19th-, and early 20th-century paintings and sculptures. Works by Cézanne, Rodin, Degas, and one of Germany's most famous portrait artists, Max Liebermann, are part of the permanent exhibition. Its Galerie der Romantik (Gallery of Romanticism) collection has masterpieces from such 19th-century German painters as Karl Friedrich Schinkel and Caspar David Friedrich, the leading members of the German Romantic school. The **Altes Museum** (Old Museum), a red-marble, neoclassical building abutting the green Lustgarten, was Prussia's first structure purpose-built to serve as a museum. Designed by Karl Friedrich Schinkel, it was completed in 1830. The permanent collection of the Altes Museum consists of everyday utensils from ancient Greece as well as vases and sculptures from the 6th to 4th century BC. Etruscan art is its highlight, and there are a few examples of Roman art. Antique sculptures, clay figurines, and bronze art of the Antikensammlung (Antiquities Collection) are also housed here; the other part of the collection is in the Pergamonmuseum. At the northern tip of Museum Island is the **Bode-Museum,** a somber-looking gray edifice graced with elegant columns. The museum presents the state museums' stunning collection of German and Italian sculptures since the Middle Ages, the Museum of Byzantine Art, and a huge coin collection. Even if you think you aren't interested in the ancient world, make an exception for the **Pergamonmuseum** (entrance on Am Kupfergraben), one of the world's greatest museums. The museum's name is derived from its principal display, the Pergamon Altar, a monumental Greek temple discovered in what is now Turkey and dating from 180 BC. The altar was shipped to Berlin in the late 19th century. Equally impressive are the gateway to the Roman town of Miletus and the Babylonian pro-

cessional way. Museum Island's new shining star, however, is the **Neues Museum** (New Museum), which reopened in 2009. Originally designed by Friedrich August Stüler in 1843–55, the building was badly damaged in World War II and has only now been elaborately redeveloped by British star architect David Chipperfield, who has been overseeing the complete restoration of Museum Island. Instead of completely restoring the Neues Museum, the architect decided to integrate modern elements into the historic landmark, while leaving many of its heavily bombed and dilapidated areas untouched. The result is a stunning experience, considered by many to be one of the world's greatest museums. Home to the Egyptian Museum, including the famous bust of Nefertiti (who, after some 70 years, has returned to her first museum location in Berlin), it also features the Papyrus Collection and the Museum of Prehistory and Early History. If you get tired of antiques and paintings, drop by any of the museums' cafés. ⊠ *Museumsinsel, Mitte* 🕾 *030/2664–24242* ⊕ *www.smb.museum* 🖾 *All Museum Island museums: €18* ☉ *Pergamonmuseum: Fri.–Wed. 10–6, Thurs. 10–8. Alte Nationalgalerie: Tues., Wed., and Fri.–Sun. 10–6; Thurs. 10–8. Altes Museum: Tues., Wed., and Fri.–Sun. 10–6; Thurs. 10–8. Neues Museum: Fri.–Wed. 10–6, Thurs. 10–8. Bode-Museum: Tues., Wed., and Fri.–Sun. 10–6; Thurs. 10–8* Ⓜ *Hackescher Markt (S-bahn).*

Neue Synagoge (*New Synagogue*). This meticulously restored landmark, built between 1859 and 1866, is an exotic amalgam of styles, the whole faintly Middle Eastern. Its bulbous, gilded cupola stands out in the skyline. When its doors opened, it was the largest synagogue in Europe, with 3,200 seats. The synagogue was damaged on November 9, 1938 (*Kristallnacht*—Night of the Broken Glass), when Nazi looters rampaged across Germany, burning synagogues and smashing the few Jewish shops and homes left in the country. It was destroyed by Allied bombing in 1943, and it wasn't until the mid-1980s that the East German government restored it. The effective exhibit on the history of the building and its congregants includes fragments of the original architecture and furnishings. ■TIP→ **Sabbath services are held in a modern addition.** ✉ *Oranienburger Str. 28–30, Mitte* ☎ *030/8802–8300* ⊕ *www.zentrumjudaicum.de* ☐ *€3.50* ☼ *Apr.–Sept., Sun.–Mon. 10–8, Tues.–Thurs. 10-6, Fri. 10–5; Nov.-Feb., Sun.–Thurs. 10–6, Fri. 10–2; Mar. and Oct., Sun.–Mon. 10-8, Tues.–Thurs. 10–6, Fri. 10–2. English/Hebrew audio guides €3* Ⓜ *Oranienburger Tor (U-bahn), Oranienburger Strasse (S-bahn).*

Neugerriemschneider. One of Berlin's heavy hitters, this Mitte gallery with a seemingly unpronounceable name (it's actually the names of the two founders combined), has either represented or hosted shows by such art world luminaries as Olafur Eliasson, Ai Weiwei, Billy Childish, and Keith Edmier. ✉ *Linenstr. 155, Mitte* ☎ *030/2887–7277* ⊕ *www.neugerriemschneider.com* ☼ *Tues.–Sat. 11–6* Ⓜ *Oranienburger Strasse (S-bahn) and Oranienburger Tor (U-bahn).*

Nikolaiviertel (*Nicholas Quarter*). Renovated in the 1980s and a tad concrete-heavy as a result, this tiny quarter grew up around Berlin's oldest parish church, the medieval, twin-spire **St. Nikolaikirche** (St. Nicholas's Church), now a museum, dating from 1230. The adjacent Fischerinsel (Fisherman's Island) area was the heart of Berlin 765 years ago, and retains a bit of its medieval character. At Breite Strasse you'll find two of Berlin's oldest buildings: No. 35 is the **Ribbeckhaus,** the city's only surviving Renaissance structure, dating from 1624, and No. 36 is the early baroque **Marstall,** built by Michael Matthais between 1666 and 1669. The area feels rather artificial, but draws tourists to its gift stores, cafés, and restaurants. ✉ *Church: Nikolaikirchpl., Mitte* ☎ *030/2400–2162* ⊕ *www.stadtmuseum.de* Ⓜ *Alexanderplatz (U-bahn and S-bahn).*

Fodor's Choice ★ **Reichstag** (*Parliament Building*). After last meeting here in 1933, the Bundestag, Germany's federal parliament, returned to its traditional seat in the spring of 1999. British architect Sir Norman Foster lightened up the gray monolith with a glass dome, which quickly became one of the city's main attractions: you can circle up a gently rising ramp while taking in the rooftops of Berlin and the parliamentary chamber below. At the base of the dome is an exhibit on the Reichstag's history, in German and English. Completed in 1894, the Reichstag housed the imperial German parliament and later served a similar function during the ill-fated Weimar Republic. On the night of February 27, 1933, the Reichstag burned down in an act of arson, a pivotal event in Third Reich history. The fire led to state protection laws that gave the Nazis a pretext to arrest their political opponents. The Reichstag was rebuilt but again badly damaged in 1945. The graffiti of the victorious Russian soldiers can still be seen on some of the walls in the hallways. After terrorism warnings at the end of 2010, the Reichstag tightened its door policy, asking all visitors to register their names and birthdates in advance and reserve a place on a guided tour. Since then, the crowds that used to snake around the outside of the building have subsided, and a visit is worth the planning. ■TIP→ As always, a reservation at the pricey rooftop Käfer restaurant (☎ *030/2262–9933*) will also get you in. Those with reservations can use the doorway to the right of the Reichstag's main staircase. The building is surrounded by ultramodern federal government offices, such as the boxy, concrete **Bundeskanzleramt** (Federal Chancellery), which also has a nickname of course: the "Washing Machine." Built by Axel Schultes, it's one of the few new buildings in the government district by a Berlin architect. Participating in a guided tour of the Chancellery is possible if you apply

WORD OF MOUTH

"If you make restaurant reservations for the Reichstag you skip the line. It's nice to eat up there. Don't expect any bargains, though." —lincasanova

in writing several weeks prior to a visit. A riverwalk with great views of the government buildings begins behind the Reichstag. ⊠ *Platz der Republik 1, Mitte* ☎ *030/2273–2152 Reichstag* ⊕ *www.bundestag.de* 🖃 *Free with prior registration* ⊙ *Daily 8 am–11 pm* Ⓜ *Unter den Linden (S-bahn), Bundestag (U-bahn).*

Sammlung Boros. This private collection has become one of Berlin's star attractions, thanks to its unusual location inside a hulking WWII bunker in Mitte. Contemporary art collector Christian Boros bought the bunker in 2003 to house his art, and built a glass penthouse on top to house his family. The best works are those created specifically for the space by well-known artists such as Ai Weiwei, Olafur Eliasson, and Tomás Saraceno. ∎**TIP**➔ **Since this is a private home, admission is only allowed on guided tours, which take place Thursday to Sunday and can be booked online. The tours are popular, so book as early as you can.** ⊠ *Reinhardtstr. 20, Mitte* ⊕ *www.sammlung-boros.de/* ⊙ *Thurs.–Sun. by prebooked tour* Ⓜ *Oranienburger Tor (U-bahn) and Friedrichstrasse (S-bahn and U-bahn).*

Fodors Choice
★
Topographie des Terrors (*Topography of Terror*). Before 2010, Topographie des Terrors was an open-air exhibit, fully exposed to the elements. Now, in a stunning new indoor exhibition center at the same location, you can view photos and documents explaining the secret state police and intelligence organizations that planned and executed Nazi crimes against humanity. The fates of both victims and perpatrators are given equal attention here. The cellar remains of the Nazis' Reich Security Main Office (composed of the SS, SD, and Gestapo) where the main exhibit used to be, are still open to the public and now contain other exhibitions, which typically run from April to October as the remains are open air. ⊠ *Niederkirchnerstr. 8, Mitte* ☎ *030/2545–0950* ⊕ *www. topographie.de* 🖃 *Free* ⊙ *Daily 10–8.*

Unter den Linden. The name of this historic Berlin thoroughfare, between the Brandenburg Gate and Schlossplatz, means "under the linden trees," and it was indeed lined with fragrant and beloved lindens until the 1930s. Imagine Berliners' shock when Hitler decided to fell the trees in order to make the street more parade-friendly. The grand boulevard began as a riding path that the royals used to get from their palace to their hunting grounds (now the central Berlin park called Tiergarten). It is once again lined with linden trees planted after World War II. ⊠ *Mitte.*

WORTH NOTING

Alexanderplatz (*Alex*). This bleak square, bordered by the train station, the Galeria Kaufhof department store, and the 37-story Park Inn Berlin-Alexanderplatz hotel, once formed the hub of East Berlin and was originally named in 1805 for czar Alexander I. German writer Alfred Döblin dubbed it the "heart of a world metropolis" (text from his 1929 novel *Berlin Alexanderplatz* is written on a building across the northeastern side of the square). Today it's a basic center of commerce and the occasional demonstration. The unattractive modern buildings are a reminder not just of the results of Allied bombing but also of the ruthlessness practiced by East Germans when they demolished what remained. A famous meeting point in the south corner is the World Time Clock (1969), which even keeps tabs on Tijuana. ⊠ *Mitte.*

WORD OF MOUTH

"Like New York City and Paris, Berlin is a city I can visit over and over again and never get bored. . . . An enjoyable trip to Alexanderplatz reminds me of some of the reasons I love this city. Surrounded by restaurants, shops and beautiful buildings like the Berliner Dom this is a nice area to spend some time on a summer afternoon." —DMBTraveler

FAMILY **AquaDom & Sea Life Berlin.** These commercially run, giant indoor tanks showcase local marine life, beginning with the Spree River, moving on to Berlin's lakes, and then taking you from fresh- to saltwater. Waterfront city scenes are part of the decor, which gradually give way to starfish-petting beds, overhead tanks, and a submarine-like room. Don't come looking for sharks or colorful tropical fish: the most exotic creatures here are perhaps the tiny sea horses and spotted rays. The aquarium's finale is the Aquadom, a state-of-the-art glass elevator that brings you through a silo-shaped fish tank to the exit. Young children love this place, but the timed wait for the elevator can be frustrating for all ages. Be prepared for a line at the entrance, too. ⊠ *Spandauer Str. 3, Mitte* ☎ *030/992–800* ⊕ *www.sealife.de* ☞ *€17.50, €11.35 online/in advance* ☉ *Daily 10–7; last admission at 6* Ⓜ *Hackescher Markt (S-bahn).*

Berliner Rathaus (*Berlin Town Hall*). Nicknamed the "*Rotes Rathaus*" (Red Town Hall) for its redbrick design, the town hall was completed in 1869. Its most distinguishing features are its neo-Renaissance clock tower and frieze that depicts Berlin's history up to 1879 in 36 terracotta plaques, each 20 feet long. Climb the grand stairwell to view the coat-of-arms hall and a few exhibits. ■TIP→ **The Rathaus has a very inexpensive, cafeteria-style canteen offering budget lunches. The entrance is inside the inner courtyard.** ⊠ *Rathausstr. 15, Mitte* ☎ *030/90260* ☞ *Free* ☉ *Weekdays 9–6* Ⓜ *Alexanderplatz (U-bahn and S-bahn).*

Brecht-Weigel-Gedenkstätte (*Brecht-Weigel Memorial Site*). You can visit the former working and living quarters of playwright Bertolt Brecht and his wife, actress Helene Weigel, and scholars can browse through the Brecht library (by appointment only). The downstairs restaurant serves Viennese cuisine using Weigel's recipes. Brecht, Weigel, and more than 100 other celebrated Germans are interred in the **Dorotheenstädtischer Friedhof** (Dorotheenstadt Cemetery) next door. ■TIP→ **The house can only be visited on tours, which take place every half-hour, in German. Call ahead to schedule an English tour.** ⊠ *Chausseestr. 125, Mitte* ☎ *030/20057-1844* ☞ *Apartment €3, library free.*

Deutscher Dom. The Deutscher Dom holds an extensive exhibition on the emergence of the democratic parliamentary system in Germany since the late 1800s. The free museum is sponsored by the German parliament. Leadership and opposition in East Germany are also documented. ■ TIP→ **An English-language audio guide covers a portion of the exhibits on the first three floors.** Floors four and five have temporary exhibitions with no English text or audio. ⊠ *Gendarmenmarkt 1, Mitte* ☎ *030/2273–0431* 🎟 *Free* 🕙 *Oct.–Apr., Tues.–Sun. 10–6; May–Sept., Tues.–Sun. 10–7.*

Hamburger Bahnhof - Museum für Gegenwart (*Museum of Contemporary Art*). This light-filled, remodeled train station is home to a rich survey of post-1960 Western art. The permanent collection includes installations by German artists Joseph Beuys and Anselm Kiefer, as well as paintings by Andy Warhol, Cy Twombly, Robert Rauschenberg, and Robert Morris. An annex presents the hotly debated Friedrich Christian Flick Collection, the largest and most valuable collection of the latest in the world's contemporary art. The 2,000 works rotate, but you're bound to see some by Bruce Naumann, Rodney Graham, and Pipilotti Rist. ⊠ *Invalidenstr. 50–51, Mitte* ☎ *030/39783411* ⊕ *www.smb. museum* 🎟 *€12* 🕙 *Tues., Weds., Fri. 10–6, Thurs. 10–8, Sat.–Sun. 11–6* Ⓜ *Naturkundemuseum (U-bahn), Hauptbahnhof (S-bahn).*

Humboldt-Universität. Running the length of the west side of Bebelplatz, the former royal library is now part of Humboldt-Universität, whose main campus is across the street on Unter den Linden. The university building was built between 1748 and 1766 as a palace for Prince Heinrich, the brother of Frederick the Great. With its founding in 1810, the university moved in. The fairy-tale-collecting Grimm brothers taught here, and political philosophers Karl Marx and Friedrich Engels studied within its hallowed halls. Albert Einstein taught physics from 1914 to 1929, when he left Berlin for the United States. ⊠ *Unter den Linden 6, Mitte.*

The Kennedys. In West Berlin in 1963, John F. Kennedy surveyed the recently erected Berlin Wall, and said "Ich bin ein Berliner"—I am one with the people of Berlin. And with that, he secured his fame throughout Germany. He's honored in this small but intriguing museum, which used to reside opposite the American embassy on Pariser Platz, but has since found a new home in the Ehemalige Jüdische Mädchenschule. With photographs, personal memorabilia, documents, and films, the collection traces the fascination JFK and the Kennedy clan evoked in Berlin and elsewhere. ⊠ *Auguststr. 11-13, in the Ehemalige Jüdische Mädchenschule, Mitte* ☎ *030/2065–3570* ⊕ *www.thekennedys.de* 🎟 *€5* 🕙 *Daily 11–7* Ⓜ *Oranienburger Strasse (S-bahn).*

Märkisches Museum (*Brandenburg Museum*). This redbrick attic includes exhibits on the city's theatrical past, its guilds, its newspapers, and the March 1848 revolution. Paintings capture the look of the city before it crumbled in World War II. ■ TIP→ **On Sunday at 3 pm, fascinating mechanical musical instruments from the collection are played.** ⊠ *Am Köllnischen Park 5, Mitte* ☎ *030/2400–2162* ⊕ *www.stadtmuseum.de* 🎟 *€5* 🕙 *Tues.–Sun. 10–6* Ⓜ *Märkisches Museum (U-bahn).*

Neue Wache (*New Guardhouse*). One of many Berlin projects by the early-19th-century architect Karl Friedrich Schinkel, this building served as both the Royal Prussian War Memorial (honoring the dead of the Napoleonic Wars) and the royal guardhouse until the kaiser abdicated in 1918. In 1931 it became a memorial to those who fell in World War I. Badly damaged in World War II, it was restored in 1960 by the East German state and rededicated as a memorial for the victims of militarism and fascism. After unification it regained its Weimar Republic appearance and was inaugurated as Germany's central war memorial. Inside is a copy of Berlin sculptor Käthe Kollwitz's *Pietà*, showing a mother mourning over her dead son. The inscription in front of it reads, "to the victims of war and tyranny." ⊠ *Unter den Linden, Mitte* ⊙ *Daily 10–6.*

St. Hedwigs-Kathedrale (*St. Hedwig's Cathedral*). The green-patina dome belongs to St. Hedwigskathedrale. Begun in 1747, it was modeled after the Pantheon in Rome, and was the first Catholic church built in resolutely Protestant Berlin since the 16th-century Reformation. It was Frederick the Great's effort to appease Prussia's Catholic population after his invasion of Catholic Silesia (then Poland). A treasury lies inside. ⊠ *Bebelpl., Mitte* ☎ *030/203–4810* ⊕ *www.hedwigs-kathedrale.de* ⊙ *Weekdays 10–5, Sun. 1–5* Ⓜ *Französische Strasse (U-bahn)* ⚲ *Tours (€3) available in English, call ahead.*

St. Marienkirche (*St. Mary's Church*). This medieval church, one of the finest in Berlin, is best known for its late-Gothic, macabre fresco *Der Totentanz* (*Dance of Death*), which is in need of restoration. Tours on Tuesday at 2 pm highlight the fresco. ⊠ *Karl-Liebknecht-Str. 8, Mitte* ☎ *030/3024-759510* ⊙ *Daily 10–9. Organ recital Thurs., Fri. at 1:30pm and Sat. at 4:30 pm* Ⓜ *Alexanderplatz (U-bahn and S-bahn), Hackescher Markt (S-bahn).*

TIERGARTEN

The Tiergarten, a bucolic 630-acre park with lakes, meadows, and wide paths, is the "green heart" of Berlin. In the 17th century it served as the hunting grounds of the Great Elector (its name translates into "animal garden"). Now it's the Berliners' backyard for sunbathing and barbecuing.

The government district, Potsdamer Platz, and the embassy district ring the park from its eastern to southern edges.

TIMING

A leisurely walk from Zoo Station through the Tiergarten to the Brandenburger Tor and the Reichstag will take at least 90 minutes.

TOP ATTRACTIONS

Tiergarten (*Animal Garden*). The quiet greenery of the 630-acre Tiergarten is a beloved oasis, with some 23 km (14 mi) of footpaths, meadows, and two beer gardens. The inner park's 6½ acres of lakes and ponds were landscaped by garden architect Joseph Peter Lenné in the mid-1800s. ⊠ *Tiergarten.*

Café am Neuen See. On the shore of the lake in the southwest corner of the park, you can relax at the Café am Neuen See, a café and beer garden. ■TIP→ For a particularly nice walk here from the S-bahn stop at Zoologischer Garten, take the path into the Tiergarten, then turn right at Schleusenkrug to follow the Landwehrkanal around the back of the zoo. Sneak a peek at the owls, flamingoes, and ostriches for free. ✉ *Lichtensteinallee 2, Tiergarten* ☎ *030/254–4930* ⊕ *www.cafe-am-neuen-see. de/* ☉ *Open daily 9–late*

Haus der Kulturen der Welt. Off the Spree River and bordering the Kanzleramt (Chancellery) is the former congress hall, now serving as the Haus der Kulturen der Welt. It is fondly referred to as the "pregnant oyster" because the sweeping, 1950's design of its roof resembles a shellfish opening. Thematic exhibits, festivals, and concerts take place here, and it's also a boarding point for Spree River cruises. ✉ *House of World Cultures, John-Foster-Dulles Allee 10, Tiergarten* ☎ *030/397–870* ⊕ *www.hkw.de* ☉ *Daily, 10 - 7*

FAMILY **Zoologischer Garten** (*Zoological Gardens*). Even though Knut, the polar bear cub who captured the heart of the city, is sadly no longer with us, there are 14,000 other animals to see here, many of whom may be happy to have their time in the spotlight once again. There are 1,500 different species (more than any other zoo in Europe), including those rare and endangered, which the zoo has been successful at breeding. New arrivals in the past years include a baby rhinoceros. The animals' enclosures are designed to resemble their natural habitats, though some structures are ornate, such as the 1910 Arabian-style Zebra House. Pythons, frogs, turtles, invertebrates, Komodo dragons, and an amazing array of strange and colorful fish are part of the three-floor aquarium. ■TIP→ Check the feeding times posted to watch creatures such as seals, apes, hippos, crocodiles, and pelicans during their favorite time of day. ✉ *Hardenbergpl. 8 and Budapester Str. 32, Tiergarten* ☎ *030/254–010* ⊕ *www.zoo-berlin.de* ✉ *Zoo or aquarium €13, combined ticket €20* ☉ *Zoo: Oct.–mid-Mar., daily 9–5; mid-Mar.–Aug., daily 9–7; Sept.-Oct., daily 9–6:30; Aquarium: daily 9–6* Ⓜ *Zoologischer Garten (U-bahn and S-bahn).*

■ NEED A BREAK?

Schleusenkrug. Forget the fast-food options at Zoo Station. Instead, follow the train tracks to the back of the taxi and bus queues, where you'll enter Tiergarten and within 100 yards come upon the best hideaway in the area: Schleusenkrug. In warmer weather you can order at the window and sit in the beer garden or on the back patio, watching pleasure ships go through the lock. Inside is a casual restaurant with a changing daily menu. Between November and mid-March the Krug closes at 7 pm. ✉ *Tiergarten, Müller-Breslau-Str., Tiergarten* ☎ *030/313–9909* ⊕ *www.schleusenkrug. de/* ☉ *Daily 10 - 12 am.*

WORTH NOTING

Siegessäule (*Victory Column*). The 227-foot granite, sandstone, and bronze column is topped by a winged, golden goddess and has a splendid view of Berlin. It was erected in front of the Reichstag in 1873 to

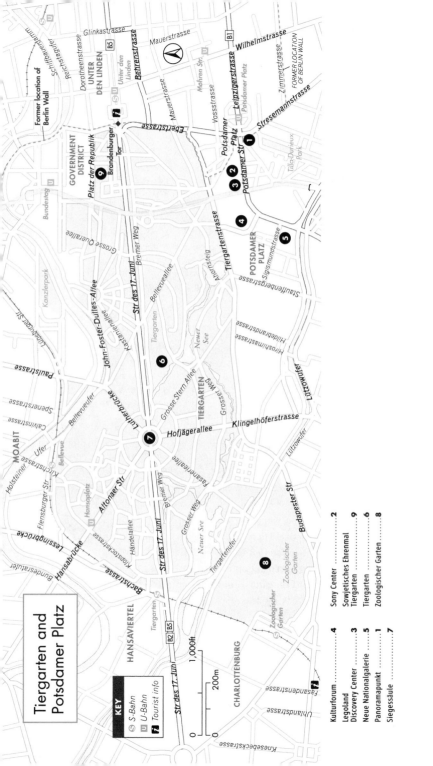

Tiergarten and Potsdamer Platz

KEY

Ⓢ S-Bahn
Ⓤ U-Bahn
🛈 Tourist info

0   200m
0   1,000ft

Kulturforum 4
Legoland
Discovery Center 3
Neue Nationalgalerie 5
Panoramapunkt 1
Siegessäule 7

Sony Center 2
Sowjetisches Ehrenmal
Tiergarten 9
Tiergarten 6
Zoologischer Garten 8

commemorate Prussia's military successes and then moved to the Tiergarten in 1938–39. You have to climb 270 steps up through the column to reach the observation platform, but the view is rewarding. The gold-tipped cannons surrounding the column are those the Prussians captured from the French in the Franco-Prussian War. ☒ *Strasse des 17. Juni/Am Grossen Stern, Mitte* ☎ *030/391–2961* ☒ *€2.20* ☉ *Nov.–Mar., weekdays 10–5, weekends 10–5:30; Apr.–Oct., weekdays 9:30–6:30, weekends 9:30–7; last admission ½ hr before closing.* Ⓜ *Tiergarten (S-bahn), Bellevue (S-bahn).*

Sowjetisches Ehrenmal Tiergarten (*Soviet Memorial*). Built immediately after World War II, this monument stands as a reminder of the Soviet victory over the shattered German army in Berlin in May 1945. The Battle of Berlin was one of the deadliest on the European front. It's one of several memorials in Berlin erected by the Soviet Union to commemorate its war dead. A hulking bronze statue of a soldier stands atop a marble plinth taken from Hitler's former Reichkanzlei (headquarters). The memorial is flanked by what are said to be the first two T-34 tanks to have fought their way into the city. ☒ *Str. des 17. Juni, Tiergarten* Ⓜ *Unter den Linden (S-bahn).*

POTSDAMER PLATZ

The once-divided Berlin is rejoined at Potsdamer Platz, which now links Kreuzberg with the former East once again. Potsdamer Platz was Berlin's inner-city center and Europe's busiest plaza before World War II. Bombings and the Wall left this area a sprawling, desolate lot, where tourists in West Berlin could climb a wooden platform to peek into East Berlin's death strip. After the Wall fell, various international companies made a rush to build their German headquarters on this prime real estate. In the mid-1990s, Potsdamer Platz became Europe's largest construction site. Today's modern complexes of red sandstone, terracotta tiles, steel, and glass have made it a city within a city.

A few narrow streets cut between the hulking modern architecture, which includes two high-rise office towers owned by Daimler, one of which was designed by star architect Renzo Piano. The round atrium of the Sony Center comes closest to a traditional square used as a public meeting point. Farther down Potsdamer Strasse are the state museums and cultural institutes of the Kulturforum.

TOP ATTRACTIONS

Fodor'sChoice **Kulturforum** (*Cultural Forum*). This unique ensemble of museums, galleries, and the Philharmonic Hall was long in the making. The first
★ designs were submitted in the 1960s and the last building completed in 1998. Now it forms a welcome modern counterpoint to the thoroughly restored Prussian splendor of Museum Island, although Berliners and tourists alike hold drastically differing opinions on the area's architectural aesthetics. Whatever your opinion, Kulturforum's artistic holdings are unparalleled and worth at least a day of your time, if not more. The Kulturforum includes the **Gemäldegalerie** (Picture Gallery), the **Kunstbibliothek** (Art Library), the **Kupferstichkabinett** (Print Cabinet), the **Kunstgewerbemuseum** (Museum of Decorative Arts), which

is closed until at least 2014 for renovations, the **Philharmonie**, the **Musikinstrumenten-Museum** (Musical Instruments Museum), and the **Staatsbibliothek** (National Library). ⊠ *Potsdamer Platz.*

Gemäldegalerie (*Picture Gallery*). The Kulturforum's Gemäldegalerie reunites formerly separated collections from East and West Berlin. It's one of Germany's finest art galleries, and has an extensive selection of European paintings from the 13th to 18th century. Seven rooms are reserved for paintings by German masters, among them Dürer, Cranach the Elder, and Holbein. A special collection has works of the Italian masters—Botticelli, Titian, Giotto, Lippi, and Raphael—as well as paintings by Dutch and Flemish masters of the 15th and 16th centuries: Van Eyck, Bosch, Brueghel the Elder, and van der Weyden. The museum also holds the world's second-largest Rembrandt collection. ⊠ *Kulturforum, Matthäikirchplatz, Potsdamer Platz* ☎ *030/2664–24242* ⊕ *www. smb.museum* ⊠ *€10* ⊙ *Tues., Wed., and Fri.–Sun. 10–6; Thurs. 10–8* Ⓜ *Potsdamer Platz [U-bahn and S-bahn]*

Kunstbibliothek (*Art Library*). With more than 400,000 volumes on the history of European art, the Kunstbibliothek (art library), in the Kulturforum, is one of Germany's most important institutions on the subject. It contains art posters and advertisements, examples of graphic design and book design, ornamental engravings, prints and drawings, and a costume library. Visitors can view items in the reading rooms, but many samples from the collections are also shown in rotating special exhibitions. ⊠ *Kulturforum, Matthäikirchpl., Potsdamer Platz* ☎ *030/2664–24242* ⊕ *www.smb.museum* ⊠ *Varies according to exhibition* ⊙ *Tues.–Fri. 10–6, weekends 11-6; reading room weekdays 9–8*

Kupferstichkabinett (*Drawings and Prints Collection*). One of the Kulturforum's smaller museums, Kupferstichkabinett has occasional exhibits, which include European woodcuts, engravings, and illustrated books from the 15th century to the present (highlights of its holdings are pen-and-ink drawings by Dürer and drawings by Rembrandt). You can request to see one or two drawings in the study room. Another building displays paintings dating from the late Middle Ages to 1800. ⊠ *Kulturforum, Matthäikirchpl. 4, Potsdamer Platz* ☎ *030/2664–24242* ⊕ *www. smb.museum* ⊠ *€6* ⊙ *Tues.–Fri. 10–6, weekends 11–6*

Musikinstrumenten-Museum (*Musical Instruments Museum*). Across the parking lot from the Philharmonie, the Kulturforum's Musikinstrumenten-Museum has a fascinating collection of keyboard, string, wind, and percussion instruments. ■TIP→ **These are demonstrated during an 11 am tour on Saturday, which closes with a 20-minute Wurlitzer organ concert for an extra €2.** ⊠ *Kulturforum, Ben-Gurion-Str. 1, Potsdamer Platz* ☎ *030/2548–1178* ⊕ *www.sim.spk-berlin.de/* ⊠ *€6* ⊙ *Tues., Wed., and Fri. 9–5; Thurs. 9–8; weekends 10–5*

Staatsbibliothek (*National Library*). The Kulturforum's Staatsbibliothek is one of the largest libraries in Europe, and was one of the Berlin settings in Wim Wenders's 1987 film *Wings of Desire.* ⊠ *Kulturforum, Potsdamer Str. 33, Potsdamer Platz* ☎ *030/2664-32333* ⊕ *staatsbibliothek-berlin.de* ⊙ *Weekdays 9–9, Sat. 10–7*

Neue Nationalgalerie (*New National Gallery*). Bauhaus member Mies van der Rohe originally designed this glass-box structure for Bacardi Rum in Cuba, but Berlin became the site of its realization in 1968. The main exhibits are below ground. Highlights of the collection of 20th-century paintings, sculptures, and drawings include works by expressionists Otto Dix, Ernst Ludwig Kirchner, and Georg Grosz. Special exhibits often take precedence over the permanent collection. ✉ *Potsdamer Str. 50, Potsdamer Platz* ☎ *030/2664–24242* ⊕ *www.smb. museum* 🖼 *Varies according to exhibition* ⊙ *Tues., Wed., and Fri. 10–6; Thurs. 10–8; weekends 11–6* Ⓜ *Potsdamer Platz (U-bahn and S-bahn).*

Panoramapunkt. Located 300 feet above Potsdamer Platz at the top of one of its tallest towers, the new Panoramapunkt (Panoramic Viewing Point) not only features the world's highest-standing original piece of the Berlin wall, but also a fascinating, multimedia exhibit about the dramatic history of Berlin's former urban center. A café and a sun terrace facing west make this open-air viewing platform one of the city's most romantic. ✉ *Potsdamer Pl. 1, Potsdamer Platz* ☎ *030/2593–7080* ⊕ *www.panoramapunkt.de* 🖼 *€5.50* ⊙ *Summer daily 10–8, Winter daily 10-5, last entrance 30 minutes before closing.*

Sony Center. This glass-and-steel construction wraps around a spectacular circular forum. Topping it off is a tentlike structure meant to emulate Mount Fuji. The architectural jewel, designed by German-American architect Helmut Jahn, is one of the most stunning public spaces of Berlin's new center, filled with restaurants, cafés, movie theaters, and apartments. A faint reminder of glorious days gone by is the old **Kaisersaal** (Emperor's Hall), held within a very modern glass enclosure, and today a pricey restaurant. The hall originally stood 75 yards away in the Grand Hotel Esplanade (built in 1907) but was moved here lock, stock, and barrel. Red-carpet glamour returns every February with the Berlinale Film Festival, which has screenings at the commercial cinema within the center. ✉ *Potsdamer Platz.*

Deutsche Kinemathek Museum für Film und Fernsehen. Within the Sony Center is the small but fun Museum für Film und Fernsehen, which presents the groundbreaking history of German moviemaking with eye-catching displays. Descriptions are in English, and there's an audio guide as well. Memorabilia includes personal belongings of Marlene Dietrich and other German stars, while special exhibitions go into depth about outstanding directors, movements, and studios. A good selection of films, from the best classics to the virtually unknown art house finds, are shown in the theater on the lower level. During the Berlinale film festival in February, this place becomes one of the centers of the action. ✉ *Sony Building, Potsdamer Str. 2, Potsdamer Platz* ☎ *030/300–9030* ⊕ *www.deutsche-kinemathek.de* 🖼 *€7* ⊙ *Tues., Wed., and Fri.–Sun. 10–6, Thurs. 10–8*

WORTH NOTING

FAMILY **Legoland Discovery Centre.** A must-see when traveling with children is the Legoland Discovery Centre, the Danish toy company's only indoor park. Children can build their very own towers while their parents live out their urban development dreams, even testing if the miniature construction would survive an earthquake. In a special section, Berlin's landmarks are presented in a breathtaking miniature world made up of thousands of tiny Lego bricks. ⊠ *Potsdamer Str. 4, Potsdamer Platz* ☎ *030/301–0400* ⊕ *www.legolanddiscoverycentre.de* 🎫 *€15.95, €7 online* ⊗ *Daily 10–7; last admittance 5 pm.*

FRIEDRICHSHAIN

The cobblestone streets of Friedrichshain, bustling with bars, cafés, and shops, give it a Greenwich Village feel. There's plenty to see here including Karl-Marx-Allee, a long, monumental boulevard lined by grand Stalinist apartment buildings (conceived of as "palaces for the people" that would show the superiority of the Communist system over the Capitalist one); the area's funky parks; the East Side Gallery; and lively Simon-Dach-Strasse. It's cool, it's hip, it's historical. If you're into street art, this is a good place to wander.

TOP ATTRACTIONS

Fodor'sChoice ★ **East Side Gallery.** This 1-km (½-mi) stretch of concrete went from guarded border to open-air gallery within three months. East Berliners breached the Wall on November 9, 1989, and between February and June of 1990, 118 artists from around the globe created unique works of art on its longest-remaining section. Restoration in 2010 renewed the old images with a fresh coat of paint, but while the colors of the artworks now look like new, the gallery has lost a bit of its charm. One of the best-known works, by Russian artist Dmitri Vrubel, depicts Brezhnev and Honnecker (the former East German leader) kissing, with the caption "My God. Help me survive this deadly love." The stretch along the Spree Canal runs between the Warschauer Strasse S- and U-bahn station and Ostbahnhof. The redbrick Oberbaumbrücke (an 1896 bridge) at Warschauer Strasse makes that end more scenic. Just past the bridge there's also a man-made beach with a bar, restaurant, and club popular with the after-work crowd, called Strandgut (⊕ www.strandgut-berlin.com). ⊠ *Mühlenstr., Friedrichshain* Ⓜ *Warschauer Strasse (U-bahn and S-bahn), Ostbahnhof (S-bahn).*

KREUZBERG

Hip Kreuzberg, stretching from the West Berlin side of the border crossing at Checkpoint Charlie all the way to the banks of the Spree next to Friedrichshain, is home base for much of Berlin's famed nightclub scene and a great place to get a feel for young Berlin. A large Turkish population shares the residential streets with a variegated assortment of political radicals and bohemians of all nationalities. In the minds of most Berliners, it is split into two even smaller sections: Kreuzberg 61 is a little more upscale, and contains a variety of small and elegant shops and restaurants, while Kreuzberg 36 has stayed grittier, as exemplified by the garbage-strewn, drug-infested, but much-beloved Görlitzer Park. Oranienstrasse, the spine of life in the Kreuzberg 36 district, has mellowed from hardcore to funky since reunification. When Kreuzberg literally had its back against the Wall, West German social outcasts, punks, and the radical left made this old working-class street their territory. Since the 1970s the population has also been largely Turkish, and many of yesterday's outsiders have turned into successful owners of shops and cafés. The most vibrant stretch is between Skalitzer Strasse and Oranienplatz. Use Bus M29 or the Görlitzer Bahnhof or Kottbusser Tor U-bahn stations to reach it.

TIMING

Owing to its small size and popularity, you may experience a wait or slow line at the Checkpoint Charlie Museum. Monday is a popular day for this museum—and for the nearby, must-see Jüdisches Museum—since the state museums are closed that day.

TOP ATTRACTIONS

Blain|Southern. The Berlin branch of a swish London gallery, Blain|Southern occupies a breathtaking loft space that once housed the printing presses of Tagesspiegel, the daily Berlin newspaper. Since opening in 2010, the gallery has highlighted star artists like Douglas Gordon, Lawrence Weiner, and Jannis Kounellis. ⊠ *Potsdamerstr. 77–87, Kreuzberg* ☎ *030/6449–31510* ⊕ *www.blainsouthern.com* ۞ *Tues.–Sat. 11–6* Ⓜ *Kurfürstenstrasse (U-bahn).*

Galeria Plan B. In March 2012, Romanian gallery Plan B moved into an industrial space deep within the Tagesspiegel building complex. This is the place to see offbeat Eastern European art. ⊠ *Potsdamerstr. 77–87, Bldg. G, 2nd courtyard, Kreuzberg* ☎ *030/3980–5236* ⊕ *www.plan-b. ro* ۞ *Tues.–Sat. noon–6* Ⓜ *Kurfürstenstrasse (U-bahn).*

Galerie Isabella Bortolozzi. Bortolozzi consistently spots and cultivates the hottest young talent in the city (like Danh Vo), showing their work in a quirky, wood-paneled space. ⊠ *Schöneberger Ufer 61, Kreuzberg* ☎ *030/2639–4985* ⊕ *www.bortolozzi.com* ۞ *Tues.–Sat. noon–6 pm* Ⓜ *Potsdamer Platz (U-bahn and S-bahn) or Mendelsohn-Bartholdy Park (U-bahn).*

Galerie Verein Berliner Künstler. Founded in 1841, this is the oldest artist association in Germany. Its lavish townhouse gallery spaces often highlight the work of its 120-odd artist members. ⊠ *Schöneberger Ufer 57, Kreuzberg* ☎ *030/261–2399* ⊕ *vbk-art.de* ۞ *Tues.–Fri. 3–7 pm, weekends 2–6 pm* Ⓜ *Potsdamer Platz (U-bahn and S-bahn) or Mendelssohn-Bartholdy Park (U-bahn).*

Helga Maria Klosterfelde Edition. This gallery exhibits and sells multiples and editions by Matt Mullican, Jorinda Voigt, Hanne Darboven, and other art stars. ⊠ *Potsdamerstr. 97, Kreuzberg* ☎ *030/9700–5099* ⊕ *www.helgamariaklosterfelde.de* ۞ *Tues.–Sat. 11–6* Ⓜ *Kurfürstenstrasse (U-bahn).*

Fodor's Choice ★ **Mauermuseum-Museum Haus am Checkpoint Charlie.** Just steps from the famous crossing point between the two Berlins, the Wall Museum-House at Checkpoint Charlie presents visitors with the story of the Wall and, even more riveting, the stories of those who escaped through, under, and over it. An infamous hot spot during the Cold War, this border crossing for non-Germans was manned by the Soviet military in East Berlin's Mitte district and, several yards south, by the U.S. military in West Berlin's Kreuzberg district. Tension between the superpowers in October 1961 led to an uneasy standoff between Soviet and

Symbols and Shifts in East and West

The year 2009 marked the 20th anniversary of the fall of the Berlin Wall, and a year later, Berlin celebrated the 20th year of German unity. In fact, most of today's young Berliners, both from East and West, are *Einheitskinder,* children of German reunification, and have no recollection of the troubled days of division. But even though the Wall may be gone, its consequences are still keenly felt by both sides.

Ask Berliners old enough to remember the days of the Wall, and a certain percentage of them, mostly "Ossis" (East Germans), may admit that they prefer their GDR lifestyle, a yearning known as Ostalgie ("nostalgia for the East"). Some West Germans remain resentful of the tax money poured into Berlin postreunification in order to get it back on its feet economically.

Meanwhile, Berlin's economy is still fumbling. Unresolved problems such as high unemployment, overstretched city budgets, and a huge debt are still worrying.

In many areas now, such as Prenzlauer Berg and northern Mitte, two proud eastern districts, the former population has all but vanished: first affluent West Berlin families moved in, and then West German or foreign "invaders" took over leases. Today, luxury condos are popping up in popular residential areas in an effort to lure ever more wealthy buyers.

As Berlin gains in popularity, rents are going up (they've doubled in the past decade) and the empty spaces that drew artists and creative types are starting to disappear. The next years will see the German capital making some tough decisions: will it retain its vibe as a city that is "poor but sexy," (the phrase coined by mayor Klaus Wowereit)? Will it be able, as Wowereit later said, to "become richer, but remain sexy?" Only time will tell.

American tanks. Today the touristy intersection consists of a replica of an American guardhouse and signage, plus cobblestones that mark the old border.

This homespun museum reviews the events leading up to the Wall's construction and, with original tools and devices, plus recordings and photographs, shows how East Germans escaped to the West (one of the most ingenious contraptions was a miniature submarine). Exhibits about human rights and paintings interpreting the Wall round out the experience. ■ TIP→ **Come early or late in the day to avoid the multitudes dropped off by tour buses.** Monday can be particularly crowded because the state museums are closed on Mondays. ✉ *Friedrichstr. 43–45, Kreuzberg* ☎ *030/253-7250* ⊕ *www.mauermuseum.com* ✑ *€12.50* ☉ *Daily 9 am–10 pm* Ⓜ *Kochstrasse (U-bahn).*

Museum der Dinge. The Museum der Dinge or "Museum of Things" is exactly that—a collection of stuff that represents the best, the worst, and the quirkiest in 20th century and contemporary design. Although there are a lot of things here, a museum for hoarders, this is not. The objects here come from the archive of the Deutsches Werkbund (DWB), a hundred-year-old, quasi-utopian consortium that sought perfection in everyday construction and design. The thousands of things are housed in a former factory building on Kreuzberg's busy Oranienstrasse and arranged beautifully by color, material, or use. Browsing the exhibition, one is hit not only by the sheer volume of what was created in the last cenutry, but also by the impressive range—Soviet kitsch toys stand near mobile phones, delicate dishware next to industrial tools. Don't miss the so-called "Frankfurt Kitchen" a space-saving prototype kitchen from the 1920s that was meant to be replicated

over 10,000 times in various housing estates. ✉ *Oranienstr. 25, Kreuzberg* ☎ *030/9210–6311* ⊕ *www.museumderdinge.de* 🎫 *€5* ⊙ *Open Thurs.-Mon. 12–7* Ⓜ *Kottbusser Tor (U-bahn)*.

Sommer & Kohl. In what was once a mattress factory, Patricia Kohl and Salome Sommer show mostly young, international artists. ✉ *Kurfürstenstr. 13/14, Kreuzberg* ☎ *030/2300–5581* ⊕ *www.sommerkohl.com* ⊙ *Wed.–Sat. 11–6, Sun.–Tues. by appt.* Ⓜ *Kurfürstenstrasse and Bülowstrasse (U-bahn)*.

Supportico Lopez. Recently joining Sommer + Kohl's courtyard (in the empire owned by Scottish artist Douglas Gordon, whose studio is upstairs), Supportico Lopez is a curator and art-lover's dream. No wonder: it started as a curatorial project in Naples, and reflects curator's Gigiotto Del Vecchio and Stefania Palumbo's concepts. ✉ *Kurfürstenstr. 14/b, Kreuzberg* ☎ *030/3198–9387* ⊕ *www.supporticolopez.com* ⊙ *Tues.–Sat. 11–6* Ⓜ *Kurfürstenstrasse and Bülowstrasse (U-bahn)*.

Thomas Fischer. One of the hottest young dealers in town, Thomas Fischer shows thought-provoking exhibitions in a gorgeously renovated townhouse apartment space. ✉ *Potsdamerstr. 77–87, Haus H, Kreuzberg* ☎ *030/7478–0385* ⊕ *www.galeriethomasfischer.de* ⊙ *Tues.–Sat. 11–6* Ⓜ *Kurfürstenstrasse (U-bahn)*.

WORTH NOTING

Berlinische Galerie. Talk about site-specific art: all the modern art, photography, and architecture models and plans here, created between 1870 and the present, were made in Berlin (or in the case of architecture competition models, intended for the city). Russians, secessionists, Dadaists, and expressionists all had their day in Berlin, and individual works by Otto Dix, George Grosz, and Georg Baselitz, as well as artists' archives such as the Dadaist Hannah Höch's, are highlights. There's a set price for the permanent collection, but rates vary for special exhibitions, which are usually well-attended and quite worthwhile. ■**TIP→** Bus M29 to Waldeckpark/Oranienstrasse is the closest transportation stop. ✉ *Alte Jakobstr. 124–128, Kreuzberg* ☎ *030/7890–2600* ⊕ *www. berlinischegalerie.de* 🎫 *€8* ⊙ *Wed.–Mon. 10–6* Ⓜ *Kochstrasse (U-bahn)*.

Deutsches Technikmuseum (*German Museum of Technology*). A must if you're traveling with children, this musem will enchant anyone who's

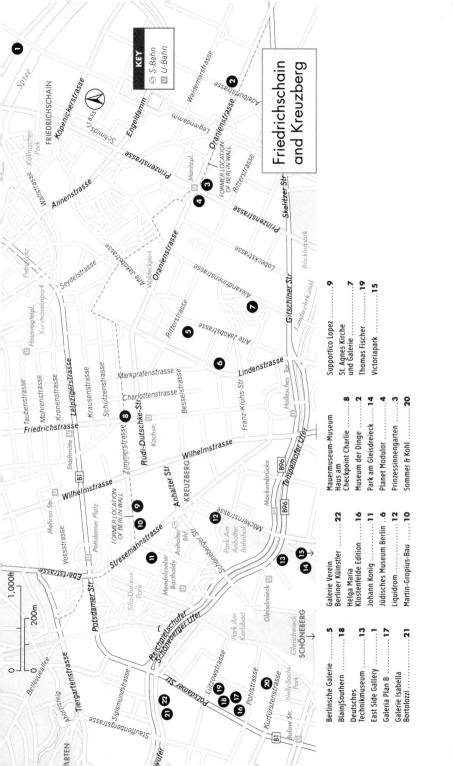

Friedrichschain and Kreuzberg

interested in technology or fascinated with trains, planes, and automobiles. Set in the remains of Anhalter Bahnhof's industrial yard and enhanced with a newer, glass-enclosed wing, the museum has several floors of machinery, including two airplane rooms on the upper floors crowned with a "Rosinen-bomber," one of the beloved airplanes that delivered supplies to Tempelhof Airport during the Berlin Airlift of 1948. Don't miss the train sheds, which are like three-dimensional, walkable timelines of trains throughout history, and the historical brewery, which has a great rooftop view of today's trains, U-bahn lines U1 and U2, converging at the neighboring Gleisdreieck station. ⊠ *Trebbiner Str. 9, Kreuzberg* ☎ *030/902–540* 🎫 *€6* ⊙ *Tues.–Fri. 9–5:30, weekends 10–6* Ⓜ *Gleisdreieck (U-bahn), Anhalter Bahnhof (S-bahn).*

NEED A BREAK?

Golgatha. This beloved local watering hole has taken up space in Viktoriapark since 1928. Open all day long and late into the night, it's the perfect place to while away the hours with a cup of coffee during the day, or sip a cocktail or beer during the evening, when a DJ is spinning. It's also a reliable lunch spot, with salads, grilled meats, and the "German pizzas" known as *Flammkuchen* on the menu. ⊠ *Dudenstr. 40–64, in Viktoriapark, closest entrance at Katzbachstr., Kreuzberg* ☎ *030/785–2453* ⊕ *www.golgatha-berlin.de* ⊙ *Apr.–Oct., 9 am–late* ⊙ *Closed Nov.–Mar.* Ⓜ *Yorckstrasse (S-bahn and U-bahn).*

Johann König. Located in a decidedly unartistic stretch of Kreuzberg south of Potsdamer Platz, this gallery displays work across a wide range of media (video and sound in addition to the more traditional painting, photography, and sculpture) in an attractive, formerly industrial atelier space. Represented artists include Alicja Kwade, Jeremy Shaw, and Justin Matherly. ⊠ *Dessauerstr. 6–7, Kreuzberg* ☎ *030/2610–3080* ⊕ *www.johannkoenig.de* ⊙ *Tues.–Sat. 10–6* Ⓜ *Potsdamer Platz (S-bahn and U-bahn), Anhalter Bahnhof (S-bahn), and Mendelssohn-Bartholdy-Park (U-bahn).*

Jüdisches Museum Berlin (*Jewish Museum*). The history of Germany's Jews from the Middle Ages through today is chronicled here, from prominent historical figures to the evolution of laws regarding Jews' participation in civil society. A few of the exhibits document the Holocaust itself, but this museum celebrates Jewish life and history far more than it focuses on the atrocities committed during WWII. An attraction in itself is the highly conceptual building, designed by Daniel Libeskind, where various physical "voids" in the oddly constructed and intensely personal modern wing of the building represent the idea that some things can and should never be exhibited when it comes to the Holocaust. Libeskind also directed the construction of the recently opened "Akademie" of the museum just across the street, which offers a library and temporary exhibitions, as well as space for workshops and lectures.

■ TIP→ **Reserve at least three hours for the museum and devote more time to the second floor if you're already familiar with basic aspects of Judaica, which are the focus of the third floor.** ⊠ *Lindenstr. 9–14, Kreuzberg* ☏ *030/2599–3300* ⊕ *www.jmberlin.de* ✆ *€7* ☉ *Mon. 10–10, Tues.–Sun. 10–8* Ⓜ *Hallesches Tor (U-bahn).*

Liquidrom. Germans love their thermal baths and saunas, and this is one of the classiest around. The dramatic main thermal pool lies under a vaulted ceiling, where glowing lights and soothing music that can be heard underwater enhance a feeling of calm. In addition to several saunas and a steam room, take advantage of the outdoor hot tub in the enclosed courtyard, best at night under stars. There's a bar and a healthy snack menu, just in case all that relaxation leaves you hungry. Full nudity is to be expected here, even in coed areas. ⊠ *Möckernstr. 10, Kreuzberg* ☏ *030/2580–0782–0* ⊕ *www.liquidrom-berlin.de* ✆ *€19.50 for 2 hrs, €24.50 for 4 hrs, €29.50 whole day* ☉ *Sun.–Thurs. 10 am–midnight, Fri. and Sat. 10 am–1 am* Ⓜ *Anhalter Bahnhof (S-bahn).*

Martin-Gropius-Bau. This magnificent palazzo-like exhibition hall first opened in 1881, and once housed Berlin's Arts and Crafts Museum. Its architect, Martin Gropius, was the great-uncle of Walter Gropius, the Bauhaus architect who also worked in Berlin. The international, changing exhibits on art and culture have recently included Aztec sculptures, Henri Cartier-Bresson's photographs, an expansive Frida Kahlo retrospective, and works from Anish Kapoor and Meret Oppenheim. ⊠ *Niederkirchnerstr. 7, Kreuzberg* ☏ *030/254–860* ⊕ *www.gropiusbau. de* ✆ *Varies with exhibit* ☉ *Wed.–Mon. 10–7* Ⓜ *Kochstrasse (U-bahn), Potsdamer Platz (U-bahn and S-bahn).*

Park am Gleisdreieck. Like the more glamorous Tempelhof Park, Gleisdreieck, one of Berlin's newest green spaces, was until recently neglected space—in this case, abandoned and overgrown WWII railyards. In between the Kreuzberg and Schöneberg neighborhoods, the park includes playgrounds and open meadows, paths for running and biking, pits for skateboarding, and even a community garden. Most interesting, however, are the remnants of the park's past: train tracks, signs, and switches have been left intact (if a bit rusty), making this park an urban paradise of the sort Berliners love—one with history hiding in the grass. ⊠ *Kreuzberg* ⊕ *www.gruen-berlin.de* Ⓜ *Gleisdreieck (U-bahn) and Yorckstrasse (S-bahn and U-bahn).*

Planet Modulor. Billed as a creative center, this complex of shops, offices, and meeting spaces on Moritzplatz is a step toward revitalizing the once-shabby and still fairly empty square. Its unusual, hulking shape seems designed to attract attention; it may also inspire some local disdain. But one visit is all it takes to appreciate how well the complex represents the Berlin aesthetic: small and mid-size companies share space with craft and designer workshops, an art bookstore, a café, an outpost of the beloved kitchenware company Coledampf's, and even a kindergarten. ⊠ *Prinzenstr. 85, Kreuzberg* ☎ *030/690–360* ⊕ *www.modulor. de* ⊙ *Weekdays 9–8, Sat. 10–6* Ⓜ *Moritzplatz (U-bahn).*

Prinzessinnengarten. This charming urban garden on the bustling Kreuzberg hub of Moritzplatz perfectly encapsulates the Berlin DIY spirit. Starting with little more than 100 wooden packing crates and an idea, the founders of the Prinzessinnengarten have created an entirely movable source of fruit, vegetables, flowers, and herbs. The café on the premises serves a daily menu of small dishes sourced directly from the garden, while a series of lectures and events facilitate interaction between gardening experts and local enthusiasts. Whether you come just to look, to taste, or to grab a bunch of gardening tools and dig in, the gardens offer a chance to stop, breathe, and enjoy a bit of open space in one of the city' most densely packed quarters. ⊠ *Prinzenstr. 35–38/Prinzessinnenstr. 15, Kreuzberg* ⊕ *www.prinzessinnengarten.net/* ⊙ *Daily, May–Oct.* Ⓜ *Moritzplatz (U-bahn).*

St. Agnes Kirche und Galerie. Hidden away in a part of Kreuzberg most visitors don't reach, St. Agnes, a Catholic church turned contemporary art gallery, is hardly a looker—unless you like the bulky, boxy concrete shapes that characterize Brutalist architecture. Gallerist Johann König took over the 1960s building in 2012 and opened it as an exhibition center; OMA, the architectural firm of Rem Koolhaas, curated the first show. ⊠ *Alexandrinenstr. 118–121, Kreuzberg* ☎ *030/2610–3080* ⊕ *www.st-agnes.net* ⊙ *Thurs.–Sun. 11–6 during exhibitions* Ⓜ *Prinzenstrasse (U-bahn).*

Viktoriapark. A neighborhood favorite, the small Viktoriapark offers one of the highest lookout points in the city center—and definitely the best place to get a free panoramic view. Beginning at the edge of the park, all trails gradually slope upward; at the top stands an elaborate cast-iron monument designed by Karl Friedrich Schinkel in 1821 to commemorate the so-called liberation wars against Napoleon of 1813–15. On the way back down, take the path heading down to Kreuzbergstrasse, next to which a lovely little waterfall trips and burbles over rocks and boulders—a favorite splashing spot for local children. ⊠ *Kreuzberg* Ⓜ *Yorckstrasse (S-bahn and U-bahn).*

SCHÖNEBERG

Long known as Berlin's gay neighborhood, these days Schöneberg is yet another burgeoning hip area, filled with artists and creative types and young families.

NEUKÖLLN

If you missed Prenzlauer Berg's heyday, you can still get a good feel for its raw charm and creative flair if you head to ultrahip Neukölln. Just southeast of Kreuzberg below the Landwehrkanal, Neukölln was an impoverished, gritty West Berlin neighborhood until the hip crowd discovered it a few years ago. It's since been almost completely transformed. Makeshift bars/galleries brighten up semi-abandoned storefronts, and vintage café or breakfast spots put a new twist on old concepts. Everything has a salvaged feel, and the crowds are young and savvy. If you're looking for nightlife, there are bars galore.

WORTH NOTING

Britzer Garten. Named after the surrounding neighborhood of Britz in southern Neukölln, this garden is really more of a large park—albeit one where flowers take centerstage year-round in stunning seasonal exhibitions, like the Tulipan tulip festival in April and May or the dahlia festival in late August. Small brooks, streams, and other waterways surround the lake in the center of the park, while hills and meadows provide ample space to amble and play. The rose garden and so-called "witches' garden" (actually a traditional herb garden) are year-round pleasures. ⊠ *Buckower Damm 146, Neukölln* ☎ *030/700–9060* ⊕ *www.gruen-berlin.de* ⊴ *€2, €3 during flower shows* ☉ *Daily 9–sunset* Ⓜ *Sangerhauser Weg (Bus).*

Gutshof Britz. The current incarnation of the Museum Neukölln has set up shop in the former cow stalls of the Gutshof Britz, a sprawling country estate consisting of a beautiful early-18th-century manor house and grounds complete with a working farm, which provides quite a contrast to the stark, modernist 1960s and 1970s housing that fills the Britz neighborhood. Don't miss the small research library in the museum's attic or the restaurant located in the so-called Schweizer Haus, the old dairyman's living quarters, and manned by Matthias Buchholz, a Michelin-starred chef who left a career in Berlin's top restaurants to make something of this local outpost. ⊠ *Alt-Britz 73, Neukölln* ☎ *030/6097–9230* ⊕ *www.schlossbritz.de* ⊴ *Schloss: €3* ☉ *Schloss open Tues.–Sun. 11–6* Ⓜ *Parchimer Allee (U-bahn).*

Körnerpark. Two blocks west of gritty, noisy Karl-Marx-Strasse, this small, beautifully landscaped park, built in the 1910s, resembles a French chateau garden. Today it remains something of a hidden treasure, cherished by locals but barely known to outsiders. At one end of the park, water cascades down several steps of a multitiered fountain into a round pool; at the other end you'll find the stately former orangerie, which now houses a gallery and café, and presents a concert every Sunday in summer. ⊠ *Schierkerstr. 8, Neukölln* ☎ *030/9023–92876* ⊕ *www.körnerpark.de* ☉ *Gallery: summer: Tues.–Sun. 10–8, winter: Tues.–Sun. 10–6* Ⓜ *Neukölln (S-bahn and U-bahn).*

Museum Neukölln. Every Berlin neighborhood has a *Heimatmuseum*, which literally translates as "homeland museum" and which acts as a repository for local lore and history. Most are dusty, ill-frequented places, but not the Museum Neukölln, which not only has gone above and beyond in terms of design and organization, but also might be

Berlin's most technologically advanced museum. Its permanent exhibition, "99 x Neukölln" is a wonderful grab-bag of objects, both old and new, that represent the neighborhood, displayed in cases equipped with touchscreen computers that tell the each object's history, context, and connection to other objects in the room. ⊠ *Gutshof Britz, Alt-Britz 81, Neukölln* 🕾 *030/6272–77727* ⊕ *www.museum-neukoelln.de* 🖃 *Free* ⊙ *Tues.–Sun. 10–6* Ⓜ *Parchimer Allee (U-bahn).*

Richardplatz. Back when this part of Neukölln was a Bohemian village, Richardplatz was its center, and today the square appears virtually untouched by time. Half-timbered houses lie on one side, and some of the grandest turn-of-the-century apartment buildings lie on the other. It's worth exploring the lanes and alleyways running off the square and its extension, Richardstrasse; you'll turn up some secret gardens and hidden buildings along the way. ■ TIP→ **This square is the location of one of the city's most charming Christmas markets, which takes place annually on the second weekend of Advent (usually either the first or second weekend in December). There, craftsmen and churches sell knitwear, candles, and all sorts of edible goodies under the light of old-fashioned gas lamps.** ⊠ *Neukölln.*

Stadtbad Neukölln. In a city dotted with lakes, pools, and thermal baths, this is one of the most attractive public bathing spots, a neoclassical beauty built in 1914 and renovated in 2009. Even if you don't plan on taking a dip, it's worth a peek: the unremarkable, gray concrete exterior, which seems designed to ward off tourists, conceals two stunning swimming halls, their pristine pools lined with columns and decorated with elaborate mosaics and gargoyles spouting water. If it proves hard to resist, get a day pass for the pools and multiple saunas. ■ TIP→ **Monday is women-only day in the sauna.** ⊠ *Ganghoferstr. 3, Neukölln* 🕾 *030/682–4980* ⊕ *www.berlinerbaeder.de* 🖃 *€4.50* ⊙ *Varies between halls and saunas; check website* Ⓜ *Rathaus Neukölln (U-bahn) and Karl-Marx-Strasse (U-bahn).*

Tempelhofer Park. Of all Berlin's many transformations, this one—from airport to park—might be the quickest. The iconic airport (it was the site of the 1948/49 Berlin airlift) had its last flight in 2008. Only two years later, it opened as a park, complete with untouched runways. It has quickly become one of the city's most beloved and impressive outdoor spots, where bikers, skaters, kite flyers, urban gardeners, picnickers, and grillers all gather. ■ TIP→ **Although the Nazi-era airport buildings are not open for wandering, you can explore them on a two-hour tour (book online).** ⊠ *Bordered by Columbiadamm and Tempelhoferdamm, Neukölln* 🕾 *030/2000–37400* ⊕ *www.tempelhoferfreiheit.de* ⊙ *Open daily sunrise–sunset.*

TREPTOW

Verdant, nearly suburban Treptow is best known for its park, but the canalside residential district of Alt-Treptow, with its ornate, century-old buildings, is also worth a stroll; it's poised to become the next Trendbesirk, or trendy neighborhood, after Neukölln.

WORTH NOTING

Arena Badeschiff. In summer, a trip to the Arena Badeschiff is a must. The outdoor pool is set on a boat anchored on the river Spree, offering great views of the Kreuzberg skyline. It's open May 1 to late August/September, daily 8–midnight. In winter (September–March) the pool is transformed into an indoor sauna. The Arena will be closed for renovations winter 2013–2014. ⊠ *Eichenstr. 4, Treptow* ☎ *0152/059-45752* ⊕ *www.arena-berlin.de/badeschiff/* ⊠ *5 Euro* ⊙ *Daily 8–midnight* Ⓜ *Schlesisches Tor [U-bahn].*

Insel der Jugend. The name of this tiny island is translated as "Island of Youth." Nestled into a bend in the Spree river between Treptow and the Alt-Stralau peninsula, it was the scene of a youth club during GDR times. Although its heyday is past, there is something dreamy, if not a bit creepy, about the island. It can only be accessed via a narrow, arched footbridge from Treptower Park, so it's devoid of cars, noise, and even much foot traffic. Visitors can enjoy a picnic on the docks, or rent paddleboats and canoes. In the evening, the club Insel Berlin hosts concerts, film screenings, and parties (the club also runs the beer garden and café). ⊠ *Alt-Treptow 6, Treptow* ☎ *030/8096–1850* ⊕ *www.inselberlin.de* Ⓜ *Treptower Park (S-bahn) and Plänterwald (S-bahn).*

Sowjetisches Ehrenmal Treptower Park. The Sowjetisches Ehrenmal in Treptower Park just might take the hard-earned title of most impressively bombastic memorial in Berlin. The size of several city blocks, this memorial celebrates the Soviet victory with inscriptions in both Russian and German, accompanying a series of Socialist realist reliefs lining both sides of an elaborate plaza. At one end stands an enormous bronze of a Russian soldier cradling a child in one arm and wielding a sword with the other, while stomping on a crumpled swastika. Well-placed text and photos educate on the history and importance of the monument, as well as explaining why it was preserved after the fall of the Wall. ⊠ *Treptower Park, Treptow.*

Treptower Park. Perhaps best known for the Soviet War Memorial located in it, this Spree-side park is a lovely place for a stroll. True to their outdoorsy reputations, hardy German families don snow boots even during winter's darkest days and traipse around the park's fields and paths, perhaps with a dog in tow, just to get some fresh air. Stick to the waterside promenade for the best people-watching: the elaborate, eccentric houseboats moored there are a glimpse into yet one more alternative Berlin lifestyle. ⊠ *Treptow.*

PRENZLAUER BERG

Once a spot for edgy art spaces, squats, and all manner of alternative lifestyles, Prenzlauer Berg has morphed into an oasis of artisanal bakeries, cute kids clothes stores (where the prices could knock your socks off) and genteel couples with baby strollers. That said, it's a beautiful area, with gorgeous, perfectly renovated buildings shaded by giant plantain and chestnut trees. If you're in the mood for an upscale, locally made snack and a nice stroll, this is the place to be. You'll find a denser

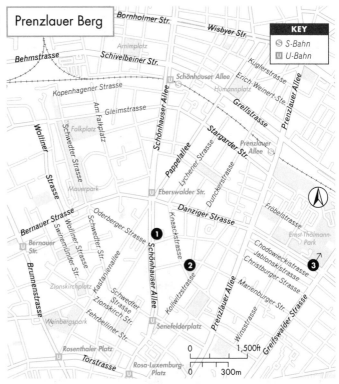

concentration of locals and long-settled expats in Prenzlauer Berg than in other parts of the city like the Scheunenviertel.

WORTH NOTING

Jüdischer Friedhof Weissensee (*Jewish Cemetery*). More than 150,000 graves make up Europe's largest Jewish cemetery in Berlin's Weissensee district, Europe's largest Jewish cemetery. The grounds and tombstones are in excellent condition—a seeming impossibility, given its location in the heart of the Third Reich—and wandering through them is like taking an extremely moving trip back in time through the history of Jewish Berlin. To reach the cemetery, take the M4 tram from Hackescher Markt to Albertinenstrasse and head south on Herbert-Baum-Strasse. At the gate you can get a map from the attendant. The guidebook is in German only. ⊠ *Herbert-Baum-Str. 45, Weissensee* ☎ *030/925–3330* ⊙ *Summer, Mon–Thurs 7:30–5, Fri. 7:30–2:30, Sun 8–5; Winter., Mon–Thurs 7:30–4, Fri. 7:30–2:30, Sun 8–4.*

Kollwitzplatz (*Kollwitz Square*). Named for the painter, sculptor, and political activist Käthe Kollwitz (1867–1945), who lived nearby, the square is the center of the old working-class district of Prenzlauer Berg. Kollwitz, who portrayed the hard times of area residents, is immortalized here in a sculpture based on a self-portrait. Ironically, this image of the artist now has a view of the upwardly mobile young families who have transformed the neighborhood since reunification. Bars and restaurants peal off from the square, and one of the best organic markets in town takes over on weekends. ⊠ *Prenzlauer Berg.*

Kulturbrauerei (*Culture Brewery*). The redbrick buildings of the old Schultheiss brewery are typical of late-19th-century industrial architecture. Parts of the brewery were built in 1842, and at the turn of the 20th century the complex expanded to include the main brewery of Berlin's famous Schultheiss beer, then the world's largest brewery. Today, the multiplex cinema, pubs, clubs, and a concert venue that occupy it make up an arts and entertainment nexus (sadly, without a brewery). Pick up information at the Prenzlauer Berg tourist office here, and come Christmastime, visit the Scandinavian-themed market, which includes children's rides. ⊠ *Schönhauser Allee 36, Entry at Sredzkistr. 1 and Knaackstr. 97, Prenzlauer Berg* ☎ *030/4431–5152* ⊕ *www.kulturbrauerei-berlin.de* Ⓜ *Eberswalder Strasse (U-bahn).*

WEDDING

While much of Berlin has gentrified rapidly in recent years, Wedding, north of Mitte, is still an old-fashioned, working-class district. Because rents are still relatively low, it will probably be the next hot spot for artists and other creative types looking for cheap studios and work places. If you want to be on the cutting edge, ferret out an underground show or two in this ethnically diverse neighborhood.

For a historical perspective on the years of Berlin's division, head to the excellent Berlin Wall Memorial Site. This illuminating museum (some of which is open-air) is located along one of the few remaining stretches of the wall, and chronicles the sorrows of the era.

WORTH NOTING

Brunnenplatz. When you see it for the first time, it can be hard to believe: just steps away from one of Wedding's busiest shopping stretches, Dracula's castle looms, with multiple pointy turrets, gables, and elaborate stone work. Although this imposing neo-Gothic structure was purportedly inspired by a real castle, the Albrechtsburg in the town of Meissen, it is actually the Wedding Amtsgericht or district courthouse, and the centerpiece of the lovely, leafy, and quite unexpected Brunnenplatz. After decades of unrealized development plans, Brunnenplatz was finally made into a local park in the 1980s, with mosaics, ornamental flower beds, and a central fountain. ⊠ *Wedding.*

Gedenkstätte Berliner Mauer (*Berlin Wall Memorial Site*). This site combines memorials and a museum and research center on the Berlin Wall. The division of Berlin was particularly heart-wrenching on Bernauer Strasse, where neighbors and families on opposite sides of the street were separated overnight. The Reconciliation Chapel, completed in 2000, replaced the community church dynamited by the Communists in 1985. The church had been walled into the "death strip," and was seen as a hindrance to patrolling it. A portion of the Wall remains on Bernauer Strasse, along with an installation meant to serve as a memorial, which can be viewed 24/7. The documentation center will be closed until late 2014 for renovation and the addition of a new permanent

Jewish Berlin Today

As Berlin continues to grapple with the past, important steps toward celebrating Jewish history and welcoming a new generation of Jews to Berlin are in the making.

Somber monuments have been built in memory of victims of the Holocaust and National Socialism. An especially poignant but soft-spoken tribute is the collection of **Stolpersteine** (stumbling blocks) found all over Berlin, imbedded into sidewalks in front of the pre-Holocaust homes of Berlin Jews, commemorating former residents simply with names and dates. German artist Gunter Demnig has personally installed these tiny memorials in big cities and small towns across Germany and Austria, and continues to do so as requests come in from communities across Europe.

The **Ronald S. Lauder Foundation** has gone a step further. Along with **Lauder Yeshurun,** Berlin's Jewish communities have been further strengthened by building housing for Jews in the city center, founding a Yeshiva, a rabbinical school, and offering special services for returning Jews.

It's difficult to say how many Jews live in Berlin today, but an official estimate puts the number at 22,000–27,000.

About 12,000 members of the Jewish community are practicing Jews, mostly from the former Soviet Union, who belong to one of several synagogues. Berlin is also gaining in popularity among young Israelis, and today, some estimates say there may be as many as 20,000 Israelis who call Berlin home. These numbers don't include the secular and religious Jews who wish to remain anonymous in the German capital.

The government supports Jewish businesses and organizations with funding, keeps close ties with important members of the community, and, perhaps most visibly, provides 24-hour police protection in front of any Jewish establishment that requests it. Two recent events proved that Jewish Berlin is thriving once again. On November 4, 2010, three young rabbis were ordained at the Pestalozzi Strasse synagogue, the first ceremony of its kind to occur in Berlin since before the Holocaust. Also in 2010, Charlotte Knobloch, a Holocaust survivor and the president of the German Jewish Council at the time, showed the ultimate faith in Germany's recovery and reparation efforts by declaring the country "once again a homeland for Jews."

exhibition. ⊠ *Bernauer Str. 111, Wedding* ☎ *030/467-9866-66* ⊕ *www.berliner-mauer-gedenkstaette.de* 🎟 *Free, tours €3* ⊙ *Memorial: 24/7 access. Visitor center: Apr.–Oct., Tues.–Sun. 9:30–7; Nov.–Mar., Tues.–Sun. 9:30–6* Ⓜ *Bernauer Strasse (U-bahn), Nordbahnhof (S-bahn).*

FAMILY **Labyrinth Kindermuseum.** Rare is the children's museum that inspires parents to join in the exploring—and even arouses the curiosity of childless adults. The Labyrinth Kindermuseum in Wedding, which occupies a large old match factory, is truly worthy of its name: a labyrinthine hall of hands-on amusements, funded by the Senate Administration for Education, Science and Research to encourage maximum child development. Rotating thematic exhibitions allow children to play, build, create, and, of course, run around. ⊠ *Osloerstr. 12, Wedding*

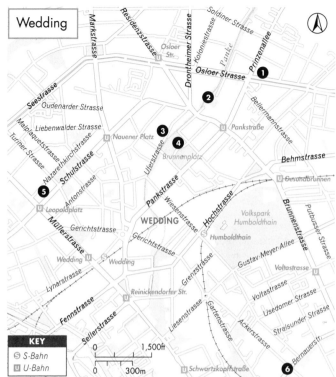

☎ *030/8009–31150* ⊕ *www.labyrinth-kindermuseum.de* 🎫 *€4.50*
⊘ *Fri.–Sat. 1–6, Sun. 11–6* Ⓜ *Osloer Strasse/Prinzenallee (Tram) and
Grüntaler Strasse (Tram).*

Leopoldplatz. The spiritual and commercial heart of Wedding, this square
is anchored by churches: the Alte Nazareth Kirche (designed by Karl
Friedrich Schinkel in the 1830s, when the square was first developed)
and the Neue Nazarethkirche, erected in the 1890s. Long considered
the center of one of the city's most downtrodden areas, Leopoldplatz
has received a makeover, and the area's residents find it a welcome
respite from some of Berlin's more hip and hyped districts. The square
is a good starting point for a neighborhood stroll: you'll find beautiful (though still slightly run down) turn-of-the-century buildings, residential parks, and interesting multicultural (or *multi-kulti*) shops and
cafés. ⊠ *Wedding.*

Panke Canal. Long neglected in favor of Kreuzberg's more hyped Landwehrkanal, the Wedding waterway known as the Panke is no less scenic.
A walk along this tiny inlet, which flows north through Wedding after
splitting off from the larger Spandauer Schifffahrtskanal above Hauptbahnhof, is something of an urban treasure hunt, revealing glimpses
of the neighborhood's history along with local street life and beautiful
scenery. At Wiesenstrasse, where the regional train lines pass overhead,

you'll spot the ruins of an old brick pump station, now housing and artists' workshops. The canal runs just behind Brunnenplatz, flanked on both sides by the Uferhallen. Where the canal crosses Badstrasse you can spot one of the city's most beautiful courtyards, including the Bibliothek am Luisenbad (a modern library hidden behind an ornamental facade). If you walk far enough, you'll arrive at a noticeable widening of the canal. This is the Franzosenbecken or French Basin, a pond so quiet and green, it seems easy to believe you've left the city behind. ■ TIP→ **Start where the canal intersects with Schulzendorfer Strasse, not far from the Reinickendorfer Strasse U-bahn station, and head north.** ✉ *Wedding.*

Uferhallen. This complex, constructed in 1873, was originally part of the Grosse Berliner Pferdeeisenbahn (Great Berlin Horse Railway), then used for electronic trolleys at the beginning of the 20th century, and finally became a bus terminal and repair shop after WWII. In 2010, the Uferhallen were transformed into a series of artists' studios and work-shops along the tiny Panke canal. Nowadays, Wedding residents and intrepid visitors can catch a contemporary dance performance at the Uferstudios, an intimate piano concert at the Piano Salon Christophori, or a meal at Café Pförtner. If you're feeling adventurous, just wander around and knock on a few doors. There's a large exhibition hall here, as well as a Bonsai company; the owner of popular Mitte ramen res-taurant Cocolo has an experimental kitchen here, too. ✉ *Uferstr. 8–11, Wedding* ☎ *030/4690–6871* ⊕ *www.uferhallen.de* ☉ *Varies according to business* Ⓜ *Pankstrasse (U-bahn).*

CHARLOTTENBURG

An important part of former West Berlin but now a western district of the united city, Charlottenburg has retained its old-world charm. Elegance is the keyword here. Whether you're strolling and shopping around Savignyplatz or pausing for a refreshment at the LiteraturHaus, you'll be impressed with the dignity of both the neighborhood's archi-tecture and its inhabitants. Kurfürstendamm (or Ku'damm, as the locals call it) is the central shopping mile, where you'll find an international clientele browsing brand-name designers, or drinking coffee at side-walk cafés.

TOP ATTRACTIONS

C/O Berlin. The C/O Berlin gallery recently moved across town from their long-standing headquarters in Mitte; they're scheduled to open in spring 2014. In the past, the gallery's shows have focused on the con-temporary, such as portraits by Annie Leibovitz or 1980s photographs of the New York City subway by Bruce Davidson. Now, while they complete renovations of their new home, the Amerika Haus, they will present a series of outdoor exhibitions, including a study of the changes taking place in Charlottenburg by the German photography agency OSTKREUZ. ✉ *Amerika Haus, Hardenbergstr. 22–24, Charlottenburg* ☎ *030/2809–1925* ⊕ *www.co-berlin.info/* ☉ *Outdoor exhibitions open 24/7* Ⓜ *Zoologischer Garten (S-bahn and U-bahn).*

Kaiser-Wilhelm-Gedächtnis-Kirche (*Kaiser Wilhelm Memorial Church*). A dramatic reminder of World War II's destruction, the ruined bell tower is all that remains of this once massive church, which was completed in 1895 and dedicated to the emperor, Kaiser Wilhelm I. The Hohenzollern dynasty is depicted inside in a gilded mosaic, whose damage, like that of the building, will not be repaired. The exhibition revisits World War II's

devastation throughout Europe. On the hour, the tower chimes out a melody composed by the last emperor's great-grandson, the late Prince Louis Ferdinand von Hohenzollern. In stark contrast to the old bell tower (dubbed the "Hollow Tooth"), which is in sore need of restoration now, are the adjoining Memorial Church and Tower, designed by the noted German architect Egon Eiermann and finished in 1961. These ultramodern octagonal structures, with their myriad honeycomb windows, have nicknames as well: the "Lipstick" and the "Powder Box." Brilliant, blue stained glass designed by Gabriel Loire of Chartres, France dominates the interiors. Church music and organ concerts are presented in the church regularly, which is slated for restoration in the near future. ⊠ *Breitscheidplatz, Charlottenburg* ☎ *030/218–5023* ⊕ *www.gedaechtniskirche-berlin.de* ⊠ *Free* ⊙ *Memorial Church daily 9–7* Ⓜ *Zoologischer Garten (U-bahn and S-bahn).*

Käthe-Kollwitz-Museum. Right next door to the Literaturhaus, this small but lovingly curated museum in a formerly private home pays homage to one of Berlin's favorite artists, the female sculptor, print-maker, and painter Käthe Kollwitz. Perhaps best known for her harrowing sculpture of a mother mourning a dead child inside the Neue Wache on Unter den Linden, she also lent her name to one of the city's most beautiful squares, the posh, leafy Kollwitzplatz, which contains a sculpture of her. ⊠ *Fasanenstr. 24, Charlottenburg* ☎ *030/882–5210* ⊕ *www.kaethe-kollwitz.de* ⊠ *€6* ⊙ *Daily 10–6* Ⓜ *Uhlandstrasse (U-bahn).*

Fodor'sChoice
★

Kurfürstendamm. This busy thoroughfare began as a riding path in the 16th century. The elector Joachim II of Brandenburg used it to travel between his palace on the Spree River and his hunting lodge in the Grunewald. The Kurfürstendamm (Elector's Causeway) was transformed into a major route in the late 19th century, thanks to the initiative of Bismarck, Prussia's Iron Chancellor.

Even in the 1920s, the Ku'damm was still relatively new and by no means elegant; it was fairly far removed from the old heart of the city, Unter den Linden in Mitte. The Ku'damm's prewar fame was due mainly to its rowdy bars and dance halls, as well as the cafés where the cultural avant-garde of Europe gathered. Almost half of its 245 late-19th-century buildings were completely destroyed in the 1940s, and the remaining buildings were damaged to varying degrees. As in most of western Berlin, what you see today is either restored or newly constructed. Many of the 1950s buildings have been replaced by high-rises, in particular at the corner of Joachimstaler Strasse. Although Ku'damm is still known as the best shopping street in Berlin, its establishments have declined in elegance and prestige over the years. Nowadays you'll

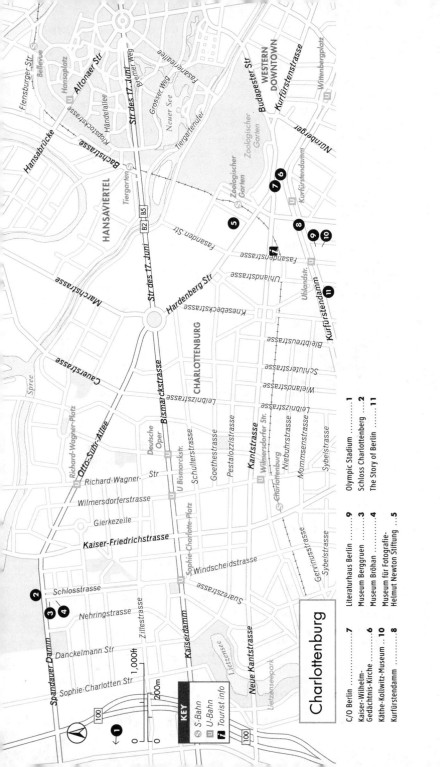

Charlottenburg

KEY

Ⓢ S-Bahn
Ⓤ U-Bahn
ⓘ Tourist info

want to visit just to check it off your list, but few of the mostly down-market chain stores will impress you with their luxury.

Literaturhaus Berlin. This grand, 19th-century villa on one of West Berlin's prettiest streets, is best known for its café, which approximates a Viennese coffeehouse in both food and atmosphere. It also serves as an intellectual meeting place for high-minded and well-to-do Berliners. The house hosts readings, literary symposia, exhibitions and writing workshops year-round, and has a cozy and comprehensive

WORD OF MOUTH

"And strolling around the neighborhoods, even in winter, is still the done thing in Berlin, despite it being a cold old hole sometimes. If Berliners let the weather dictate everything, they'd never leave the house! Plus, if you're strolling, and get too cold, there are plenty of cafes and pubs/bars to pop into along the way to warm up, so don't let winter deter you from exploring." —madamtrashheap

bookstore (one of the city's best) on the lower level. ⊠ *Fasanenstr. 23, Charlottenburg* ☎ *030/887–2860* ⊕ *www.literaturhaus-berlin.de/* ⊗ *Bookshop weekdays 10:30–7:30, Sat. 10:30–6; café daily 9–midnight* Ⓜ *Uhlandstrasse (U-bahn).*

Museum Berggruen. This small modern-art museum just reopened in 2013 after extensive renovations. It holds works by Matisse, Klee, Giacometti, and Picasso, who is particularly well represented with more than 100 works. Heinz Berggruen (1914–2007), a businessman who left Berlin in the 1930s, collected the excellent paintings. He narrates portions of the free audio guide, sharing anecdotes about how he came to acquire pieces directly from the artists, as well as his opinions of the women portrayed in Picasso's portraits. ⊠ *Schlossstr. 1, Charlottenburg* ☎ *030/2664-24242* ⊕ *www.smb.museum* €10 ⊗ *Tues.–Sun. 10–6* Ⓜ *Sophie-Charlotte-Platz (U-bahn), Richard-Wagner-Platz (U-bahn).*

Museum für Fotografie–Helmut Newton Stiftung. Native son Helmut Newton (1920–2004) pledged this collection of 1,000 photographs to Berlin months before his unexpected death. The man who defined fashion photography in the 1960s through the 1980s was an apprentice to Yva, a Jewish fashion photographer in Berlin in the 1930s. Newton fled Berlin with his family in 1938, and his mentor was killed in a concentration camp. The photographs, now part of the state museum collection, are shown on a rotating basis in the huge Wilhelmine building behind the train station Zoologischer Garten. You'll see anything from racy portraits of models to serene landscapes. ⊠ *Jebensstr. 2, Charlottenburg* ☎ *030/2664-24242* ⊕ *www.helmutnewton.com* €10 ⊗ *Tues.–Sun. 10–6 (Thurs. until 8)* Ⓜ *Zoologischer Garten (U-bahn and S-bahn).*

Fodor'sChoice
★
Schloss Charlottenburg (*Charlottenburg Palace*). A grand reminder of imperial days, this showplace served as a city residence for the Prussian rulers. The gorgeous palace started as a modest royal summer residence in 1695, built on the orders of King Friedrich I for his wife, Sophie-Charlotte. In the 18th century Frederick the Great made a number of additions, such as the dome and several wings designed in the rococo style. By 1790 the complex had evolved into a massive royal

domain that could take a whole day to explore. Behind heavy iron gates, the Court of Honor—the front courtyard—is dominated by a baroque statue of the Great Elector on horseback. ■TIP→ **Buildings can be visited separately for different admission prices, or altogether as part of a €19 Tageskarte (day card).**

The **Altes Schloss** is the main building of the Schloss Charlottenburg complex, with the ground-floor suites of Friedrich I and Sophie-Charlotte. Paintings include royal portraits by Antoine Pesne, a noted court painter of the 18th century. A guided tour visits the Oak Gallery, the early-18th-century palace chapel, and the suites of Friedrich Wilhelm II and Friedrich Wilhelm III, furnished in the Biedermeier style. Tours leave hourly from 9 to 5. The upper floor has the apartments of Friedrich Wilhelm IV, a silver treasury, and Berlin and Meissen porcelain and can be seen on its own.

The **Neuer Flügel** (New Building), where Frederick the Great once lived, was designed by Knobbelsdorff, who also built Sanssouci. It is closed for restoration until 2015. ✉ *Spandauer Damm 20–24, Charlottenburg* ☎ *030/331–9694–200* ⊕ *www.spsg.de* ✉ *A Tageskarte (day card) for €19 covers admission for all buildings, excluding tour of Altes Schloss baroque apartments* Ⓜ *Richard-Wagner-Platz (U-bahn).*

Schlosspark Charlottenburg. The park behind the Charlottenburg Palace was laid out in the French baroque style beginning in 1697, and was transformed into an English garden in the early 19th century. In it stand the Neuer Pavillon by Karl Friedrich Schinkel and Carl Langhan's Belvedere Pavillon, which overlooks the lake and the Spree River and holds a collection of Berlin porcelain. ⊕ *www.spsg.de* ✉ *€3* ☉ *Park open daily, Belvedere Apr.-Oct., Tues.-Sun. 10-6; Nov.-Mar. Weekends 10-5*

WORTH NOTING

Museum Bröhan. This enjoyable, lesser-known museum of art deco, art nouveau, and functionalist furniture, dishware, jewelry, and paintings is hidden away in plain sight, just across the street from Schloss Charlottenburg. It provides a lovely glimpse into a time when every object was made with great care and artistic creativity—and when artists in booming creative cities like Berlin and Vienna were at the top of their game. ✉ *Schlossstr. 1a, Charlottenburg* ☎ *030/3269–0600* ⊕ *www.broehanmuseum.de* ✉ *€6* ☉ *Tues.–Sun. 10–6* Ⓜ *Richard-Wagner-Platz (U-bahn).*

Olympic Stadium. Berlin's famous sports attraction is the 1936 Olympic Stadium, which received a thorough modernization in 2004. American sprinter Jesse Owens won his stunning four gold medals in 1936; these days, the Berlin Thunder, a mixed nationality team playing American football in the European league, and the local soccer team Hertha BSC are the stars in the arena. The stadium hosted the World Cup soccer final match in July 2006 and served as a spectacular backdrop to the Athletics World Championship in 2009. Different themed tours are offered throughout the year; one option is touring on your own with an audio guide, but only a guided tour will show you the nonpublic areas. Tours in English are offered less frequently, so check the website or call ahead for the schedule. ✉ *Olympischer Pl. 3, Charlottenburg* ☎ *030/2500–2322* ⊕ *www.olympiastadion-berlin.de* ✉ *€7, tours €10*

⊘ *Daily general tour at 11, 1, 3, and 5 in summer months but open times vary on days before and after major sports events, so call ahead.* Ⓜ *Olympiastadion (U-bahn).*

FAMILY **The Story of Berlin.** You can't miss this multimedia museum for the airplane wing exhibited outside. It was once part of a "Raisin bomber," a U.S. Air Force DC-3 that supplied Berlin during the Berlin Airlift in 1948 and 1949. Eight hundred years of the city's history, from the first settlers casting their fishing lines to Berliners heaving sledgehammers at the Wall, are conveyed through hands-on exhibits, film footage, and multimedia devices in this unusual venue. The sound of footsteps over broken glass follows your path through the exhibit on the *Kristallnacht* pogrom, and to pass through the section on the Nazis' book-burning on Bebelplatz, you must walk over book bindings. Many original artifacts are on display, such as the stretch Volvo that served as Erich Honnecker's state carriage in East Germany. ■TIP➜ **The eeriest relic is the 1974 nuclear shelter, which you can visit by guided tour on the hour.** Museum placards are also in English. ✉ *Ku'damm Karree, Kurfürstendamm 207–208, Charlottenburg* ☎ *030/8872–0100* ⊕ *www.story-of-berlin. de* 🖾 *€12* ⊘ *Daily 10–8; last entry at 6* Ⓜ *Uhlandstrasse (U-bahn).*

FRIEDENAU

Just south of Charlottenburg, Friedenau is a residential neighborhood, with quiet tree-lined streets and a handful of cafés.

GRUNEWALD

The lush Grunewald forest, where tony villas peep out between the trees is in southwest Berlin. Nearby, you can swim in bucolic Schlachtensee Lake.

TOP ATTRACTIONS

Teufelsberg. When it comes to the strange history of this man-made hill, it's hard to separate truth from rumor and legend. Constructed from the rubble leftovers from WWII bombings, the hill became the site of an important U.S. listening station during the Cold War, the otherworldly ruins of which still stand today, topped with globular, mosque-like roofs. Until recently, sneaking in was the only way to explore, but now tour company Berlin Sight Out offers tours weekends at 1 pm (€15). ✉ *Grunewald* ☎ *0163/858–5096* ⊕ *www.berliner-teufelsberg. com* Ⓜ *Grunewald (S-bahn) and Heerstrasse (S-bahn).*

ZEHLENDORF

After the war, Zehlendorf—especially the suburb of Dahlem—was a headquarters of sorts for American forces. The Freie Universität (Free University) is here, as is the citizen services branch of the American Embassy.

WANNSEE

Most tourists come to leafy, upscale Wannsee to see the House of the Wannsee Conference, where the Third Reich's top officials met to plan the "final solution." Beyond this dark historical site, however, there are parks, lakes, and islands to explore. Leave a day for a trip here, especially in warm weather: the Wannsee lake is a favorite spot for a summer dip.

TOP ATTRACTIONS

Gedenkstätte Haus der Wannsee-Konferenz (*Wannsee Conference Memorial Site*). The lovely lakeside setting of this Berlin villa belies the unimaginable Holocaust atrocities planned here. This elegant edifice hosted the fateful conference held on January 20, 1942, at which Nazi leaders and German bureaucrats, under SS leader Reinhard Heydrich, planned the systematic deportation and mass extinction of Europe's Jewish population. Today this so-called *Endlösung der Judenfrage* ("final solution of the Jewish question") is illustrated with a chilling exhibition that documents the conference and, more extensively, the escalation of persecution against Jews and the Holocaust itself. A reference library offers source materials in English. ⊠ *Am Grossen Wannsee 56–58, from the Wannsee S-bahn station, take Bus 114, Wannsee* ☎ *030/805–0010* ⊕ *www.ghwk.de* ☞ *Free, tour €2* ⊙ *Daily 10–6; library weekdays 10–6* Ⓜ *Wannsee (S-bahn)*.

Haus am Waldsee. Built in the 1920s, when an earlier Berlin art scene was at its peak, this villa officially became an exhibition space in 1946, just as Germany was recovering from the war. Today, it stays true to its mission as both a museum for contemporary art and an expansive sculpture park—albeit one a good many Berlin visitors don't know about. The Haus presents a wide range of work by contemporary artists of international acclaim who are from Berlin or live here in up to five exhibitions each year. The juxtaposition of the contemporary and avant-garde and the nearly 100-year-old villa is well worth the trek out from the center of town. ⊠ *Argentinische Allee 30, Wannsee* ☎ *030/801–8935* ⊕ *www.hausamwaldsee.de/i* ☞ *€7* ⊙ *Tues.–Sun. 11–6* Ⓜ *Krumme Lanke (U-bahn)*.

Mutter Fourage. After a trip out to Pfaueninsel or a long walk around the Wannsee lake, refuel at this café, which is also a garden and gourmet foods shop and an event space. In warm weather, grab a table in the courtyard. ⊠ *Chausseestr. 15a, Wannsee* ☎ *030/8058-3283* ⊕ *www. hofcafe-berlin.de/* ⊙ *May.–Sept., daily 9–7; Oct.–Apr., daily 10–6* Ⓜ *Wannsee (S-bahn)*.

WORTH NOTING

Pfaueninsel (*Peacock Island*). Prussian king Friedrich Wilhelm II whisked his mistresses away to this small island oasis on the Great Wannsee. **Schloss Pfaueninsel,** the small white palace, erected in 1794 according

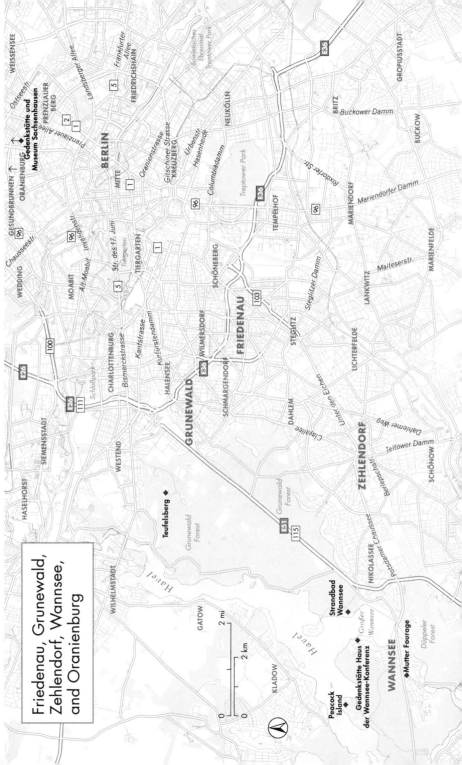

Friedenau, Grunewald,
Zehlendorf, Wannsee,
and Oranienburg

to the ruler's plans—and in accordance with the taste of the era—was built as a fake ruin. The simple building looks strangely cartoonlike; you can see the interior on half-hour tours. In the early 19th-century garden architect Joseph Peter Lenné designed an English garden on the island, which ultimately became western Berlin's favorite summer getaway. ✉ *Wannsee* ✛ *From the Wannsee S-bahn station, take Bus 118, 218, or 316 (leaving every 20 mins) and then a ferry* ☎ *030/8010–9742* ⊕ *www.spsg.de* 🖃 *€3 to the castle, €3 ferry service* ☉ *Palace Apr.–Oct., Tues.–Sun. 10–6; ferry to Pfaueninsel yr-round* Ⓜ *Wannsee (S-bahn).*

Strandbad Wannsee. The huge Strandbad Wannsee attracts as many as 40,000 Berliners to its fine, sandy beach on summer weekends. ✉ *Wannseebadweg 25, Wannsee.*

ORANIENBURG

In this little village a short drive north of Berlin, the Nazis built one of the first concentration camps (neighbors claimed not to notice what was happening there). After the war, the Soviets continued to use it. Only later did the GDR regime turn it into a memorial site. If you feel like you've covered all the main sites in Berlin, this is worth a day trip.

EXPLORING

Fodor's Choice
★
Gedenkstätte und Museum Sachsenhausen (*Sachsenhausen Memorial and Museum*). This concentration camp was established in 1936 and held 200,000 prisoners from every nation in Europe, including British officers and Joseph Stalin's son. It is estimated that tens of thousands died here, among them more than 12,000 Soviet prisoners of war.

Between 1945 and 1950 the Soviets used the site as a prison, and malnutrition and disease claimed the lives of 20% of the inmates. The East German government made the site a concentration camp memorial in April 1961. Many original facilities remain; the barracks and other buildings now hold exhibits.

To reach Sachsenhausen, take the S-bahn 1 to Oranienburg, the last stop. The ride from the Friedrichstrasse Station will take 50 minutes. Alternatively, take the Regional 5 train, direction north, from one of Berlin's main stations. From the Oranienburg Station it's a 25-minute walk (follow signs), or you can take a taxi or Bus 804 (a 7-minute ride, but with infrequent service) in the direction of Malz. ■TIP→ **An ABC zone ticket will suffice for any type of train travel and bus transfer. Allow three hours at the memorial, whose exhibits and sites are spread apart.** Oranienburg is 35 km (22 mi) north of Berlin's center. ✉ *Str. der Nationen 22, Oranienburg* ☎ *03301/200–200* ⊕ *www.stiftung-bg.de* 🖃 *Free, audio guide €3* ☉ *Visitor's center and grounds: Mid-Mar.–mid-Oct., daily 8:30–6; mid-Oct.–mid-Mar., daily 8:30–4:30; last admission ½ hr before closing. Museum closed Mon., all other days open according to above* . Ⓜ *Oranienburg (S-bahn).*

WHERE TO EAT

Updated by
Giulia Pines

Berlin has plenty of unassuming neighborhood restaurants serving old-fashioned German food but happily, the dining scene in this thriving city has expanded to incorporate all sorts of international cuisine, as well as healthier, more contemporary versions of the German classics.

As in many other destinations around the world, eating locally sourced and organic food is more and more the rage in Berlin. Restaurants are beginning to understand that although they could import ingredients from other European countries, fresh farm resources are closer to home. Surrounding the city is the rural state of Brandenburg, whose name often comes before *Ente* (duck) or *Schwein* (pork) on a menu. In spring the Weisser*Spargel,* white asparagus from Beelitz, are all the rage, showing up as main courses with a variety of sauces, pastas, soups, and even desserts.

When it comes to international cuisine, Italian food is abundant, from relatively mundane "red sauce" pizza and pasta establishments to restaurants offering specific regional Italian delicacies. Asian food, in particular, has made a big entrance, with Charlottenburg's Kantstrasse leading the way as Berlin's unofficial "Asiatown." Turkish food continues to be popular, too, especially the beloved *döner* shops selling pressed lamb or chicken in flat-bread pockets with a variety of sauces and salads—always great for a quick meal, and a perennial late-night favorite. *Wurst,* especially *Currywurst—curry-flavored* pork sausage served with a mild curry ketchup—is also popular if you're looking for a quick meal on the go.

Old-fashioned German and especially Berlin cuisine is getting a bit tougher to find, as most restaurants aim to attract customers by reinventing the classics in the so-called *Neue Deutsche Küche* (new German cuisine) movement. But real, old Berlin classics are still lurking around town if you know where to look. Berlin's most traditional four-part meal is *Eisbein* (pork knuckle), always served with sauerkraut, pureed peas, and boiled potatoes. Other old-fashioned Berlin dishes include *Rouladen* (rolled, stuffed beef), *Spanferkel* (suckling pig), *Berliner Schüsselsülze* (potted meat in aspic), *Hackepeter* (ground beef), and *Berliner Leber* (calf's liver with cooked apples and onions).

It's worth noting that Berlin is known for its curt, slow service, except at high-end restaurants. Also keep in mind that many of the top restaurants are closed Sunday.

PLANNING

A *Tageskarte* lists the menu of the day. Seasonal menus, or *Saisonkarten,* feature seasonal dishes, like white asparagus or red cabbage.

In most restaurants it is not customary to wait to be seated. Simply walk in and take any unreserved space.

German restaurants do not automatically serve water. If you order water, you will be served mineral water and be expected to pay for it. The concept of free refills or the bottomless cup of coffee is also completely foreign.

Cash or Credit? While German restaurants will occasionally accept credit cards, most expect you to pay cash (even for large and expensive meals). If you are having something small, like coffee and cake, you will definitely need to pay in cash.

Tipping: When you get the check for something small, like a cup of coffee, round up to the next even euro. For larger amounts, tip 10%. Also, instead of leaving the tip on the table, add it to the total amount when you pay. For example, if the bill is €14, and you want to tip €2, when the waitress comes to collect the bill, tell her the total amount (cost plus tip) you want to pay ("€16, please").

German waitstaff are more than happy to split the check so that everyone can pay individually. Remember to pay the waiter directly; do not place the money on the table and leave.

RESTAURANT REVIEWS

Restaurants are listed alphabetically by neighborhood. Use the coordinates *(⊕ 1:B3)* at the end of each listing to locate a site on the corresponding map.

MITTE

If you're looking for innovative food at restaurants both hip and cozy, trendy and non, at any price point, offering any cuisine, Berlin's city center delivers. Don't expect a quiet meal, though: as exciting as the food is here, half the fun is mingling with the crowd and indulging in the see-and-be-seen atmosphere. Dinner at a restaurant in Mitte is all too often only a precursor for an evening out, so pace yourself: you'll want enough time and energy left to make a stop at that bar you spotted on your way out, and maybe enough time for a bit of dancing later on. The best areas for restaurants are the Scheunenviertel just north of Hackescher Markt, and Friedrichstrasse just south of Unter den Linden.

$ ╳ **Altes Europa.** By day, this is a quiet café reminiscent of a classic Viennese coffeehouse, shabby but trendy, with fashionable Mitte-ites chatting in while middle-aged intellectuals page through newspapers and magazines. At night, it turns into a comfortable but bustling neighborhood pub, just crowded enough to look like a scene, but never too packed. And throughout it all, Altes Europa ("Old Europe") manages to construct a daily menu of six or seven tasty dishes like classic German *knödel* (dumplings) baked with mushrooms and spinach or *tafelspitz* (boiled beef) with potatoes. The food is inventively prepared and served in record time. ⑤ *Average main: €8* ⌧ *Gipsstr. 11, Mitte: Scheunenviertel* ☎ *303/2809–3840* ▭ *No credit cards* ⊕ *1:A5.*

GERMAN

$ ╳ **Bandol sur Mer.** This tiny, 20-seat eatery serves French classics. The foie gras, tartar, and entrecôte are standouts, and desserts like crème

FRENCH

BEST BETS FOR BERLIN DINING

With hundreds of restaurants to choose from, how will you decide where to eat? Fodor's writers and editors have selected their favorite restaurants by price, cuisine, and experience in the Best Bets lists below. In the first column, Fodor's Choice properties represent the "best of the best" in every price category. You can also search by neighborhood for excellent eats—just peruse our reviews on the following pages.

Fodor'sChoice ★

Café Einstein Stammhaus, $$, p. 90
Cookies Cream, $$, p. 78
Curry 36, $, p. 85
Die Henne, $, p. 86
Facil, $$$$, p. 84
Hartmanns, $$$$, p. 86
Paris-Moskau, $$$, p. 82
Pauly Saal, $$$$, p. 80
Restaurant Reinstoff, $$$$, p. 80
Weinbar Rutz, $$$$, p. 81

Best by Price

$
Cocolo, p. 77
Hot Spot, p. 100
Lubitsch, p. 101
Maria Bonita, p. 95
Mariona, p. 89
Monsieur Vuong, p. 80

Nansen, p. 92
Sasaya, p. 96

$$
Café Einstein Stammhaus, p. 90
Engelbecken, p. 98
Renger-Patzsch, p. 91

$$$
Francucci's, p. 100
Lutter & Wegner, p. 79
Richard, p. 89

$$$$
Facil, p. 84
Pauly Saal, p. 80

Best By Cuisine

ASIAN
Hot Spot, $, p. 100
Kushinoya, $$$, p. 101
ULA, $$, p. 81

AUSTRIAN
Lutter & Wegner, $$$, p. 79

Ottenthal, $$, p. 101

FRENCH
Bandol sur Mer, $, p. 75
Richard, $$$, p. 89

GERMAN
Florian, $$, p. 100
Renger-Patzsch, $$, p. 91
Restaurant Reinstoff, $$$$, p. 80

ITALIAN
Da Baffi, $, p. 97
Francucci's, $$$, p. 100
Lavanderia Vecchia, $$$$, p. 91

Best By Experience

BUSINESS DINING
Café Einstein Stammhaus, $$, p. 90

Lubitsch, $, p. 101
Sra Bua, $$$ p. 82

CHILD-FRIENDLY
Engelbecken, $$, p. 98
Markthalle IX, $, p. 89

HIDDEN HISTORY
Die Henne, $, p. 86
La Soupe Populaire, $$, p. 95
Lavanderia Vecchia, $$$$, p. 91
Paris-Moskau, $$$, p. 82
Zur Letzten Instanz, $, p. 82

LATE-NIGHT DINING
Aroma China Restaurant $, p. 98
Habel Weinkultur, $$$, p. 78
Lubitsch, $, p. 101
Lutter & Wegner, $$$, p. 79

MOST ROMANTIC
Facil, $$$$, p. 84
Hartmanns, $$$$, p. 86
Katz Orange, $$$, p. 79

QUIET MEAL
Defne, $, p. 85
Ottenthal, $$, p. 101
ULA, $$, p. 81

brûlée round out the menu. The wine selection is good and the atmosphere is comfortable, though ever since Brad Pitt paid Bandol a visit, getting a table has gotten much more difficult. Its location, right in the middle of bustling Torstrasse, makes it a magnet for the hip and fashionable. ■TIP→ **If you can't get a reservation here, try their sister restaurant next door: the larger and slightly more casual 3 Minutes Sur Mer is also open for lunch.** Ⓢ *Average main: €15* ⊠ *Torstr. 167, Mitte: Scheunenviertel* ☎ *030/6730–2051* ⌔ *Reservations essential* ⊟ *No credit cards* ☉ *Closed Sun. No lunch weekdays* Ⓜ *Rosenthaler Platz (U-bahn)* ✛ *1:A4.*

$ ✕ **The Barn Coffee Shop.** The Barn's original, smaller location in Mitte's
CAFÉ Scheunenviertel. Ⓢ *Average main: €3* ⊠ *Auguststr. 58, Corner of Koppenplatz, Mitte* ⊕ *www.barn.bigcartel.com* ⊟ *No credit cards* Ⓜ *Rosenthaler Platz (U-bahn)* ✛ *1:A5.*

$$ ✕ **Borchardt.** The menu changes daily at this celebrity meeting place—the
BRASSERIE location near Gendarmenmarkt makes it a popular power lunch spot for politicians and influential people, though the food and service are not what you'd expect from the high prices. The high ceiling, plush maroon benches, art nouveau mosaic (discovered during renovations), and marble columns make the atmosphere feel like the 1920s. The cuisine is French-German and there are generally several fish dishes and oyster choices on the menu, as well as carnivorous classics like veal schnitzel or beef fillet. The courtyard garden is lively in warm weather, and fills with a rotating cast of wealthy regulars. Beware, though: this restaurant tends to treat customers better when they appear well-heeled and well-connected. Ⓢ *Average main: €19* ⊠ *Französischestr. 47, Mitte* ☎ *030/8188–6262* ⊕ *www.borchardt-restaurant.de* ⌔ *Reservations essential* Ⓜ *Französische Strasse (U-bahn)* ✛ *1:C4.*

$ ✕ **Chén Chè.** Tucked into a courtyard behind the bflat jazz club, this
ASIAN elegant restaurant benefits from fresh ingredients, expert cooking, and an enticing exotic tea list. It has a lovely location; the outdoor space is adorned with paper lamps and canopies. You'll find the usual suspects, like fresh summer rolls and skewered meats with peanut sauce, but there are also some excellent original dishes, like the pickled Vietnamese eggplant and the rice "burger" with smoked tofu and lotus root. Brunch is served on the weekends. Ⓢ *Average main: €8* ⊠ *Rosenthalerstr. 13, Mitte: Scheunenviertel* ☎ *030/2888–4282* ⊕ *www.chenche-berlin.de* ⊟ *No credit cards* ✛ *1:A5.*

$ ✕ **Cocolo.** The most surprising thing about this authentic ramen joint
RAMEN is the fact that the owner and chef is German, not Japanese. When it comes to the narrow, blink-and-you-miss-it Cocolo, Oliver Prestele has obviously done something right; the noodle kitchen is packed almost every night of the week and has gained a devoted following. Soups come with a variety of pork-based broths, like creamy Tonkotsu, salty Shio, or soy-based Shoyu, along with flavorful toppings like tender pork or chicken, vegetables, bonito flakes, and an egg. Dishes are served in nubby clay bowls made by Prestele in his Wedding workshop, with a long-handled wooden spoon for easy slurping. Ⓢ *Average main: €10* ⊠ *Gipsstr. 3, Mitte* ☎ *0172/304–7584* ⊕ *www.oliverprestele.de*

3

⚐ *Reservations not accepted* 🚭 *No credit cards* Ⓜ *Rosenthaler Platz, Weinmeisterstrasse (U-bahn), Hackescher Markt (S-bahn)* ✛ *1:A5.*

$ ✕ **Confiserie Orientale.** If you think the döner kebab is the pinnacle of
TURKISH   Turkish food in Berlin, a visit to this exquisite sweets boutique will surely bring you to your senses. The gleaming, all-white shop interior mimics nearby art galleries, all the better to show off jewel-like offerings: multicolor and –flavor marzipan and *lokum* (Turkish delight), produced by Cemilzade, a more than 100-year-old confectionary business in Istanbul. The beautifully wrapped and beribboned boxes make for a perfect gift (even if it's only to yourself), while the homemade cakes and pastries can be eaten in-house, along with a samovar of tea or a tiny cup of Turkish coffee. ⓢ *Average main: €3* ✉ *Linienstr. 113, Mitte* ☎ *030/6092–5957* ⊕ *www.confiserie-orientale.com/* 🚭 *No credit cards* ⊗ *Closed Mon.* Ⓜ *Oranienburger Tor (U-bahn), Oranienburger Strasse (S-bahn)* ✛ *1:A4.*

$$ ✕ **Cookies Cream.** With three restaurants, a club, and a bar to his name,
VEGETARIAN   Berlin nightlife "mogul" Cookie is a fixture on the Mitte scene and
Fodor'sChoice   Cookies Cream, the vegetarian fine-dining establishment above the club
★   Cookies, is his crowning achievement. The restaurant is accessible only via a dingy alleyway between the Westin Grand Hotel and the Komische Oper next door, and its entrance seems designed to deter would-be visitors but once you're through the door the service is friendly and casual, and the vibe not at all intimidating. Chef Stephan Hentschel makes a point of never serving pasta or rice dishes, saying that would be too easy in a vegetarian restaurant. Instead, he focuses on innovative preparations like kohlrabi turned into ravioli-esque pockets filled with lentils, or celery that's wrapped canneloni-style around potato puree and chanterelle mushrooms. ⓢ *Average main: €18* ✉ *Behrenstr. 55, Mitte: Unter den Linden* ☎ *030/2749–2940* ⚐ *Reservations essential* ⊗ *Closed Sun. and Mon., no lunch* ✛ *1:C4.*

$$ ✕ **Das Lokal.** This popular restaurant, located on the corner of one of
GERMAN   Berlin's prettiest streets, serves locally sourced dishes like Brandenburg wild boar, lake trout, or venison on stylish long wooden tables to an equally stylish crowd. Kantine, the owners' older restaurant, once occupied this very spot before being torn down in a renovation. The unfussy German standards here (*spätzle*, chicken leg, baked potato) became fast favorites with local gallerists and shop owners. Now the owners have reclaimed the old courtyard spot, so Berliners and visitors get to enjoy eateries. Das Lokal itself is nearby in Mitte, at Joachimstrasse 11, in the courtyard, open for breakfast and lunch, from Monday to Friday. ⓢ *Average main: €18* ✉ *Linienstr. 160, Mitte* ☎ *030/2844–9500* ⊕ *www.lokal-berlinmitte.de* 🚭 *No credit cards* ⊗ *Dinner daily; open for lunch Tues.–Fri. only* Ⓜ *Oranienburger Tor (U-bahn), Oranienburger Strasse (S-bahn)* ✛ *1:A4.*

$$$ ✕ **Habel Weinkultur.** Under the arches of the S-bahn tracks connecting
GERMAN   Friedrichstrasse with Hauptbahnhof, Habel Weinkultur seems unassuming from outside, but inside you'll find a typical old Berlin ambience melding elegance with industrial chic: leather banquettes, crystal chandeliers dangling from the arched brick ceilings, and rumbling trains overhead. The no-nonsense waiters serve local classics, like lamb,

Wiener schnitzel, *weisser spargel* (asparagus), and *knödel* (dumplings) with mushrooms and ham. There's a huge wine selection. Ⓢ *Average main: €24* ✉ *Luisenstr. 19, Mitte: Unter den Linden* ☎ *030/2809–8484* ⊕ *www.wein-habel.de* ☟ *No dinner Sun.* Ⓜ *Brandenburger Tor (S- and U-bahn)* ✛ *1:B3.*

$$ ✕**Hackescher Hof.** This huge-yet-cozy German restaurant is in the middle

GERMAN of the action at bustling Hackesche Höfe, and one of the best places to munch on internationally flavored German food while doing some excellent people-watching. The Hackescher Hof—which sports the walking green man symbol from East Berlin's stoplights—is a mix of *Ostalgie* (nostalgia for the East), solid cooking (if available, go for the regional country dishes like Brandenburg wild boar), and an intriguing clientele made up of tourists, intellectuals, artists, and writers, in a beautiful, wood-paneled but always smoky dining hall—there are also some outside tables in the courtyard, too. It's usually packed in the evening, so reservations are strongly recommended. Ⓢ *Average main: €16* ✉ *Rosenthalerstr. 40–41, inside Hackesche Höfe, Mitte: Scheunenviertel* ☎ *030/283–5293* ⊕ *www.hackescher-hof.de* Ⓜ *Hackescher Markt (S-bahn)* ✛ *1:B5.*

$$$ ✕**Katz Orange.** This cozy restaurant, hidden in a courtyard off a quiet,

CONTEMPORARY residential street, is both elegant enough for a special occasion and homey enough to become a favorite local haunt. Katz Orange takes pride in sourcing the tastiest local ingredients to create dishes that are both fresh and inventive (local suppliers are listed on the back of the menu). Try the *melonen kaltschale,* a peppery melon soup that can be ordered with or without lobster, or the colorful "open ravioli" with green peas and red beet sauce. The real stunners, however, are the slow-cooked meats for two: choose pork, short ribs, or lamb shoulder, along with fresh veggy sides like Beluga lentils, caramelized onions, or kohlrabi with lovage. Ⓢ *Average main: €23* ✉ *Bergstr. 22, Mitte* ☎ *030/9832–08430* ⊕ *www.katzorange.com* ☟ *Closed Sun.* Ⓜ *Nordbahnhof (S-bahn)* ✛ *1:A4.*

$$$ ✕**Lutter & Wegner.** One of the city's oldest vintners (*Sekt,* German cham-

GERMAN pagne, was first conceived here in 1811 by actor Ludwig Devrient), Lutter & Wegner has returned to its historic location across from Gendarmenmarkt. The dark-wood-panel walls, parquet floor, and multiple rooms take diners back to 19th-century Vienna, and the food, too, is mostly Austrian, with superb game dishes in winter and, of course, the classic Wiener schnitzel with potato salad. The sauerbraten (marinated pot roast) with red cabbage is a national prizewinner. ◼**TIP➔ In the Weinstube, a cozy room lined with wine shelves meat and cheese plates are served until 3 am.** There are several other locations around Berlin but this one is widely considered the best. Ⓢ *Average main: €23* ✉ *Charlottenstr. 56, Mitte: Unter den Linden* ☎ *030/2029–5417* ⊕ *www.l-w-berlin.de* Ⓜ *Französische Strasse and Stadtmitte (U-bahn)* ✛ *1:D4.*

$ ✕**Mädchenitaliener.** This cozy Mitte spot has two different spaces: the

MODERN ITALIAN bustling and sometimes drafty front room with high tables where they put walk-ins, and a darker, more romantic back room for those who remember to reserve ahead—so you should, too. The short but well-thought-out menu includes small and large antipasti plates with grilled vegetables, olives, cheeses, and meats, and unusual pastas like tagliatelle with crawfish in a lemon-mint sauce, or with pine nuts and balsamic-roasted figs. Chestnut-filled ravioli with pears is a favorite in winter. The lunch menu, with an appetizer and a pasta dish for only €8.50, is a great deal, especially for the area. $ *Average main: €11* ⊠ *Alte Schönhauserstr. 12, Mitte: Scheunenviertel* ☎ *030/4004–1787* ▭ *No credit cards* ☽ *Lunch served Mon.–Sat.* ✛ *1:A5*

$ ✕ **Mogg & Melzer.** In the renovated Ehemalige Jüdische Mädchenschule
CAFÉ (Old Jewish Girls' School), this deli-style café pays homage to the building's roots in the best way possible: with delectable Jewish delicacies that are hard to find elsewhere in Berlin—think matzoh ball soup or pastrami on rye. At breakfast there is a delicious *shakshuka* (tomato stew with eggs) and the classic New York bagel with cream cheese and lox. More standard fare like a beet and goat cheese salad and French onion soup round out the menu. The space is comfortable, too, with a simple interior featuring wooden floors and tables, light blue walls, and low, deep purple banquettes. $ *Average main: €10* ⊠ *Auguststr. 11-13, Ehemalige Jüdische Mädchenschule, Mitte: Scheunenviertel* ☎ *030/3300-60770* ⊕ *www.moggandmelzer.com* ▭ *No credit cards* Ⓜ *Tucholskystrasse (S-bahn)* ✛ *1:B4.*

$ ✕ **Monsieur Vuong.** This hip Vietnamese eatery is a convenient place to
VIETNAMESE meet before hitting Mitte's galleries or clubs, or for a light lunch after browsing the area's popular boutiques. The atmosphere is always lively, and the clientele is an entertaining mix of tech geeks on their lunch breaks from the area's many start-ups, fashionistas with multiple shopping bags, tourists lured in by the crowd, or students from the nearby Goethe Institut, Germany's most prestigious language school. There are only five items and two specials to choose from, but the delicious *goi bo* (spicy beef salad) and *pho ga* (chicken noodle soup) keep the regulars coming back. The teas and shakes are also excellent. $ *Average main: €7* ⊠ *Alte Schönhauserstr. 46, Mitte* ☎ *030/9929–6924* ⊕ *www.monsieurvuong.de* ⌖ *Reservations not accepted* Ⓜ *Weinmeister Strasse, Rosa-Luxemburg-Platz (U-bahn)* ✛ *1:A6.*

$$$$ ✕ **Pauly Saal.** A new meeting point for the hip Mitte set, Pauly Saal is
GERMAN in the newly renovated and converted Ehemalige Jüdische Mädchen-
Fodor's Choice schule (Old Jewish Girls' School), a worthy destination in its own right
★ due to its beautifully restored interior and several noteworthy galleries. With indoor seating in what used to be the school gym, and outdoor tables taking over the building's expansive courtyard, the setting alone is a draw, but the food is also some of the most exquisite in this part of Mitte. The focus is on artful presentation and local ingredients, like meat sourced directly from Brandenburg. ■TIP➔ **The lunch prix-fixe (€28) is a great way to sample the restaurant's best dishes.** $ *Average main: €34* ⊠ *Auguststr. 11-13, Ehemalige Jüdische Mädchenschule, Mitte: Scheunenviertel* ☎ *030/3300-6070* ⊕ *www.paulysaal.com* ☽ *Closed Sun.* Ⓜ *Tucholskystrasse (S-bahn)* ✛ *1:B4.*

$$$$ ✕ **Restaurant Reinstoff.** One of the top newcomers of the past few years,
CONTEMPORARY the Michelin-starred Reinstoff is a delight. The perfectly crafted and cre-
Fodor's Choice ative haute cuisine, prepared by renowned chef Daniel Achilles, focuses
★ on traditional German ingredients but gives them an avant-garde twist

and often playful presentations. The competent yet relaxed service and great atmosphere make this one of the most enjoyable dining destinations. Guests choose from five-, six-, or eight-course menus (there is no à la carte) that are carefully orchestrated to create an unforgettable dining experience. The wine selection is heavy on German and Spanish wines. $ *Average main: €50* ✉ *Schlegelstr. 26c, in Edison Höfe, Mitte: Scheunenviertel* ☎ *030/3088–1214* ⊕ *www.reinstoff.eu* ⚓ *Reservations essential* ✆ *Closed Sun. and Mon.* Ⓜ *Nordbahnhof (S-bahn)* ✛ *1:A3.*

Rosenthaler Grill und Schlemmerbuffet. *Döner kebab* aficionados love this restaurant for the delicious food; the fact that it's in the middle of the city and open 24 hours a day is an added bonus. The friendly staff expertly carve paper-thin slices of perfectly cooked meat from the enormous, revolving spit. If you like things spicy, ask for the red sauce. ✉ *Torstr. 125, Mitte: Scheunenviertel* ☎ *030/283-2153* Ⓜ *Rosenthaler Platz (U-bahn)* ✛ *1:A5.*

$$$$
GERMAN
Fodor's Choice
★

✕ **Weinbar Rutz.** Rutz might be the most unassuming Michelin-starred restaurant in the world. Its narrow facade is tucked away on a sleepy stretch of Chausseestrasse, but the elegant and enjoyable interior matches the quality of the food, with surprising combinations like roe deer with stinging nettle puree, or monkfish with a ginger and radish ragout. The restaurant's "Inspiration" tasting menus of 6, 8, or 10 courses (starting at 115 euros) offer dual interpretations (labeled "experiences") of luxury ingredients like goose liver or Wagyu beef, though there are à la carte options as well. For those wishing for just a taste of the magic rather than a multicourse affair, the separate weinbar (downstairs) has a more reasonably priced à la carte menu. Sommelier and owner, Billy Wagner, is usually in-house to recommend wines from a list of more than 1,000 vintages. $ *Average main: €60* ✉ *Chausseestr. 8, Mitte: Scheunenviertel* ☎ *030/2462–8760* ⊕ *www.weinbar-rutz.de* ✆ *Closed Sun. and Mon.* Ⓜ *Oranienburger Tor (S-bahn)* ✛ *1:A3.*

$$
JAPANESE

✕ **ULA.** For those who equate Japanese food with sushi, this restaurant is an eye opener. Sushi is a small part of the menu here, which includes cooked dishes and some outstanding desserts. Start with the appetizer trio and one of the unusual rolls, like seaweed wrapped in silky tofu skins with peanut sauce. For vegetarians, the sizzling lotus root steak is a satisfying main course, while omnivores might enjoy Japanese beef cooked at the table, or seared sesame tuna with wasabi mashed potato. ULA is also on a mission to introduce Berliners to the world of sake; the two-page sake menu might seem intimidating, but the gracious, well-informed staff is there to help. $ *Average main: €19* ✉ *Anklamerstr. 8, Mitte* ☎ *030/8937–9570* ⊕ *www.ula-berlin.com* ⊘ *No credit cards* ✆ *Closed Mon.* Ⓜ *Bernauer Strasse (U-bahn)* ✛ *1:A5.*

$$$$
GERMAN

✕ **VAU.** Trendsetter VAU defined hip in the Mitte district years ago and remains a favorite even as it ages. The excellent German fish and game dishes prepared by chef Kolja Kleeberg have earned him endless praise and awards. Menu options might include duck with red cabbage, quince, and sweet chestnuts, or turbot with veal sweetbread with shallots in red wine. The six-course dinner menu is €120, but there are also dishes you can order á la carte. The best bargain is a lunch entrée at €18. The cool interior was designed by Meinhard von Gerkan, one of Germany's leading industrial architects. $\boxed{\$}$ *Average main: €40* ✉ *Jägerstr. 54/55, Mitte: Unter den Linden* ☎ *030/202–9730* ⊕ *www. vau-berlin.de* ✍ *Reservations essential* ⊗ *Closed Sun.* Ⓜ *Französische Strasse (U-bahn), Stadmitte (U-bahn)* ✛ *1:C4.*

$$$
THAI

✕ **Sra Bua.** There aren't many Thai restaurants in Berlin but even if the competition was fierce, this exciting addition to the city's high-end dining scene would stand out. The service is attentive and the setting is lavish at this fourth Sra Bua location (after Bangkok, Switzerland, and St. Moritz). Spicy, flavorful curries are front and center on the menu, excellently complemented by salads and raw fish starters that play with some of the freshest ingredients around. Save room for the "deconstructed" yuzu cheesecake dessert, and make sure to sample the cocktails, which also pay homage to Southeast Asia with ingredients like chili, ginger, mango, and sesame oil. $\boxed{\$}$ *Average main: €24* ✉ *Adlon Kempinski Hotel, Behrenstr. 72, Mitte: Unter den Linden* ☎ *030/2261–1590* ⊕ *www.srabua-adlon.de* ✍ *Reservations essential* Ⓜ *Brandenburger Tor (S- and U-bahn)* ✛ *1:C3.*

$
GERMAN

✕ **Zur Letzten Instanz.** Berlin's oldest restaurant (established in 1621) lies half hidden in a nest of medieval streets, though it's welcomed some illustrious diners: Napoléon is said to have sat alongside the tile stove, Mikhail Gorbachev sipped a beer here in 1989, and Chancellor Gerhard Schröder treated French president Jacques Chirac to a meal here in 2003. The small menu focuses on some of Berlin's most traditional specialties, including *Eisbein* (pork knuckle), and takes its whimsical dish titles from classic legal jargon—the national courthouse is around the corner, and the restaurant's name is a rough equivalent of the term "at the 11th hour." Inside, the restaurant is cozy, and while the service is always friendly it can sometimes feel a bit erratic. $\boxed{\$}$ *Average main: €11* ✉ *Waisenstr. 14–16, Mitte: Alexanderplatz* ☎ *030/242–5528* ⊕ *www.zurletzteninstanz.de* ✍ *Reservations essential* ⊗ *Closed Sun.* Ⓜ *Klosterstrasse (U-bahn)* ✛ *1:C6.*

TIERGARTEN

As a food destination, Tiergarten has yet to really be discovered. Flanked by Potsdamer Platz to the south and Moabit to the north, Tiergarten has comfortable local restaurants offering solid German and international cuisine at affordable prices.

$$$
ECLECTIC
Fodor's Choice
★

✕ **Paris-Moskau.** If you're looking for a one-of-a-kind dining experience, head to the rather barren stretch of land between Hauptbahnhof and the government quarter, where a single half-timbered house stands, now dwarfed by a government complex going up around it: The restaurant Paris-Moskau was built more than 100 years ago as a pub and guesthouse along the Paris-Moscow railway. Today, it serves dishes so intricately prepared they look like works of art, with refreshing flavor combinations such as smoked eel with pork belly ray, or guinea hen with beetroots and dates. In addition to the à la carte menu, there are a variety of set menus in the evening menu—you can choose four, five, six, or eight courses. The well-edited wine list and attentive service help

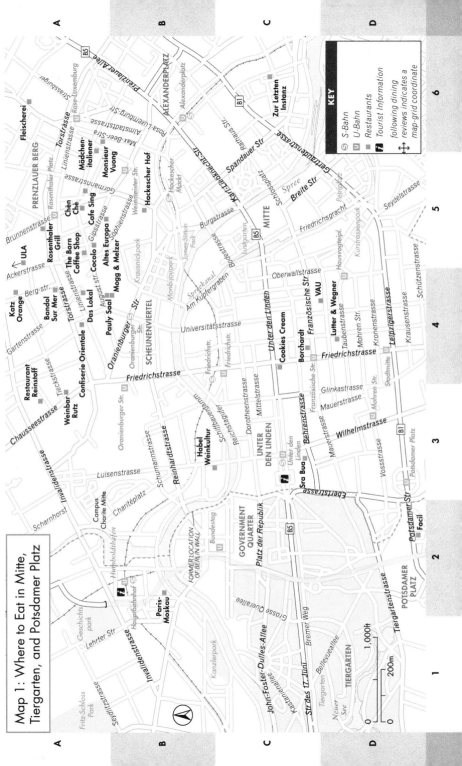

Map 1: Where to Eat in Mitte, Tiergarten, and Potsdamer Platz

KEY

Ⓢ S-Bahn
Ⓤ U-Bahn
▪ Restaurants
🛈 Tourist Information
↔ *following dining reviews indicates a map-grid coordinate*

PRENZLAUER BERG

Fleischerei
Torstrasse
Mädchen-italiener
Monsieur Vuong
Rosenthaler Platz
Rose-Luxemburg
Rosa-Luxemburg-Str
Max-Beer-Str.
Almstadtstrasse
Linienstrasse
Gormannstrasse
ALEXANDERPLATZ
Alexanderplatz

ULA →
Rosenthaler Grill
The Barn Coffee Shop
Chén Chè
Cafe Sing
Cocolo
Altes Europa
Weinmeister Str.
Sophienstrasse
Hackescher Hof
Hackescher Markt
Spandauer Str

Katz Orange
Bandol Sur Mer
Das Lokal
Pauly Saal
Mogg & Melzer
August. str.
Oranienburger Str
Krausnickpark
SCHEUNENVIERTEL
Burgstrasse
MITTE
Breite Str
Spree
Schlossplatz
Zur Letzten Instanz
Gertraudenstrasse
Friedrichsgracht
Petriplatz

Restaurant Reinstoff
Weinbar Rutz
Confiserie Orientale
Torstrasse
Linienstrasse
Chausseestrasse
Tieckstrasse
Gartenstrasse
Berg-str.
Ackerstrasse
Brunnenstrasse
Oranienburger Str.
Friedrichstrasse
Monbijoupark
James-Simon-Park
Spreekanal Am Kupfergraben
Universitätsstrasse
Bodestrasse
Lustgarten
Oberwallstrasse
Französische Str
VAU
Hausvogteipl.
Kunstrassenpark
Seydelstrasse
Schützenstrasse

Habel Weinkultur
Reinhardtstrasse
Schumannstrasse
Luisenstrasse
Friedrichstr.
Friedrichstr.
Dorotheenstrasse
Mitte/strasse
Am Weidendamm
Reichstagufer
Schiffbauerdamm
Unter den Linden
UNTER DEN LINDEN
Unter den Linden
Cookies Cream
Borchardt
Lutter & Wegner
Friedrichstrasse
Taubenstrasse
Mohren Str.
Kronenstrasse
Leipzigerstrasse
Krausenstrasse
Stadtmitte

Scharnhorst
Invalidenstrasse
Campus Charité Mitte
Charitéplatz
FORMER LOCATION OF BERLIN WALL
Bundestag
GOVERNMENT QUARTER
Platz der Republik
Ebertstrasse
Behrenstrasse
Glinkastrasse
Mauerstrasse
Wilhelmstrasse
Mohren Str.
Vossstrasse
Potsdamer Platz
Sra Bua

Geschichts park
Lehrter Str
Humboldthafen
Hauptbahnhof Ⓢ
Paris-Moskau
Kanzlerpark
Kronprinzenbrücke
John-Foster-Dulles-Allee
Grosse Querallee
Bremer Weg
Str des 17. Juni
Bellevueallee
Tiergartenstrasse
POTSDAMER PLATZ
Potsdamer Str
Facil

Fritz-Schloss Park
Seydlitzstrasse
Invalidenstrasse
Kästanienallee
Neuer See
Tiergarten
TIERGARTEN

0 ____ 1,000ft
0 ____ 200m

Berlin's Coffee Culture

As in many other world cities, Berlin has developed a discerning coffee culture. Artisanal coffee bars have appeared all over the city, brewing tasty caffeine beverages, offering plenty of fair trade beans, world-class latte art, and sometimes roasting on the premises using highly professional equipment. Locally baked cakes and pastries usually provide the accompanying sugar jolt. These coffee bars have become a home-away-from-home for Berlin's creative set, although there is, not surprisingly, debate among the coffee fanatics about which are best. These are some of our top picks; full reviews are in the listings.

The Barn has two locations in central Berlin: there is a coffee shop in Mitte's Scheunenviertel, while their large roaster is just a few steps north at the foot of Prenzlauer Berg on Schönhauser Allee. Tiny Bonanza Coffee Heroes manages to fit its roasting machines and a small coffee bar in its space on Oderberger Strasse near Mauerpark, while Godshot holds down the fort in hip Prenzlauer Berg just off of Prenzlauer Allee. Five Elephant is at the sleepy end of Reichenberger Strasse just south of Görlitzer Park in Kreuzberg.

make this restaurant a standout. $\boxed{\$}$ *Average main: €25* $\boxtimes$ *Alt-Moabit 141, Tiergarten* $\boxed{\text{☎}}$ *030/394–2081* $\oplus$ *www.paris-moskau.de* $\lessapprox$ *Reservations essential* $\odot$ *Closed Wed., no lunch weekends* $\oplus$ *1:B2.*

POTSDAMER PLATZ

Potsdamer Platz is a bustling commercial center, full of high-rise office buildings and hotels, most of which have extremely high-end—and usually quite good—restaurants serving multicourse meals by renowned chefs.

$$$$
ECLECTIC
Fodor's Choice
★

✕ **Facil.** One of Germany's top restaurants, Facil is also one of the more relaxed of its class. The elegant, minimalist setting—it's in the fifth-floor courtyard of the Mandala Hotel, with exquisite wall panels and a glass roof that opens in summer—and impeccable service give the place an oasislike feel. Diners can count on a careful combination of German classics and Asian inspiration; the options are to choose from the four- to eight-course set meals, or order à la carte. Seasonal dishes include goose liver with celery and hazelnuts, char with an elderflower emulsion sauce, or roasted regional squab. The wine list is extensive but the staff can provide helpful advice. $\boxed{\$}$ *Average main: €40* $\boxtimes$ *Mandala Hotel, Potsdamerstr. 3, Tiergarten* $\boxed{\text{☎}}$ *030/5900–51234* $\oplus$ *www.facil.de* $\odot$ *Closed weekends* $\boxed{\text{M}}$ *Potsdamer Platz (U-bahn and S-bahn)* $\oplus$ *1:D2.*

KREUZBERG

Exciting, gritty, artistic, ever-changing, and multicultural, Kreuzberg has found the spotlight in recent years and its restaurant scene is catching up now, too. You won't find glitz and glamour here: the neighborhood takes its leftist, student, and working-class image quite seriously. Of course, that doesn't mean you won't find truly spectacular cuisine, just that it will probably be hiding in what appears at first to be a shabby café or a comfy local hangout. Kreuzberg is all about looking past the surface, and its restaurants dutifully follow suit. It's hard to end up in an area that doesn't have something to offer, but the best restaurant are clustered around Lausitzer Platz in Kreuzberg's northern half, and Bergmanstrasse in its southern section.

WORD OF MOUTH

Regarding currywurst, Berlin's signature street food: "Even I, a certified ketchup hater, had to admit that the marriage of the tomato-y sauce with curry spices, slathered over a grilled bratwurst was top-rate street eats. And when paired with perfectly crispy fried potatoes and a Berliner Pilsner . . . it became a rather civilized street food."   —fourfortravel

$ ✕ **Café Morgenland.** Within view (and earshot) of the elevated U1 line,

MIDDLE EASTERN Café Morgenland is a relatively unremarkable neighborhood haunt on weekdays but on Sunday it devotes an entire room to its extremely popular brunch buffet, which means table space can be scarce. The Turkish-inspired dishes (an ode to the home country of many a Kreuzberg native) are the perfect alternative to more traditional brunches in town. $ *Average main: €10* ✉ *Skalitzerstr. 35, Kreuzberg* ☎ *030/611–3291* ⊕ *www.morgenland-berlin.de* ▭ *No credit cards* Ⓜ *Görlitzer Bahnhof (U-bahn)* ✛ *2:B5.*

$ **Curry 36.** This currywurst stand in Kreuzberg has a cult following and

GERMAN anytime of day or night you'll find yourself amid a crowd of cab drivers,

Fodor'sChoice students, and lawyers while you have your currywurst *mit Darm* (with

★ skin) or *ohne Darm* (without skin). Most people order their sausage with a big pile of crispy fries served *rot-weiss* (red and white)—with ketchup and mayonnaise. Curry 36 stays open until 5 in the morning. ✉ *Mehringdamm 36, Kreuzberg* ☎ *030/251–7368* Ⓜ *Mehringdamm (U-bahn)* ✛ *2:C3.*

$ ✕ **Defne.** In a city full of Turkish restaurants, Defne stands out for its

TURKISH exquisitely prepared food, friendly service, and pleasant setting. Beyond simple kebabs, the fresh and healthy menu here includes a great selection of hard-to-find fish dishes from the Bosphorus, such as *acili ahtapot* (spicy octopus served with mushrooms and olives in a white-wine-and-tomato sauce), as well as a selection of delicious mezes small plates and typical Turkish dishes like "the Imam Fainted," one of many eggplant preparations. The vegetable dishes are especially popular. Defne is near the Maybachufer, on the bank of the Landwehrkanal that runs through Berlin, and its beloved Turkish market. $ *Average main: €11* ✉ *Planufer 92c, Kreuzberg* ☎ *030/8179–7111* ⊕ *www.defne-restaurant.de* ▭ *No credit cards* ⊗ *No lunch* Ⓜ *Kottbusser Tor (U-bahn)* ✛ *2:B5.*

$ ✕ **Die Henne.** This 100-year-old Kreuzberg stalwart has survived a lot.
GERMAN   After two world wars, it found itself quite literally with its back against
Fodor's Choice   the wall: the Berlin Wall was built right next to the front door, forcing
★   it to close its front-yard beer garden. But Die Henne (which means "the
hen") has managed to stick around thanks in part to its most famous
dish, which is still just about all they serve: crispy, buttermilk fried
chicken. The rest of the menu is short: coleslaw, potato salad, a few
boulette (meat patty) options, and several beers on tap. For "dessert,"
look to their impressive selection of locally sourced brandies and fruit
schnapps. The small front yard beer garden, reopened after 1989, is
once again a lovely and lively place to sit in summer. Die Henne is full
nearly every night it's open so make reservations a few days in advance
to secure a table. $ *Average main: €8* ✉ *Leuschnerdamm 25, Kreuzberg*
☎ *030/614–7730* 🚫 *No credit cards* 🕓 *Closed Mon.* ✣ *2:A5*

$ ✕ **Five Elephant.** In addition to serving first-rate, quality, coffee from
CAFÉ   beans roasted on the premises, Five Elephant sells some of the best cakes
in town, including a cheesecake that has become something of a local
legend. Like most of its brethren, this little outfit at the quiet end of
Kreuzberg's Reichenbergerstrasse sources its own coffee directly from
growers, and makes sure interactions along every step of the chain are
fair and humane. $ *Average main: €3* ✉ *Reichenbergerstr. 101, Kreuz-
berg* ☎ *030/9608–1527* ⊕ *www.fiveelephant.com* Ⓜ *Glogauer Strasse
(Bus)* ✣ *2:B6.*

$$$$ ✕ **Hartmanns Restaurant.** Named for the acclaimed chef Stefan Hart-
GERMAN   mann, Hartmanns Restaurant is in the heart of Kreuzberg, on a resi-
Fodor's Choice   dential street that manages to be both elegant and jarringly historical
★   (a 19th-century gasometer used as a bunker in WWII sits directly opposite). The restaurant's sublevel interior, however, is all warm lighting and
white-painted walls. The changing menu uses market-fresh ingredients
to revive classic German dishes, though there are also some Mediterranean influences here and there. You can order à la carte, but the
real treat is the chef's three- to seven-course tasting menu, which costs
between 65 and 110 euros, and can be served with or without wine
pairings. Each plate is like a work of art, and the service is impeccable and friendly. $ *Average main: €30* ✉ *Fichtestr. 31, Kreuzberg*
☎ *030/6120–1003* ⊕ *www.hartmanns-restaurant.de* ⚑ *Reservations
essential* 🕓 *Closed Sun. and Mon.* Ⓜ *Südstern (U-bahn)* ✣ *2:C5.*

$ ✕ **Jolesch.** With a front bar area and a cozy, sage-color dining room,
AUSTRIAN   Jolesch is usually filled with chattering locals and the occasional dog
peeking out from under the table (pets are allowed in unexpected places
in Berlin, including many restaurants). The house specialties include
Viennese classics like Wiener schnitzel and apple strudel, but there are
surprises on the seasonal daily menu, which is full of inspiring ingredients and unusual combinations like grilled octopus with saffron sorbet
in spring, or a trio of duck, including silky foie gras, in fall. ■ TIP→ **Look
for a special menu if you're here in late April and May, during "Spargelzeit,"
the white asparagus season.** $ *Average main: €15* ✉ *Muskauerstr. 1,
Kreuzberg* ☎ *030/612–3581* ⊕ *www.jolesch.de* ✣ *2:B6.*

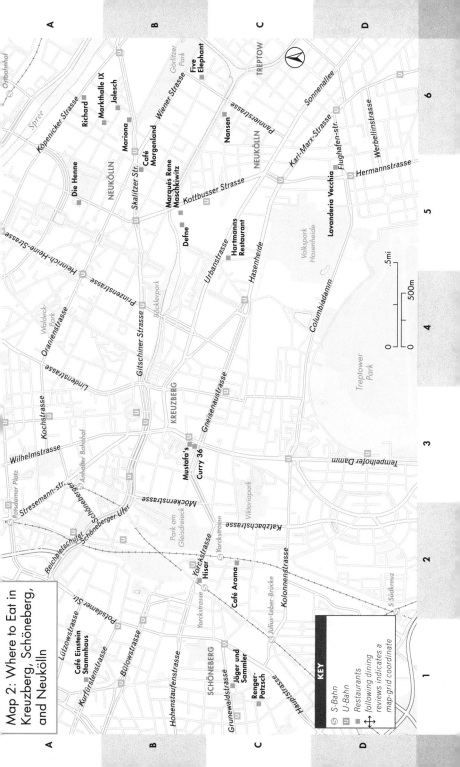

Map 2: Where to Eat in Kreuzberg, Schöneberg, and Neukölln

KREUZBERG

SCHÖNEBERG

NEUKÖLLN

TREPTOW

Die Henne

Köpenicker Strasse

Richard

Markthalle IX

Jolesch

Mariona

Café Morgenland

Skalitzer Str.

Marqués Rene Maschkiwitz

Kottbusser Strasse

Defne

Five Elephant

Görlitzer Park

Wiener Strasse

Nansen

Pannierstrasse

Sonnenallee

Karl-Marx-Strasse

Flughafen-str.

Lavanderia Vecchia

Werbellinstrasse

Hermannstrasse

Hermannstrasse

Urbanstrasse

Hartmanns Restaurant

Hasenheide

Volkspark Hasenheide

Columbiadamm

Treptower Park

Spree

Ostbahnhof

Heinrich-Heine-Strasse

Prinzenstrasse

Oranienstrasse

Lindenstrasse

Waldeck-Park

Böcklerpark

Gitschiner Strasse

Kochstrasse

Wilhelmstrasse

Anhalter Bahnhof

Stresemann-str.

Potsdamer Platz

Reichpietschufer

Schöneberger Ufer

Schöneberger

Mückernstrasse

Park am Gleisdreieck

Mustafa's

Curry 36

Gneisenaustrasse

Yorckstrasse

Katzbachstrasse

Viktoriapark

Tempelhofer Damm

Hisar

Yorckstrasse

Yorckstrasse

Café Aroma

Kolonnenstrasse

Julius-Leber-Brücke

S Südkreuz

Lützowstrasse

Café Einstein Stammhaus

Kurfürstenstrasse

Potsdamer Str.

Bülowstrasse

Hohenstaufenstrasse

Grunewaldstrasse

Jäger und Sammler

Renger-Patzsch

Hauptstrasse

.5mi

500m

0

0

A   B   C   D

1   2   3   4   5   6

Berlin's Supper Clubs

Some of Berlin's best chefs aren't found in restaurants. Instead, they're the owners and operators of private supper clubs, which may open weekly, monthly, or just every once in a while. They're often in the chef's own apartment.

Supper clubs showcase the best of what these talented chefs have to offer, perhaps authentic cuisine from an amateur chef's home country or a multicourse meal with wine pairings from a professional who has worked in Michelin-starred kitchens. Here's a taste of what's going on behind closed doors in Berlin. Supper clubs are listed with websites only. Your first contact is usually via email, and you don't receive an address until you've booked a place or, in some cases, only days before the event.

Thyme Supperclub (www.thyme-supperclub.com) was one of Berlin's first supper clubs; two talented amateur chefs serving reasonably priced, multicourse meals with international influences in their own home. The couple behind it has since teamed up with another Berlin supper club, Zuhause (www.zuhauseberlin.com), which means "at home" in German, to open the space Muse, where they host supper club events on weekends and rent out the space to other supper clubs.

The couple behind Fisk & Gröönsaken are Berliners with day jobs, so they only host a dinner once every few months. They serve fish and vegetable dishes (no meat), from a private apartment in Prenzlauer Berg. With only eight spaces per meal and prices of 25 euro or less for three courses, it sells out quickly.

Chî Fàn (www.facebook.com/chifanberlin) is run by Shanghai native Ash Lee, aka Berlin's "Dumpling Diva." She offers 10-course, family-style meals with a variety of perfectly spiced vegetable and meat dishes, and at least one dim sum, all shared at the table.

The Taiwanese chef behind Phoebe in Berlin (www.phoebe-berlin.de) was trained in French cuisine and owned a French restaurant in Taipei before moving to Berlin. She offers a rotating mixture of either Chinese or French nights at her home in Friedrichshain.

Dylan Watson-Brawn, the young chef behind Jung, Grün & Blau (www.junggrunblau.com), has worked in famous kitchens, including Noma in Copenhagen. His supper club offers exquisite 17 to 20 course meals with wine pairings in an airy Moabit loft. The fee (around 100 euro per person) might seem extravagant—until you realize you're witnessing a phenomenal up-and-coming talent.

Mother's Mother (www.facebook.com/MothersMother), run by Brit Kavita Meelu, takes family traditions and devotion to age-old recipes and turns it into a supper club: once a month or so, a guest chef is invited to develop a menu based on the foods his or her grandmother used to cook, allowing Berliners the chance to sample authentic, international, and sometimes quite obscure cuisines.

Kitchensurfing (www.kitchensurfing.com) a New York–based start-up also operating in Berlin, is a web platform for chefs without restaurants. It's also one of the original organizers of Street Food Thursday, the popular weekly street food festival at Kreuzberg's Markthalle IX.

$ ✕ **Mariona.** This bright, welcoming space just off Kreuzberg's Lausitzer
CATALAN Platz offers tasty Catalonian tapas created from locally sourced ingredients that put a bit of sunshine on the plate during the dreary months.
The colorful dishes on the menu, which changes daily, often pairs sweet
and savory unexpectedly and go perfectly with Spanish wines. Expect
at least one fresh fish dish, like octopus with potatoes and grilled toma-
toes; one soup, like the classic Spanish *salmorejo* (tomato and bread);
and a few meat dishes with at least one expertly cooked, juicy steak,
best accompanied by a glass (or bottle) of *tempranillo*. ⑤ *Average main:*
€12 ✉ *Skalitzerstr. 94b, Kreuzberg* ☎ *030/6167–1214* ⊕ *www.mariona-*
berlin.de ▭ *No credit cards* Ⓜ *Görlitzer Bahnhof (U-bahn)* ✛ *2:B6.*

$ ✕ **Markthalle IX.** Thanks to the efforts of local activists, this century-
INTERNATIONAL old market hall was saved from becoming another chain supermarket
and instead turned into a center for local food vendors, chefs, wine
dealers, and brewers. Thursday to Saturday, Big Stuff Smoked BBQ
sells scrumptious meat samplers and pulled pork sandwiches next to
Glut & Späne, which offers smoked fish platters and ceviches. Hiding
in a corner at the other end is the beloved Heidenpeters, which brews
unusual beers like Thirsty Lady and Spiced Ale in the basement. The
space also hosts a dazzling array of rotating events like the popular
Street Food Thursday or the bimonthly, sweets-only Naschmarkt. ⑤ *Av-*
erage main: €8 ✉ *Eisenbahnstr. 42/43, Kreuzberg* ☎ *030/5770–94661*
⊕ *www.markthalleneun.de/* ▭ *No credit cards* ☉ *Sellers hrs vary; check*
website ☉ *Closed Sun.* Ⓜ *Görlitzer Bahnhof (U-bahn)* ✛ *2:A6.*

$ ✕ **Marqués Rene Maschkiwitz.** In a city where 10 new restaurants seem to
PORTUGUESE open every day, this Spanish and Portugese tapas spot has been spared
much of the hype, but that's a good thing: Marqués serves high-end,
inventive food with Mediterranean wine, and without pretension. The
menu is extensive, so talk it over with friendly staff, who will serve you
delights like sizzling plates of chorizo, and salted, fried *pimientos de*
padron, the small green Spanish peppers. To sate a larger appetite, try
the beef fillets or pasta with mixed seafood—a rarity in land-locked Berlin. ⑤ *Average main: €15* ✉ *Graefestr. 92, Kreuzberg* ☎ *030/6162–5906*
Ⓜ *Schönleinstrasse (U-bahn)* ✛ *2:B5.*

$ ✕ **Mustafa's.** For a twist on the traditional *döner kebab*, head to Mus-
MEDITERRANEAN tafa's for mouthwateringly delicious vegetable kebabs. The specialty
is toasted pita bread stuffed full of roasted veggies—carrots, potatoes, zucchini—along with fresh tomato, lettuce, cucumber, and cabbage. The sandwich is topped with sauce, a generous squeeze of fresh
lemon juice, and sprinkling of the creamy feta cheese. You'll lick your
fingers and contemplate getting in line for another. ⑤ *Average main:*
€15 ✉ *Mehringdamm 32, Kreuzberg* ☎ *283/2153* Ⓜ *Mehringdamm*
(U-bahn) ✛ *2:B3.*

$$$ ✕ **Richard.** On an industrial Kreuzberg street, Richard isn't relying on
MODERN FRENCH foot traffic to bring in customers; you've got to know about this place,
which is one of Berlin's new best. The unassuming facade hides a beau-
tiful interior with stained-glass window, an intricate, carved wood ceil-
ing adorned, and modern paintings. The food is equally elegant, with
a French influence: an appetizer of clams, mussels, and octopus is per-
fectly cooked, while a simple dish of polenta with mushrooms and black

truffles really packs a punch. The service is attentive and knowledge-able, and there's a good selection of German and Austrian wine. $ *Average main: €22* ✉ *Köpenickerstr. 174, Kreuzberg* ☎ *030/4920–7242* ⊕ *www.restaurant-richard.de* ⊗ *Closed Sun. and Mon.* Ⓜ *Schlesisches Tor (U-bahn)* ✛ *2:A6.*

SCHÖNEBERG

The restaurants in Schöneberg cater to the local clientele of young fami-lies and older, more established artists and creative types. Schöneberg isn't looking to show off, but that makes its culinary offerings depend-able and solid, its restaurants the kinds of places you can rely on for both a low-key evening out and a meal on a special occasion.

$
ITALIAN
✕ **Café Aroma.** A neighborhood institution, Café Aroma sits in the curve of a small winding street in an area between Kreuzberg and Schöneberg known as *Rote Insel* or "red island" because of its location between two S-bahn tracks and its socialist, working-class history. An early advocate of the Slow Food movement, Aroma serves some of the most eclectic Italian food in town, made from locally sourced ingredients. Brunch here is on the pricier side, but well worth it: pile your plate high with Italian delicacies like stuffed mushrooms, meatballs in home-made tomato sauce, and bean salads, but leave room for the fluffy tiramisu, which, of course, they'll bring out the moment you declare yourself stuffed. $ *Average main: €13* ✉ *Hochkirchstr. 6, Schöneberg* ☎ *030/782–5821* ⊕ *www.cafe-aroma.de* ▭ *No credit cards* ⊗ *No lunch on weekdays* Ⓜ *Yorkstrasse (S-bahn)* ✛ *2:C2.*

$$
AUSTRIAN
Fodor'sChoice
★
✕ **Café Einstein Stammhaus.** The Einstein is a Berlin landmark and one of the leading coffeehouses in town. In the historic grand villa of silent movie star Henny Porten, it charmingly recalls the elegant days of the Austrian-Hungarian empire, complete with slightly snobbish waiters gliding across squeaking parquet floors. The Einstein's very own cof-fee roasting facility produces some of Germany's best java, and the cakes are fabulous, especially the fresh strawberry cake—probably best enjoyed in summer, in the shady garden behind the villa. The café also excels in preparing solid Austrian fare such as schnitzel or gou-lash for an artsy, high-brow clientele. ◼TIP➔ **Up one flight of stairs is the cocktail bar Lebensstern, which matches the restaurant in sumptu-ous, old-world feel.** $ *Average main: €18* ✉ *Kurfürstenstr. 58, Schöne-berg* ☎ *030/2639–1918* ⊕ *www.cafeeinstein.com* Ⓜ *Kurfürstenstrasse (U-bahn)* ✛ *2:A1.*

$
TURKISH
✕ **Hisar.** The lines here are often long, but they move fast and the com-bination of seasoned, salty meat, with crunchy salad and warm bread is unbeatable. If you're just stopping for a quick döner kebab, line up outside on the sidewalk and order from the window. If you prefer a more leisurely sit-down meal, head into the adjoining Turkish restau-rant for the *Dönerteller* (*döner* plate), heaped with succulent meat, rice, potatoes, and salad. $ *Average main: €18* ✉ *Yorckstr. 49, Schöneberg* ☎ *030/216–5125* Ⓜ *Yorckstrasse (U-bahn and S-bahn)* ✛ *2:B2.*

$$ ✕ **Jäger und Sammler.** The name of this small, casual restaurant, a local
GERMAN favorite, means "hunter and gatherer" in German. The short daily menu
of German classics is local and seasonal: hearty, meat-heavy winter fare
might include pork belly with Beluga lentils or spinach gnocchi with
roasted pumpkin, while spring and summer are devoted to the lighter
gifts of field and forest (German favorite white asparagus makes a big
debut in April or May). The interior is classic Berlin prewar, with long,
rough wooden tables on top of old floor boards, white-painted walls and
ceilings with ornate moldings, and a shelf full of cookbooks so visitors
can do a bit of their own hunting and gathering to gain inspiration for
their next home-cooked meal. $ *Average main: €17* ✉ *Grunewaldstr.
81, Schöneberg* ☎ *030/7009–4084* ⊕ *www.jaegerundsammler-berlin.de*
⊟ *No credit cards* ⊘ *Closed Sun.* Ⓜ *Eisenacherstrasse (U-bahn)* ✛ *2:C1.*

$$ ✕ **Renger-Patzsch.** Black-and-white photographs from German landscape
GERMAN photographer Albert Renger-Patzsch, the restaurant's namesake, deco-
rate the darkwood-paneled dining room at this beloved local gathering place. With a changing daily menu, chef Hannes Behrmann focuses
on top-notch ingredients, respecting the classics while also reinventing
them. Juicy bits of quail sit atop a bed of celery puree, and lamb is
braised in red wine and oranges with crisp polenta dumplings. Lighter
bites like a selection of *Flammküchen* (Alsatian flatbread pizzas) are
great to share. The attentive and good-humored service makes this an
excellent place to relax, even on the busiest nights. $ *Average main: €16*
✉ *Wartburgstr. 54, Schoeneberg* ☎ *030/784–2059* ✛ *2:C1.*

NEUKÖLLN

Neukölln has exploded in popularity over the last half-decade, and is
now stiff competition for neighboring Kreuzberg in the restaurant and
bar department. Most of Neukölln's trendiest spots are clustered within
the Kreuzkölln area, named for its proximity to Kreuzberg just across
the Landwehrkanal but head farther south for hip new hangouts that
were the first to open on their streets, or beloved, long established local
spots that were worthwhile destinations long before Neukölln was on
anybody's radar.

$$$$ ✕ **Lavanderia Vecchia.** Hidden away in a courtyard off a busy Neukölln
ITALIAN street, Lavanderia Vecchia is no longer the secret it was when it opened,
in 2010, in a space that used to contain an old laundrette (hence the
name, which means "old laundrette" in Italian) but it's still very much
a destination spot, and one of the best meals in the city. Come hungry,
though, as the prix-fixe-only menu includes at least 10 appetizers, a
pasta "primi," a meat or fish "secondi," and a dessert, followed by
coffee and a digestif. The open kitchen allows diners to watch as the
chef makes classics like Insalata di Polpo (octopus and potato salad)
or homemade tagliatelle with eggplant, and the contrast of the industrial space strewn with wash lines hung with vintage kerchiefs and
aprons is oh-so-Berlin. $ *Average main: €45* ✉ *Flughafenstr. 46, Neu-
kölln* ☎ *030/6272–2152* ⊕ *www.lavanderiavecchia.de* ⌕ *Reservations
essential* ⊘ *Closed Sun. and Mon.* Ⓜ *Boddinstrasse and Rathaus Neukölln (U-bahn)* ✛ *2:D5.*

$ ✕ **Nansen.** This comfortable corner pub has a secret: it happens to serve
GERMAN   some of the best food in the neighborhood. The unremarkable wooden
tables adorned with half-melted candles don't need to impress; the
dishes on the menu, which is handwritten daily and highlights local produce, speak for themselves. Past dishes include grilled perch, juicy lamb
shoulder, and vegetarian pumpkin strudel with grilled leeks and fennel.
Order off the extensive list of local *obstbrände* (fruit schnapps) for a
perfect finish to the meal. Ⓢ *Average main: €10 ⊠ Maybachufer 39, at
Nansenstr., Neukölln* ☎ *030/6630–1438* ⊕ *www.restaurant-nansen.de*
⊟ *No credit cards* Ⓜ *Schönleinstrasse (U-bahn)* ✛ *2:C6.*

PRENZLAUER BERG

Mitte's older sister, Prenzlauer Berg has become a bit more mature by
default, as it welcomes seemingly one influx after another of creative
professionals and new families with young children. There are many
restaurants here that have been around forever—or at least since the
wall fell—and have diligently cultivated a loyal clientele. Newcomers
are often trying to attract that same clientele, and as such are likely
to offer large, welcoming spaces, friendlier service, long hours, and a
more laid-back attitude. If you're looking for cheap and casual, look no
further than Kastanienallee. If you want something a bit more special
and upscale, the neighborhood's best restaurants are clustered around
Kollwitzplatz and Helmholtzplatz.

$ ✕ **The Barn Roastery.** The Barn roasts their coffee beans on the premises
CAFÉ   and offers a limited menu of near perfect brews—they take coffee seriously, and can get a bit dictatorial about how much milk or sugar you
add. You can also buy beans and brewing equipment here, as well as
pastries, but really, this is more like a showroom than a coffeeshop:
the less that distracts from the quality of the coffee, the better. Ⓢ *Average main: €3 ⊠ Schönhauser Allee 8, Prenzlauer Berg* ⊕ *www.barn.
bigcartel.com* ⊟ *No credit cards* ◷ *Closed Mon.* Ⓜ *Rosa-Luxemburg-
Platz or Senefelder Platz (U-bahn)* ✛ *3:D5.*

$ ✕ **The Bird.** Yes, it serves burgers, and yes, it's run by Americans, but
AMERICAN   the Bird, overlooking a corner of Mauerpark in Prenzlauer Berg, is
more than just an expat burger joint. Burger spots have recently been
popping up everywhere, but the Bird remains one of the best, and
is practically the only place in town where the word "rare" actually
means pink and juicy on the inside. Besides cheekily named burgers
like the "Bronx Jon" (mushrooms and swiss cheese) and "Da Woiks"
(everything, including guacamole if you ask for it), the Bird also serves
up a mean steak frites suitable for two. Your best bet is to grab a seat
at the bar, yell out the order, chow down, and be on your way unless
you're with a large group, as the place can get pretty packed. Ⓢ *Average main: €12 ⊠ Am Falkplatz 5, Prenzlauer Berg* ☎ *030/5105–3283*
⊕ *www.thebirdinberlin.com* ⌕ *Reservations essential* ⊟ *No credit cards*
◷ *Lunch on weekends* ✛ *3:B4.*

Map 3: Where to Eat in Prenzlauer Berg and Wedding

KEY

Ⓢ S-Bahn

Ⓤ U-Bahn

■ Restaurants

following dining reviews indicates a map-grid coordinate

A · B · C · D

1 · 2 · 3 · 4 · 5 · 6

Restaurants and locations shown

Wok Show

Wisbyer Strasse

Stadt Land Fluss

Sasaya

Maria Bonito

Godshot

Muse

Pasternak

Gugelhof

Konnopke's Imbiss

La Soupe Populaire

The Bird

Bonanza Coffee Heroes

The Barn Roastery

Volta

Cafe Pförtner

Da Baffi

Streets and areas

Prenzlauer Allee

Greifswalder Strasse

Grellstrasse

Ernst-Thälmann-Park

Chodowieckistrasse

Jablonskistrasse

Christburger Strasse

Marienburger Str.

Winsstrasse

Am Friedrichshain

Bötzowstrasse

Stargarder Str.

Danziger Strasse

Kollwitzstrasse

Knaackstrasse

Schönhauser Allee

Senefelderplatz

Rosa-luxemburg-Platz

Lychener Strasse

Pappelallee

Dunckerstrasse

Schwedter Strasse

Oderberger Str.

Kastanienallee

Zionskirchplatz

Zionskirch Str.

Schwedter Str.

Fehrbelliner Str.

Torstrasse

Eberswalder Str.

Kuglerstrasse

Erich-Weinert-Str.

Humannplatz

Schönhauser Allee

Bornholmer Strasse

Paul-Robeson-Straße

Arnimplatz

Schivelbeiner Str.

Esplanade

Ibsenstrasse

Bornholmer Str.

Gleimstrasse

Am Falkplatz

Folkplatz

Schwedter Strasse

Kopenhagener Str.

Mauerpark

Wolliner Strasse

Swinemünder Str.

Bernauer Str.

Brunnenstrasse

Rosenthaler Platz

Behmstrasse

Jülicher Strasse

Gesundbrunnen

Bellermannstrasse

Prinzenallee

Pankstraße

Gustav-Meyer-Allee

Hochstrasse

Volkspark Humboldthain

Humboldthain

Putbusser Strasse

Brunnenstrasse

Voltastrasse

Usedomer Strasse

Stralsunder Strasse

Ackerstrasse

Gartenstrasse

Bernauer Str.

Nordbahnhof

Invalidenstrasse

Schwartzkopffstrasse

Chausseestraße

Naturkundemuseum

MITTE

Osloer Strasse

Drontheimer Str.

Prinzenallee

Osloer Str.

Brunnenplatz

Uferstrasse

Parkstrasse

Wiesenstrasse

Grenzstrasse

Liesenstrasse

Reinickendorfer Str.

Scharnhorststrasse

Invalidenstrasse

Markstrasse

Oudenarder Str.

Liebenwalder Strasse

Malplaquet Str.

Turiner Str.

Nazarethkirchstrasse

Schulstrasse

Antonstrasse

Gerichtstrasse

Müllerstrasse

Wedding

Fennstrasse

Seestrasse

Seestrasse

Schillerpark

Leopoldplatz

Nauener Platz

Seifestrasse

WEDDING

PRENZLAUER BERG

Schönhauser Allee

Wolliner Strasse

Swinemünder Str.

Gerichtstrasse

Lynarstrasse

Frobelstrasse

0 ___ 1,500ft

0 ___ 300m

$
CAFÉ
✕ Bonanza Coffee Heroes. The name isn't an exaggeration: Bonanza really was one of the first "coffee heroes" to champion artisanal roasting and brewing methods in the German capital. From their tiny home just next to Mauerpark in Prenzlauer Berg, Bonanza roasts their own beans, runs a catering business, offers their beans wholesale to customers all over the city, and serves some of the smoothest, tastiest coffee in town. If you're lucky they'll be a croissant or pain au chocolate to enjoy as well, but don't count on it, and anyway, you won't need it: Bonanza coffee is better than most pastries and sweets. *Average main: €3 ✉ Oderbergerstr. 35, Prenzlauer Berg* ☎ *0171/5630795 ⊕ www.bonanzacoffee.de* ▭ *No credit cards* Ⓜ *Eberswalder Strasse (U-bahn)* ✛ *3:C4.*

$$
GERMAN
✕ Fleischerei. In an old butcher shop, Fleischerei (which means "butcher shop") is a meat-lover's paradise—and probably not the place to bring your vegetarian friends. The oversize, black-and-white images of pork halves dominating the room give you a hint that the emphasis is on meat, like Berlin-style calves liver (with apple, onion, and potato puree) and the famous beef fillet. Service can be slow and sometimes even unfriendly, but the atmosphere, enhanced by several elaborate chandeliers, wall mirrors, and a projection screen, is unique and stylish. *Average main: €18 ✉ Schönhauser Allee 8, Prenzlauer Berg* ☎ *030/501–82117 ⊕ www.fleischerei-berlin.com* ⌕ *Reservations essential* ☾ *No lunch weekends* Ⓜ *Rosa-Luxemburg-Platz (U-bahn)* ✛ *1:A6.*

$
CAFÉ
✕ Godshot. Godshot bills itself as the "Future Urban Coffee Klub," and indeed this tiny space has become something of a destination for those not just hoping to enjoy a good cup of coffee, but also looking to learn exactly what went into that cup. Offering barista and latte art classes as well as coffee catering, Godshot seems intent on spreading the art of brewing. *Average main: €3 ✉ Immanuelkirchstr. 32, Prenzlauer Berg* ⊕ *www.godshot.de* ▭ *No credit cards* Ⓜ *Knaackstrasse (Tram)* ✛ *3:D5.*

$
ECLECTIC
✕ Gugelhof. Although far from Alsatian France and the Mosel and Saar regions of Germany's southwest that inspire the hearty fare here, a visit to this busy but homey Kollwitzplatz restaurant will leave you pleasantly surprised—and thoroughly stuffed. The raclette for two and the "pate de canard" (Alsation duck paté) are the best you're likely to get this side of the Rhine, and classic choucroute comes with *Blutwurst* (blood sausage) provided by an award-winning Berlin butcher. The vegetarian Tarte Flambée, a crispy crust topped with creamy cheese and grilled vegetables, holds its own on the meat-centric menu. Breakfast and lunch are served only on the weekends; it's dinner only during the week. *Average main: €14 ✉ Knaackstr. 37, Kreuzberg* ☎ *030/442–9229 ⊕ www.gugelhof.de* ⌕ *Reservations essential* ✛ *3:D5.*

$ ✕**Konnopke's Imbiss.** Under the tracks of the elevated U2 subway line is
GERMAN Berlin's most beloved sausage stand. Konnopke's is a family business
that's been around for more than 70 years and it's famous for currywurst, which is served on a paper tray with a plastic prong that can
be used to spear the sauce-covered sausage slices. The location, in the
center of one of Berlin's trendiest neighborhoods, makes it super convenient. Ⓢ *Average main: €14* ✉ *Schönhauser Allee 44b, Prenzlauer Berg*
☎ *030/442–7765* Ⓜ *Eberswalderstrasse (U-bahn)* ✛ *3:C5.*

$$ ✕**La Soupe Populaire.** Berlin can't resist a glamorous ruin, and Bötzow
GERMAN Brauerei, the old brewery complex that houses this new restaurant, is
the mother of them all. Local chef Tim Raue serves reinterpreted Berlin
classics in a soaring industrial space (on the ground floor is a gallery
with rotating artists-in-residence). Try the Königsberger Klöpse—
heavy, doughy meatballs with potato mash, which Raue served Presi-
dent Barack Obama on his visit to the German capital. Finish with
the Bienenstich (literally "bee sting") cake, a classic German dessert
with a crisp honey almond topping. Here, it comes with a little choco-
late bee perched on the plate. Ⓢ *Average main: €17* ✉ *Prenzlauer Allee
242, in Bötzow Brauerei, Prenzlauer Berg* ☎ *030/4431–9680* ⊕ *www.
lasoupepopulaire.de* ⚘ *Reservations essential* ☽ *Open Thurs.–Sat.*
Ⓜ *Senefelderplatz (U-bahn)* ✛ *3:D5.*

$ ✕**Maria Bonita.** This Mexican restaurant is an unassuming space on
MEXICAN Prenzlauer Berg's Danziger Strasse. The young owners (hailing from
Mexico and Australia) had different ideas of what Mexican food could
be, but shared one dream: to bring the authentic cuisine to Berlin. The
food is authentic, as fans will attest, and the hot sauce is satisfyingly
hot in a country known for sensitive taste buds and blandly spiced
dishes. But diners also keep coming back for the sense of camarade-
rie: the restaurants host frequent parties (Cinco de Mayo is the most
raucous, of course) and have done a lot to invite the neighborhood
in. ■**TIP→** If you get a craving for Mexican food in Kreuzberg, visit the
sister restaurant Santa Maria at Oranienstrasse 170. Ⓢ *Average main:
€6* ✉ *Danzigerstr. 33, Prenzlauer Berg* ☎ *030/2025–5338* ⊕ *www.
mariabonitaberlin.wordpress.com* ⚘ *Reservations not accepted* ▭ *No
credit cards* ☽ *Closed Mon.* ✛ *3:C5*

$ ✕**Muse.** The result of a collaboration between local supper clubs, this
INTERNATIONAL lunch spot is tucked into a pleasant, tree-lined, cobblestone street just
up the hill from Alexanderplatz. Its shorter hours (noon to 3) leave the
owners time to host local chefs and nomadic supper clubs several eve-
nings a month. The scrumptious Berliner Bao sandwich, a new take on
the Vietnamese classic, is made with maple-glazed pork belly in a fluffy,
doughy steamed bun. The playfully named Das Beef is a delectable
concoction of slow-braised beef brisket and caramelized onions. The
Montreal Currywurst is a version of classic Canadian poutine. Ⓢ *Aver-
age main: €7* ✉ *Immanuelkirchstr. 31, Prenzlauer Berg* ☎ *030/4005–
6289* ⊕ *www.museberlin.com* ▭ *No credit cards* ☽ *Open for lunch only*
☽ *Closed weekends* Ⓜ *Knaackstrasse (Tram)* ✛ *3:D5.*

$ ✕ **Pasternak.** Russian-inspired treats such as deviled eggs topped with
RUSSIAN   salmon roe, blini with sour cream and dill, and pierogi, are the draw
at Pasternak. Lunch and dinner are popular, but brunch is the major
reason to come here, and it gets quite crowded. At €12 per person, it's
not the cheapest brunch in town, but it's far from the most expensive
and the food is tasty and inventive. If you nab an outside table, you'll
be eating within view of a Berlin oddity: a historic brick water tower
that is now an apartment complex. ⑤ *Average main: €13* ⊠ *Knaackstr.*
22/24, Prenzlauer Berg ☎ *030/441-3399* ⊕ *www.restaurant-pasternak.*
de ⊟ *No credit cards* Ⓜ *Senefelder Platz (U-bahn)* ✛ *3:D5.*

$ ✕ **Sasaya.** In a city that still sometimes struggles to get sushi right,
JAPANESE   Sasaya's concept can seem groundbreaking: simple, authentic Japanese
food in an equally comfortable, no-fuss atmosphere. Don't expect sushi
rolls to be the center of the menu, though—the focus is on reasonably
priced small plates made for sharing. Pickled vegetables, seaweed salad,
crispy pork belly, raw octopus, and a number of soups served with the
traditional Japanese dashi (fish and seaweed) broth are highlights. Dessert favorites include green tea ice cream and satisfyingly chewy balls
of mochi. ■TIP➡ **Reservations are essential; call early enough and you**
might score one of the low tables by the windows, where long, low couches
mean you can recline languidly during your meal. ⑤ *Average main: €12*
⊠ *Lychenerstr. 50, Prenzlauer Berg* ☎ *030/4471-7721* ⊕ *www.sasaya-*
berlin-en.tumblr.com ⚌ *Reservations essential* ⊟ *No credit cards*
⊘ *Closed Tues.–Wed.* Ⓜ *Eberswalder Strasse (U-bahn)* ✛ *3:B5.*

$$$ ✕ **Stadt Land Fluss.** This proud local restaurant, whose name means "City
GERMAN   Country River," has created an unconventional menu that reads like a
culinary introduction to Germany. Choose several small bites from the
Imis section ("tapas" in Bavarian dialect), such as *Saumagen* (cured
pig's stomach), *Schwarzwalder Schinken* (Black Forest ham), or *Rehm-*
aultasche (venison dumplings) before moving on to the complete menu,
which is split into sections for the three places in the restaurant's name.
Try river perch, braised beef ribs, or potato noodles with mushrooms
and cheese from Blomeyer's, one of the city's best cheese distributors.
Of course, an expert list of German wines is also on hand. ⑤ *Aver-*
age main: €23 ⊠ *Pappelallee 65, Prenzlauer Berg* ☎ *030/4057–4736*
⊕ *www.slf-restaurant.de* ⊘ *Closed Sun.* Ⓜ *Schönhauser Allee (U-bahn*
and S-bahn) ✛ *3:B5.*

$ ✕ **Wok Show.** This local favorite looks so nondescript from the outside,
CHINESE   you might walk up and down the street a few times before realizing
you're here. Although there's a full menu of Chinese dishes, it's the
Jiaozi you want: juicy, perfectly wrapped dumplings with veggie, pork,
or lamb fillings, to be dipped in a sour black vinegar and spicy chili
paste. Start off with addictive appetizers like tofu with crispy shrimp,
cucumber with garlic, or Kaofu–silky tofu skins with bean sprouts
and soy bean. Then dive into the dumplings, which can be ordered in
batches of 20 or 40. The friendly waitstaff is happy to accept repeat
orders; go with a group and you'll be surprised how many you'll devour
within minutes. ⑤ *Average main: €8* ⊠ *Greifenhagenerstr. 31, Prenz-*
lauer Berg ☎ *030/4391–1857* ⊘ *Dinner daily; lunch Fri.–Sun. only*
Ⓜ *Schönhauser Allee (U-bahn and S-bahn)* ✛ *3:A5.*

WEDDING

There are a few restaurant gems to be found in up-and-coming Wedding, and there are sure to be more as hungry people in ever greater numbers discover the area, known best for its cheap rents and large Turkish population (which translates to a lot of great Turkish eats). For the best collection of restaurants, cafés, and bars, head to Sprengelkiez, clustered near the Spandauer Schifffahrtskanal (Spandau Ship Canal), or Leopoldplatz, the central square off Wedding's main thoroughfare Müllerstrasse.

$ ✕ **Café Pförtner.** Though Wedding's on the rise, there are still few spots
ITALIAN for a quick meal that doesn't involve either falafel or döner. Enter Café Pförtner, located at the entrance to the Uferhallen on Wedding's Panke canal. Although quite small, the squat, brick Pförtner makes good use of the surrounding space, with long tables out front and, in a nod to the Uferhallen's previous incarnation as a BVG garage, a brightly painted bus-turned-dining-area. You'll order at the counter, but the food is some of the best in the neighborhood. Expect a couple vegetarian and meat dishes at lunch, and an expanded dinner menu that includes fresh, house-made pasta. ⑤ *Average main: €9* ✉ *Uferstr. 8–11, Wedding* ☎ *030/5036–9854* ⊕ *www.pfoertner.co* ▭ *No credit cards* ⊗ *Closed Sun.* Ⓜ *Pankstrasse (U-bahn)* ✛ *3:A2.*

$ ✕ **Da Baffi.** At the quieter end of bustling Leopoldplatz, Da Baffi is
ITALIAN a bright Italian light in Berlin. The interior is charming and casual, with white-painted wood, community tables, fresh wildflowers, and dish-towel placemats—all of which complement the fresh, seasonal menu, which is presented in a notebook and changes weekly. Favorites tend to stick around though, and that means the paper-thin octopus carpaccio and the aromatic tagliatelle with shaved black truffles are almost always available, along with cannelloni with wild boar ragout, or whole grilled fish stuffed with herbs and lemon. ■**TIP**➔ **Hungry for Italian in Kreuzberg? Da Baffi's sister café Salumeria Lamuri (Köpenicker-str. 183) is open weekdays for breakfast and lunch.** ⑤ *Average main: €15* ✉ *Nazarethkirchstr. 41, Wedding* ☎ *0175/692–6545* ⊕ *www.dabaffi. com* ⌕ *Reservations essential* ▭ *No credit cards* ⊗ *Closed Sun.–Mon.* Ⓜ *Leopoldplatz (U-bahn)* ✛ *3:B1.*

$ ✕ **Volta.** For proof that Wedding is on the rise, look no further than this
BURGER tiny, trendy restaurant, which serves high-end, beautifully presented bar food (including a burger with a reputation) along with local beers. Volta makes its unusual round space work with a central horseshoe-shape bar and wraparound banquettes. The menu varies, but aside from the burger, which comes with onion rings, barbecue sauce, and shoestring fries, look out for the miso-glazed salmon with seaweed salad, or the decadent and satisfying pork belly. A small list of cocktails and one dessert round out the short but sweet menu. ⑤ *Average main: €10* ✉ *Brunnenstr. 73, Wedding* ☎ *0178/396–5490* ⊕ *www.dasvolta. com* ▭ *No credit cards* ⊗ *Closed Sun.* Ⓜ *Voltastrasse (U-bahn)* ✛ *3:C3.*

Brunch the Berlin Way

Berliners can be lured out of bed on a Sunday morning with the promise of a Sonntagsbrunch ("Sunday brunch"), which generally means, all-you-can-eat buffet. Lingering for hours over a second, third, or fourth helping is encouraged—and you can always sneak in and survey the spreads before you make your decision.

Our top picks can be found near popular squares in less touristy neighborhoods. On warm days, patrons take over outdoor tables on Kollwitzplatz

and Helmholtzplatz in Prenzlauer Berg—check out **Pasternak** for Russian food or Restauration 1900 for a straight-up German buffet spread on one of the best corners for people-watching—or around Oranienstrasse and Wrangelstrasse in Kreuzberg—a good choice here is the Turkish food at **Café Morgenland**. For quieter meals in places that still have an air of off-the-beaten-path, head to Schöneberg, where **Café Aroma** has one of the most eclectic Italian-inspired brunches in town.

CHARLOTTENBURG

No doubt about it, Charlottenburg is the grand dame of Berlin's neighborhoods, with its high concentration of elegant, upscale joints frequented by elegant, slightly older Berliners who have made this neighborhood home for decades. A new, westward-looking spirit has been slowly creeping up on the city, and that means Charlottenburg is due for a transformation, evidenced by some daring newcomers matching wits with the established hot spots. In a city where the only constant seems to be stimulating, exciting, very often unexpected change, Charlottenburg too has waited its turn long enough. For the area's best restaurants, look to Savignyplatz or the side streets off of Kürfurstendamm. For the city's unofficial "Asiatown," head to Kanstrasse.

$ ✕**Aroma China Restaurant.** Not to be confused with the Italian Café
CANTONESE Aroma in Schöneberg, this eatery's delectable aromas come from authentic dim sum and family-style Chinese cooking, devoured by a mostly Chinese clientele. This large, casual restaurant on Kantstrasse–Charlottenburg's unofficial "Asiatown" is such a favorite that many local Asian chefs come here after their shifts to get the real deal: chickenfeet, jellyfish, and thousand-year egg, plus simple comfort food like the soy chicken noodle soup and sauteed bitter greens. The kitchen is open till 2:30 am. $ *Average main: €12 ⊠ Kantstr. 35, Charlottenburg* 🕾 *030/37591628* Ⓜ *Savignyplatz (S-bahn)* ✛ *4:C3.*

$$ ✕**Engelbecken.** The beer coasters are trading cards of the Wittelsbach
GERMAN dynasty in this relaxed restaurant that focuses on food from Bavaria and the Alps. Excellent renditions of classics like Wiener schnitzel and grilled saddle steak are made of "bio" meat and vegetable products, meaning that even the veal, lamb, and beef are the tasty results of organic and humane upbringing. The corner location facing a park on Lake Lietzensee makes this a lovely spot for open-air dining. Lunch is only served on Sunday and holidays. $ *Average main: €17 ⊠ Witzlebenstr.*

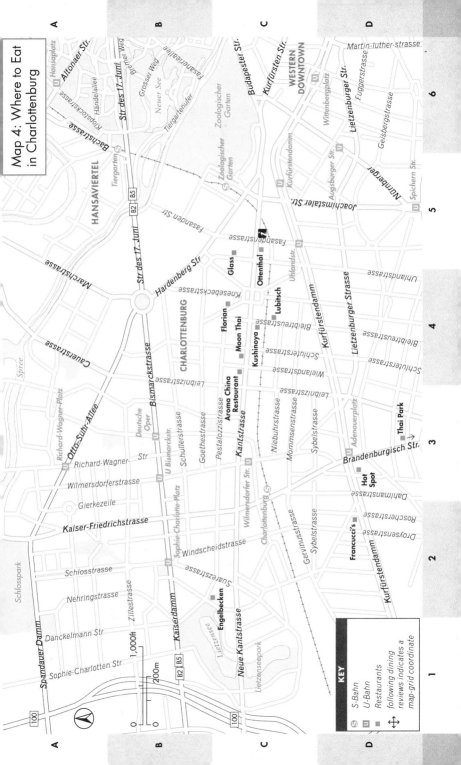

Map 4: Where to Eat in Charlottenburg

KEY
- Ⓢ S-Bahn
- Ⓤ U-Bahn
- ■ Restaurants
- ✛ following dining reviews indicates a map-grid coordinate

31, Charlottenburg ☎ *030/615–2810* ⊕ *www.engelbecken.de* ⊗ *No lunch Mon.–Sat.* Ⓜ *Sophie-Charlotte-Platz (U-bahn)* ✛ *4:C2.*

$$
GERMAN

✕ **Florian.** The handwritten menu is just one page, but everything on the menu is fresh and delicious at this well-established restaurant in the heart of the buzzing nightlife scene around Savignyplatz. *Steinbeisser,* a white, flaky fish, might be served with a salsa of rhubarb, chili, coriander, and ginger, or you can opt for some Franconian comfort cuisine such as *Kirchweihbraten* (marinated pork with baked apples and plums) or their legendary *Nürnberger Rostbratwurst* (small pork sausages) served as late-night snacks. ■ TIP➔ **The kitchen is open until 1 am, and smaller dishes are available until 2 am.** Ⓢ *Average main: €18* ⊠ *Grolmanstr. 52, Charlottenburg* ☎ *030/313–9184* ⊕ *www.restaurant-florian.de* ♨ *Reservations essential* ⊗ *No lunch* Ⓜ *Savignyplatz (S-bahn)* ✛ *4:C4.*

$$$
ITALIAN

✕ **Francucci's.** This upscale restaurant on the far western end of Kurfürstendamm is one of the best-kept Italian secrets in Berlin. You won't find many tourists here but the posh neighborhood's residents pack the cheerful, rustic dining room. The high-quality, straightforward cooking means incredibly fresh salads and appetizers (the bruschetta is excellent), as well as homemade breads and exquisite pasta dishes. More-refined Tuscan and Umbrian creations might include meat options like wild boar but there might also be Mediterranean fish classics such as grilled *loup de mer* or dorade. In warm weather there are tables on the sidewalk. Ⓢ *Average main: €24* ⊠ *Kurfürstendamm 90, at Lehniner Pl., Charlottenburg* ☎ *030/323–3318* ⊕ *www.francucci.de* Ⓜ *Adenauerplatz (U-bahn)* ✛ *4:D2.*

$$$$
ECLECTIC

✕ **Glass.** One of the only Berlin restaurants tackling the world of molecular gastronomy, Glass is also one of the newest dining establishments in Charlottenburg. Diners choose the six- or eight-course option from the regular or the vegan menu and then enjoy surprises that emerge from the kitchen burning, smoking, enveloped by a whiff of dry ice, or arranged in cubes and dustings on UFO-like dishware. Israeli chef Gal Ben Moshe has worked in top restaurants around the world, including Chicago's Alinea, and his culinary expertise is tempered by playfulness. One dish, with fruits, vegetables, and edible breadcrumb "earth" is an homage to Berlin's parks and gardens. A highlight is the wacky dessert made up of childhood sweets including marshmallows, fruit gummies, and exploding chocolate pop rocks, served directly on the tabletop. Ⓢ *Average main: €50* ⊠ *Uhlandstr. 195, Charlottenburg* ☎ *030/5471–0861* ⊕ *www.glassberlin.de* ♨ *Reservations essential* ⊗ *Closed Sun. and Mon.* Ⓜ *Savignyplatz (S-bahn)* ✛ *4:C5.*

$
CHINESE

✕ **Hot Spot.** In a city that's unfortunately full of mediocre pseudo-Asian restaurants that serve bland, tasteless versions of curries, noodles, and rice dishes, Hot Spot stands out for its daring and authenticity. The menu features recipes from the provinces of Sichuan, Jiangsu, and Shanghai, and the freshest ingredients are guaranteed—with no MSG. *Mala* (spicy) dishes are a specialty, and the mostly cold appetizers, like the beef in chili sauce, can't be found anywhere else in Berlin. Mr. Wu and his wife, who own the restaurant, have a love for German wines and offer a large selection. In summer, make a reservation for a table on the sidewalk for the added bonus of people-watching. Ⓢ *Average main:*

€14 ⊠ *Eisenzahnstr. 66, Charlottenburg* ☎ *030/8900–6878* ⊕ *www. restaurant-hotspot.de* Ⓜ *Adenauerplatz (U-bahn)* ✛ *4:D3.*

$$$ ✕ **Kushinoya.** This eatery makes art from a beloved Japanese snack,
JAPANESE *kushiage*—skewered, breaded, and fried meat, fish, veggies, and fruit,
accompanied by an array of colorful dipping sauces. The Kushinoya
team uses a special cooking process to deeply fry the skewers' doughy
exteriors without letting much oil penetrate, and offers at least 30 dif-
ferent skewers daily, using fresh, local ingredients. Ⓢ *Average main:
€25* ⊠ *Bleibtreustr. 6, Charlottenburg* ☎ *030/3180–9897* ⊕ *www.
kushinoya.de* ⊗ *Closed Mon.* Ⓜ *Savignyplatz (S-bahn)* ✛ *4:C4.*

$ ✕ **Lubitsch.** One of the few traditional, artsy restaurants left in bohe-
GERMAN mian Charlottenburg, the Lubitsch—named after the famous Berlin
film director Ernst Lubitsch—exudes an air of faded elegance and serves
hearty local fare (and lighter international options) that's hard to find
these days. Dishes like *Königsberger Klopse* (cooked dumplings in a
creamy caper sauce) and *Kassler Nacken mit Sauerkraut* (salted, boiled
pork knuckle) are examples of home-style German cooking. The local
clientele don't mind the dingy seating or good-humored, but sometimes
cheeky service. In summer the outdoor tables are perfect for people-
watching on one of Berlin's most beautiful streets. The three-course
lunch is a great bargain at €10. Ⓢ *Average main: €13* ⊠ *Bleibtreustr. 47,
Charlottenburg* ☎ *030/882–3756* ⊕ *www.restaurant-lubitsch.de* ⊗ *No
lunch Sun.* Ⓜ *Savignyplatz (S-bahn)* ✛ *4:C4.*

$ ✕ **Moon Thai.** Located on Kantstrasse–Charlottenburg's unofficial
THAI Asiatown–this spot offers tasty and affordable dishes with fresh veg-
etables, nuanced sauces, and if you request it, that long, slow burn that's
a rarity in Germany. The menu has a spice ranking system; if you ask for
Thai scharf ("Thai spicy"), you might get a chuckle or a gasp from your
waitress. The *tom yam gung* lemongrass soup with fresh mushrooms
and shrimp is a great way to start off the meal. ■ TIP➔ **Moon Thai has a
second location just around the corner at Knesebeckstrasse 15.** Ⓢ *Average
main: €12* ⊠ *Kantstr. 32, Charlottenburg* ☎ *030/5304–4054* ⊕ *www.
moonthai-restaurant.de/* ▭ *No credit cards* Ⓜ *Savignyplatz (S-bahn)*
✛ *4:C4.*

$$ ✕ **Ottenthal.** This intimate restaurant with white tablecloths is owned by
AUSTRIAN Austrians from the small village of Ottenthal, and serves as an homage
to their hometown—the wines, pumpkinseed oil, and organic ingredients on the menu all come from there. Interesting and delicious combinations might include pike perch with lobster sauce and pepper-pine-nut
risotto, or venison medallions with vegetable-potato-strudel, red cabbage, and rowanberry sauce. The huge Wiener schnitzel extends past
the plate's rim, and the pastas and strudel are homemade. ■ TIP➔ **Ottenthal opens at 5 pm, which makes it a good option for a leisurely meal
before catching a show at Theater des Westens around the corner. This is
also a good choice on Sunday evening, when many of Berlin's fine restaurants are closed.** Ⓢ *Average main: €16* ⊠ *Kantstr. 153, Charlottenburg*
☎ *030/313–3162* ⊕ *www.ottenthal.com* ⊗ *No lunch* Ⓜ *Zoologischer
Garten (U-bahn and S-bahn)* ✛ *4:C5.*

3

$ ✕ **Thai Park.** Every weekend in decent weather, the main lawn at nonde-
THAI   script Wilmersdorf park fills up with Southeast Asian families (mostly
Thai, but some Vietnamese, Malaysian, and Indonesian) who set cooking equipment and loads of authentic delicacies right on the grass, and
sell fresh bowls of beef noodle soup, skewered fried meat, and spicy
green papaya salad to walkers by. Come with a picnic blanket and a
lot of napkins, and stay for the afternoon. ■TIP➔ **Meander through
the weekend flea market at the entrance to the Ferhbelliner Platz U-bahn
station while you work up an appetite.** $ *Average main: €5* ⊠ *Preussen-
park, Charlottenburg* ⊟ *No credit cards* ⊗ *Weekends in warm weather*
Ⓜ *Fehrbelliner Platz (U-bahn)* ⊹ *4:D3.*

WHERE TO STAY

Updated by
Katherine
Sacks

Berlin's distinct personality shines through in its hotels. You'll find everything here—rooms individually designed by artists at Arte Luise Kunsthotel; funky indoor camping at Hüttenpalast; ship cabins on the Spree River at Eastern Comfort; or classic European luxury at Hotel Adlon Kempinski. There's something for everyone.

Although much of the city was destroyed during the war, many of the city's hotels are in beautiful historic buildings, from old boarding homes like the Honigmong Hotel to the neoclassical Hotel de Rome, formerly a 19th-century bank. But with tourism on the upswing, the hotel industry is happily expanding to accommodate. New buildings seem to go up every day, including the Waldorf Astoria, a 1920s-style skyscraper in West Berlin, and Monbijou Hotel, on the quiet Monbijou park, which feels more like a neighborhood spot, although it's just around the corner from a buzzing marketplace. Though prices in midrange to luxury hotels have increased, Berlin's first-class hotels still tend to be less expensive than their counterparts in Paris, London, or Rome, with comparatively spacious rooms.

Many of the city's hotels are found around the major destination areas of Mitte—home of the Berlin Cathedral, Museum Island, and many other landmarks—or West Berlin's ritzy shopping street Kurfürstendamm in Charlottenburg, and these are great places to stay if you're looking to pack in lots of sightseeing. But Berlin is an expansive city, and there are great farther-flung accommodations as well: Schlosshotel im Grunewald, near the beautiful Grunewald forest; Das Stue, in Tiergarten park, with an insider's peek into the Berlin Zoo animal dens; and artist-inspired Hotel Klee, in the low-key residential neighborhood of Friedenau, a short ride away from the bustle.

Hotels listed here as $$$$ often come down to a $$ level on weekdays or when there is low demand. You often have the option to decline the inclusion of breakfast, which can save you anywhere from €8 to €30 per person per day.

■ TIP→ The least expensive accommodations are in pensions, which are similar to bed-and-breakfasts. These basic lodgings have limited amenities but include a European breakfast spread, which usually consists of bread, jam, meats, and cheeses. These are mostly found in western districts such as Charlottenburg, Schöneberg, and Wilmersdorf.

German and European travelers often use apartment rental agencies for longer stays, and Americans on a budget should consider this as well (apartments start at €350 per month). In Berlin, double rooms with shared bathrooms in private apartments begin around €33 per day.

$ 🖼 **Wohn-Agentur Freiraum.** This
RENTAL English-speaking agency has its
own guesthouse with rooms and
apartments, as well as private room
listings all over Berlin. $ *Rooms
from: €36* ⊠ *Wiener Str. 14, Kreuzberg* ☎ *030/618–2008* ⊕ *www.frei-
raum.com* 🍽 *No meals.*

LODGING REVIEWS

For expanded hotel reviews, visit Fodors.com. Use the coordinate
(✚ 1:B3) at the end of each listing to locate a site on the corresponding map.

4

MITTE

Staying in Mitte, the heart of city, is incredibly convenient: you'll be
close to many of the major sightseeing destinations, including the Berlin
Cathedral, Museum Island, Unter den Linden, and Brandenburg Gate,
as well as the Hackershmarkt and Alexanderplatz shopping areas.

$ 🖼 **Arte Luise Kunsthotel.** The Luise is one of Berlin's most original bou-
HOTEL tique hotels, with each fantastically creative room in the 1825 building
Fodor's Choice or 2003 built-on wing—facing the Reichstag—styled by a different art-
★ ist. **Pros:** central location; historic flair; individually designed rooms.
Cons: simple rooms with limited amenities and hotel facilities; can be
noisy because of the nearby rail station. $ *Rooms from: €110* ⊠ *Luisen-
str. 19, Mitte* ☎ *030/284–480* ⊕ *www.luise-berlin.com* 🛏 *54 rooms, 36
with bath* 🍽 *No meals* Ⓜ *Friedrichstrasse (U-bahn and S-bahn)* ✚ *1:A2.*

$$ 🖼 **Casa Camper.** This boutique hotel offers a convenient location in the
HOTEL heart of Mitte, with spacious rooms and plenty of perks. **Pros:** airy,
spacious rooms with modern, clean design; 24-hour lounge; central
location near shopping and transportation. **Cons:** view is not great
except on top floor; windows do not open, though hotel is well venti-
lated. $ *Rooms from: €165* ⊠ *Weinmeisterstr. 1, Mitte* ☎ *030/200–034*
⊕ *www.casacamper.com/* 🛏 *40 rooms, 11 suites* 🍽 *Some meals* Ⓜ *Wein-
meisterstrasse (U-bahn) and Hackescher Markt (S-bahn)* ✚ *1:D2.*

$$ 🖼 **Cosmo Hotel Berlin.** This well-located hotel has spacious, airy rooms
HOTEL with large windows and a small but pleasant Finnish sauna. **Pros:** eco
bath products; spacious rooms; convenient location. **Cons:** design may
be over the top for some guests; immediate area is not great. $ *Rooms
from: €104* ⊠ *Spittelmarkt 13, Mitte* ☎ *030/5858–2222* ⊕ *www.cosmo-
hotel.de* 🛏 *76 rooms, 8 suites* 🍽 *No meals* Ⓜ *Spittelmarkt (U-bahn)*
✚ *1:D4.*

$$$ 🖼 **Grand Hyatt Berlin.** Stylish guests feel at home at Europe's first Grand
HOTEL Hyatt, which has a feng shui–approved design that combines inspira-
Fodor's Choice tions from tropical decor, thought-provoking modern art, and the city's
★ history with Bauhaus photographs. **Pros:** large rooms; excellent service;
stylish spa; large pool area. **Cons:** location can be very busy; ongoing
construction may be a nuisance for some travelers; in-room Wi-Fi is

BEST BETS FOR BERLIN LODGING

Fodor's offers a selective listing of quality lodging in every price range, from the best budget beds to the most sophisticated luxury hotels. Those properties that provide a remarkable experience in their price range are designated with the Fodor's Choice logo.

Fodor's Choice ★

Arte Luise Kunsthotel, $, p. 105

Das Stue, $$, p. 110

Ellington Hotel Berlin, $$, p. 110

Grand Hyatt Berlin, $$$, p. 105

Hotel Adlon Kempinski Berlin, $$$$, p. 107

Hotel de Rome, $$$$, p. 107

Soho House, $$$, p. 114

Best by Price

$

Arte Luise Kunsthotel, p. 105

Bleibtreu Berlin, p. 114

Eastern Comfort Boat, p. 111

Hotel Bogota, p. 115

$$

Das Stue, p. 110

Ellington Hotel Berlin, p. 110

Honigmond Hotel and Garden Hotel, p. 107

$$$

Grand Hyatt Berlin, p. 105

The Ritz-Carlton Berlin, p. 108

Soho House, p. 114

$$$$

Hotel Adlon Kempinski Berlin, p. 107

Hotel de Rome, p. 107

Best by Experience

BEST CONCIERGE

Eastern Comfort, $, p. 111

Hotel Adlon Kempinski Berlin, $$$$, p. 107

The Regent Berlin, $$$, p. 108

BEST GRANDES DAMES

Hotel Adlon Kempinski Berlin, $$$$, p. 107

The Regent Berlin, $$$, p. 108

Schlosshotel im Grunewald, $$$$, p. 116

BEST INTERIOR DESIGN

Das Stue, $$, p. 110

Grand Hyatt Berlin, $$$, p. 105

Hotel Q!, $$, p. 115

Hotel de Rome, $$$$, p. 107

Michelberger Hotel, $, p. 111

Propeller Island City Lodge, $$, p. 115

BEST-KEPT SECRET

Arte Luise Kunsthotel, $, p. 105

Bleibtreu Berlin, $, p. 114

Das Stue, $$, p. 110

Honigmond Hotel and Garden Hotel, $$, p. 107

Hotel Bogota, $, p. 115

ÏMA Loft Apartments, $, p. 112

BEST LOCATION

Ellington Hotel Berlin, $$, p. 110

Grand Hyatt Berlin, $$$, p. 105

Hotel Adlon Kempinski Berlin, $$$$, p. 107

Hotel Amano, $, p. 107

Hotel Hackescher Markt, $$, p. 107

Swissôtel Berlin, $$, p. 111

Waldorf Astoria Berlin, $$$$, p. 111

BEST SERVICE

Bleibtreu Berlin, $, p. 114

Grand Hyatt Berlin, $$$, p. 105

Hotel de Rome, $$$$, p. 107

The Regent Berlin, $$$, p. 108

Schlosshotel im Grunewald, $$$$, p. 116

BUSINESS TRAVEL

Brandenburger Hof, $$$, p. 114

Hotel Amano, $, p. 107

Sofitel Gendarmenmarkt, $$$, p. 108

Swissôtel Berlin, $$, p. 111

HIPSTER HOTELS

Hotel Q!, $$, p. 115

Michelberger Hotel, $, p. 111

Soho House, $$$, p. 114

only free for the first 30 minutes. $⑤ Rooms from: €210 ✉ Marlene-Dietrich-Pl. 2, Mitte ☎ 030/2553–1234 ⊕ www.berlin.grand.hyatt.de ⇌ 326 rooms, 16 suites ◯⃓ Breakfast Ⓜ Potsdamer Platz (U-bahn and S-bahn) ✛ 1:A5.*

$$ **Honigmond Hotel and Garden**
HOTEL **Hotel.** These two hotels are charming, quaint oases only a few steps away from the buzzing neighbor-

hoods of Mitte. **Pros:** individually designed rooms; warm, welcoming service; quiet courtyard rooms. **Cons:** front rooms can be noisy due to busy street; restaurant is expensive relative to the area's budget choices. $⑤ Rooms from: €125 ✉ Tieckstr. 12 and Invalidenstr. 122, Mitte ☎ 030/284–4550 ⊕ www.honigmond.de ⇌ 50 rooms ◯⃓ Breakfast Ⓜ Nordbahnhof (S-bahn) ✛ 1:B1.*

$$$$ ⬚ **Hotel Adlon Kempinski Berlin.** The first Adlon was considered Europe's
HOTEL ultimate luxury resort until it was destroyed in the war and the new
Fodor's Choice version, built in 1997, has a nostalgic aesthetic, and the elegant rooms
★ are furnished with turn-of-the-century photos of the original hotel, along with cherrywood trim, mahogany furnishings, and brocade silk bedspreads. **Pros:** top-notch luxury hotel; surprisingly large rooms; excellent in-house restaurants. **Cons:** sometimes stiff service with an attitude; rooms off Linden are noisy with the windows open; inviting lobby often crowded. *⑤ Rooms from: €260 ✉ Unter den Linden 77, Mitte ☎ 030/22610 ⊕ www.kempinski.com/adlon ⇌ 304 rooms, 78 suites ◯⃓ No meals Ⓜ Brandenburger Tor (U-bahn and S-bahn) ✛ 1:A3.*

$ ⬚ **Hotel Amano.** Built as a "budget design hotel," the basic rooms of
HOTEL the Amano are fairly small, and there is no real restaurant or room service, but stay here and you'll be in the center of the action. **Pros:** excellent location; happening bar scene; roof deck and garden. **Cons:** no room service; too trendy for some. *⑤ Rooms from: €85 ✉ Auguststr. 43, Mitte ☎ 030/809–4150 ⊕ www.hotel-amano.com ⇌ 71 rooms, 46 apartments ◯⃓ No meals Ⓜ Rosenthaler Platz (U-bahn) ✛ 1:D1.*

$$$$ ⬚ **Hotel de Rome.** Discreet service and a subdued but boutiquey atmo-
HOTEL sphere make the Hotel de Rome a major draw for the Hollywood jet set.
Fodor's Choice **Pros:** great location; large rooms. **Cons:** design may be over the top for
★ some guests; expensive even for five-star hotel; can be dark during the day due to low lighting. *⑤ Rooms from: €270 ✉ Behrenstr. 37, Mitte ☎ 030/460–6090 ⊕ www.hotelderome.com ⇌ 109 rooms, 37 suites ◯⃓ No meals Ⓜ Französische Strasse (U-bahn) ✛ 1:C3.*

$$ ⬚ **Hotel Hackescher Markt.** Amid the nightlife around Hackescher Markt,
HOTEL this hotel provides discreet and inexpensive top services. **Pros:** great location for shops, restaurants, and nightlife; large rooms. **Cons:** some rooms may be noisy due to tram stop; rooms in need of an update. *⑤ Rooms from: €119 ✉ Grosse Präsidentenstr. 8, Mitte ☎ 030/280–030 ⊕ www.hotel-hackescher-markt.com ⇌ 27 rooms, 5 suites ◯⃓ No meals Ⓜ Hackescher Markt (S-bahn) ✛ 1:D2.*

$$ **Monbijou Hotel.** This new Hackerschermarkt hotel offers a central location, scenic views of the Berlin Cathedral, and affordable rooms, making it a great option for business travels and sightseers. **Pros:** great, convenient location; good value. **Cons:** limited amenities; small rooms; no room service. $ *Rooms from: €100* ✉ *Monbijoupl. 1, Mitte* ☎ *030/6162–0300* ⊕ *monbijouhotel.com* ⇱ *89 rooms, 12 suites* ❍❘ *No meals* Ⓜ *Hackescher Markt (S-bahn)* ✛ *1:C2.*

HOTEL

$$ **Radisson Blu Berlin.** This hotel has an ideal location in the heart of Berlin near the Berlin Cathedral, Nikolai Church, and Unter den Linden, but you may prefer a view into the courtyard, where the world's largest cylindrical aquarium is located. **Pros:** central location; discounted entry to the adjacent Sea Life Berlin. **Cons:** location can be very busy. $ *Rooms from: €159* ✉ *Karl-Liebknecht-Str. 3, Prenzlauer Berg* ☎ *030/238–280* ⊕ *www.radissonblu.com/hotel-berlin* ⇱ *403 rooms, 24 suites* ❍❘ *No meals* Ⓜ *Hackescher Markt (S-bahn)* ✛ *1:D3.*

HOTEL

$$$ **Regent Berlin.** One of Germany's most esteemed hotels, the Regent pairs the opulence of gilt furniture, thick carpets, marble floors, tasseled settees, and crystal chandeliers with such modern conveniences as flat-screen TVs. **Pros:** Berlin's most hushed five-star hotel; unobtrusive service; very large rooms and top location off Gendarmenmarkt. **Cons:** some public areas in need of update; the primary hotel restaurant specializes in fish only. $ *Rooms from: €225* ✉ *Charlottenstr. 49, Mitte* ☎ *030/20338* ⊕ *www.regenthotels.com* ⇱ *156 rooms, 39 suites* ❍❘ *No meals* ✛ *1:C3.*

HOTEL

$$$ **The Ritz-Carlton Berlin.** Judging from the outside of this gray, high-rise hotel that soars above Potsdamer Platz, you may never guess that inside it's all luxurious, 19th-century grandeur. **Pros:** stylish and luxurious interior design; great views; elegant setting yet informal service. **Cons:** rooms surprisingly small for a luxury hotel; not family-friendly (business-oriented atmosphere). $ *Rooms from: €215* ✉ *Potsdamer Pl. 3, Mitte* ☎ *030/337–777* ⊕ *www.ritzcarlton.com* ⇱ *264 rooms, 39 suites* ❍❘ *No meals* Ⓜ *Potsdamer Platz (U-bahn and S-bahn)* ✛ *1:A4.*

HOTEL

$$$ **Sofitel Berlin Gendarmenmarkt.** This luxurious place to stay has maximized the minimalist look of East Berlin architecture. **Pros:** great location off one of the city's most beautiful squares; sumptuous breakfast buffet; great Austrian restaurant, Aigner. **Cons:** limited facilities for a luxury hotel; smallish rooms. $ *Rooms from: €200* ✉ *Charlottenstr. 50–52, Mitte* ☎ *030/203–750* ⊕ *www.sofitel.com* ⇱ *70 rooms, 22 suites* ❍❘ *No meals* Ⓜ *Französische Strasse (U-bahn)* ✛ *1:C4.*

HOTEL

WORD OF MOUTH

"I'm one who enjoys staying at the Potsdamerplatz (Hyatt, Ritz, etc.) because it's a very modern and well designed area. You can walk to the Brandenburg Gate, the Holocaust memorial and Parliament building and there are tons of restaurants, shops and entertainment center. It also gives easy direct access to the Mitte as well as the old West Berlin. Staying in the Mitte gives you the added benefit of being close to the artsy/bohemian Prenzlauerberg area. Truth to be told, everything is easily accessed with the fantastic modern transportation network that Berlin has." —dax

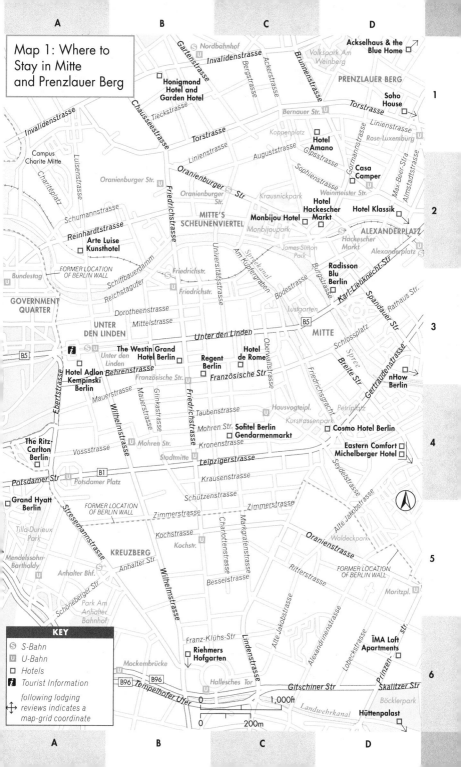

$$$$ ⬚ **The Westin Grand Hotel Berlin.** This large hotel in a renovated East
HOTEL German building has a great location at the corner of Friedrichstrasse
and Unter den Linden. **Pros:** impressive lobby; recently updated rooms;
perfect location for historic sights and shopping. **Cons:** service often
not on five-star level; no great views; may feel street vibrations in lower
rooms off Friedrichstrasse, as well as noise due to street construction.
⑤ *Rooms from: €250* ⊠ *Friedrichstr. 158–164, Mitte* ☎ *030/20270*
⊕ *www.westingrandberlin.com* ↩ *350 rooms, 50 suites* ⦿*No meals*
Ⓜ *Französische Strasse (U-bahn)* ✛ *1:B3.*

TIERGARTEN

You can't actually stay in the Tiergarten, the sprawling 520-acre park
that stretches from Brandenburg Gate to the Berlin Zoo, but if being
near the park and its scenic pathways, ponds, and lakes is a priority, the
hotels across the street are about as close as you can get.

$$ ⬚ **Das Stue.** History meets contemporary style in the heart of Berlin, in
HOTEL a building that once housed the Royal Danish Embassy and still retains
Fodor's Choice governmental grandeur—from the classical facade to the dramatic entry
★ staircase—now mixed with warming touches like cozy nooks designed
by Patricia Uriquola. **Pros:** central location; popular restaurants and
bar; Berlin Zoo views. **Cons:** small spa can book up fast. ⑤ *Rooms
from: €153* ⊠ *Drakestrasse 1, Tiergarten* ☎ *030/311–7220* ⊕ *www.
das-stue.com/en/* ↩ *80 rooms and suites* ⦿*No meals* ✛ *2:B6.*

$$ ⬚ **Ellington Hotel Berlin.** Tucked away behind the beautiful, historic
HOTEL facade of a grand Bauhaus-style office building, this sleek, modern
Fodor's Choice hotel has small but stylish rooms, accentuated with modern art. **Pros:**
★ stylish interior design with alluring 1920s touches; perfect location off
Tauentzienstrasse and great for shopping sprees; nice bar; great, green
courtyard. **Cons:** small rooms; no spa. ⑤ *Rooms from: €128* ⊠ *Nürn-
bergerstr. 50–55, Tiergarten* ☎ *030/683–150* ⊕ *www.ellington-hotel.
com* ↩ *285 rooms* ⦿*No meals* Ⓜ *Wittenbergplatz (U-bahn)* ✛ *2:C6.*

$ ⬚ **Hotel Astoria at Kurfürstendamm.** Each simple room in this small build-
HOTEL ing, which dates back to 1898, is different, and the service is exceptional. **Pros:** some rooms are individually designed with old-world style;
warm and personal service; quiet location on central Ku'damm side
street. **Cons:** furniture and rooms need update; many rooms on the
smaller side; many rooms without air-conditioning. ⑤ *Rooms from:
€94* ⊠ *Fasanenstr. 2, Tiergarten* ☎ *030/312–4067* ⊕ *www.hotelastoria.
de* ↩ *32 rooms* ⦿*No meals* Ⓜ *Uhlandstrasse (U-bahn), Zoologsicher
Garten (U-bahn and S-bahn)* ✛ *2:C5.*

$$ ⬚ **Hotel Palace.** This is one of the only privately owned first-class hotels
HOTEL in the heart of western downtown, and although it may not look like
much from the outside, inside, the friendly staff and spacious rooms
make it a popular choice. **Pros:** large rooms; quiet, central location;
impeccable service. **Cons:** interior design outdated in some areas; nearby
area of Europa-Center and Breitscheidplatz not the most interesting.
⑤ *Rooms from: €128* ⊠ *Europa-Center, Budapesterstr. 45, Tiergarten*
☎ *030/25020* ⊕ *www.palace.de* ↩ *238 rooms, 40 suites* ⦿*No meals*
Ⓜ *Zoologsicher Garten (U-bahn and S-bahn)* ✛ *2:C6.*

$$ **Swissôtel Berlin.** At the bustling corner of Ku'damm and Joachimst-
HOTEL   haler Strasse, this hotel excels with its reputable Swiss hospitality—from accompanying guests to their floor after check-in to equipping each room with an iron, an umbrella, and a Nespresso espresso machine that preheats the cups. **Pros:** large rooms; unobtrusive service; great location. **Cons:** the lobby is on the third floor, with shops on the lowers levels; mostly for business travelers. ⑤ *Rooms from: €130* ✉ *Augsburger Str. 44, Tiergarten* ☎ *030/220–100* ⊕ *www.swissotel.com* ⤳ *296 rooms, 20 suites* ⦿ *No meals* Ⓜ *Kurfürstendamm (U-bahn)* ✛ *2:C5.*

$$$$ **Waldorf Astoria Berlin.** This impressive skyscraper, a nod to the Wal-
HOTEL   dorf's original New York location, has a chic art deco look and unparalleled service. **Pros:** ideal location near Ku'damm; large, luxurious rooms and bathrooms; several eateries and bars. **Cons:** limited amenities for the price; nearby construction may bother some travelers. ⑤ *Rooms from: €230* ✉ *Hardenbergst. 28, Tiergarten* ☎ *030/814–0000* ⊕ *www. waldorfastoriaberlin.com* ⤳ *152 rooms, 50 suites* ⦿ *No meals* Ⓜ *Zoologsicher Garten (U-bahn and S-bahn)* ✛ *2:C5.*

FRIEDRICHSHAIN

The small cobblestone streets of Friedrichshain have a neighborhood feel and the hotels here are convenient to bustling bars, cafés, and shops.

$ **Hotel Klassik.** One of the best things about the Hotel Klassik is its
HOTEL   central location, walking distance to Friedrichshain's countless eating, drinking, and shopping hot spots. **Pros:** excellent location for neighborhood vibe and access to transportation; plentiful, fresh breakfast buffet; friendly and helpful staff. **Cons:** located on a loud and busy corner. ⑤ *Rooms from: €89* ✉ *Revaler Str. 6* ☎ *30/319–8860* ⊕ *www.hotelklassik-berlin.com* ⤳ *57 rooms, 2 suites* ⦿ *Breakfast* Ⓜ *Warschauer Straße (U-bahn and S-bahn)* ✛ *1:D2.*

$ **Michelberger Hotel.** Started by a group of young Berliners who
HOTEL   dreamed of a uniquely designed, artsy space, the Michelberger Hotel is part budget hotel, part clubhouse, and part bar and restaurant. **Pros:** located at the epicenter of eastern Berlin nightlife; great design and fun atmosphere; affordable prices. **Cons:** busy thoroughfare and transit hub, so front rooms can be noisy; casual service without luxury amenities; no phone in rooms. ⑤ *Rooms from: €60* ✉ *Warschauer Str. 39–40, Friedrichshain* ☎ *030/2977–8590* ⊕ *www.michelbergerhotel. com* ⤳ *113 rooms* ⦿ *No meals* Ⓜ *Warschauer Str. (S-bahn)* ✛ *1:D4.*

KREUZBERG

Stay in hip Kreuzberg if you want to be in the midst of young Berlin. Much of Berlin's famed nightclub scene is here and there are plenty of waterfront paths by the Spree River as well as cafés and restaurants to explore.

$ **Eastern Comfort.** The Spree River is one of Berlin's best assets, and at Eastern Comfort you'll wake up on it in this moored, three-level ship with simple cabins. **Pros:** unique accommodation on a boat; friendly staff; perfect location for nightclubbing in Kreuzberg and Friedrichshain.

Cons: insects may be a bother in summer; smallish rooms not pleasant in rainy or stormy weather; lack of privacy. $ *Rooms from: €62* ⊠ *Mühlenstr. 73–77, Kreuzberg* ☎ *030/6676–3806* ⊕ *www. eastern-comfort.com* ⬎ *26 cabins* ⦿ *No meals* Ⓜ *Warschauer Strasse (U-bahn and S-bahn)* ✛ *1:D4.*

WORD OF MOUTH

"I would certainly stay somewhere in Kreuzberg. I think the place has heaps of character and of course lots of restaurants and cafes. We recently spent 5 nights in Berlin and stayed at Kreuzberg."

—Shraddha

$
RENTAL
▦ **ÏMA Loft Apartments.** A comfortable cross between apartment rental and hotel, ÏMA's aim is to throw its guests into the fray of Kreuzberg's hectic, artistic, multicultural scene. **Pros:** maximum privacy (a separate entrance means you never have to interact with hotel staff and other guests unless you want to). **Cons:** minimal amenities and services. $ *Rooms from: €79* ⊠ *Ritterstr. 12–14, Kreuzberg* ☎ *030/6162–8913* ⊕ *www.imalofts.com* ⬎ *20 apartments* ⦿ *No meals* Ⓜ *Moritzplatz (U-bahn)* ✛ *1:D6.*

$$
HOTEL
▦ **nHow Berlin.** This spot bills itself as the music hotel—it hosts regular open mike nights, has two sound studios overlooking the Spree River, and will send a guitar or keyboard to your room anytime creativity strikes. **Pros:** beautiful location on the Spree River; unique music theme; convenient location in Kreuzberg. **Cons:** design isn't to everyone's taste; slightly isolated from neighborhood restaurants and bars; Wi-Fi not reliable. $ *Rooms from: €120* ⊠ *Stralauer Allee 3, Kreuzberg* ☎ *030/290-2990* ⊕ *www.nhow-hotels.com/berlin/en/* ⬎ *263 rooms, 41 suites* ⦿ *No meals* Ⓜ *Warschauer Strasse (S-bahn and U-bahn)* ✛ *1:D3.*

NEUKÖLLN

A bit removed from the hustle and bustle, this is an up-and-coming neighborhood with plenty of cafés, markets, and shops. Note that some of the streets can feel a bit desolate in the evenings.

$
B&B/INN
▦ **Hüttenpalast.** These individually decorated cabins and vintage caravans, in the heart of up-and-coming Neuköln, offer a funky take on glamping (glam indoor camping). **Pros:** unique experience; large community spaces encourage traveler interactions. **Cons:** minimal amenities and services; some campers are very small; neighborhood may feel rundown to some. $ *Rooms from: €55* ⊠ *Hobrechtstr. 66, Neukölln* ☎ *030/3730–5806* ⊕ *www.huettenpalast.de* ⬎ *46 beds, 18 cabins and caravans* ⦿ *Breakfast* Ⓜ *Hermannplatz (U-bahn)* ✛ *1:D6.*

PRENZLAUER BERG

This is an excellent alternative to staying in Mitte: the tree-lined streets and Altbau homes are charming and much quieter, and trams can get you downtown quickly. It's an upscale area with boutiques, galleries, and trendy cafés.

$$
B&B/INN
▦ **Ackselhaus & the Blue Home.** This boutique bed-and-breakfast is tucked on a quiet tree-lined street in Prenzlauer Berg and offers uniquely

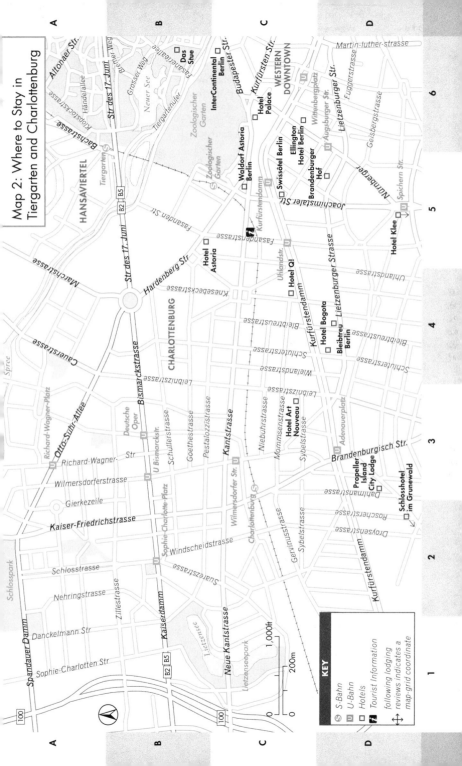

Map 2: Where to Stay in Tiergarten and Charlottenburg

KEY

- Ⓢ S-Bahn
- Ⓤ U-Bahn
- ☐ Hotels
- ⓘ Tourist Information
- *following lodging reviews indicates a map-grid coordinate*
- ⟷

designed rooms which give the feel of a finely appointed guest house rather then a stuffy hotel. **Pros:** Intimate location away from the bustle of the city but close to transportation; unique themed rooms. **Cons:** Limited amenities and services; reception is only staffed until 10pm. $ *Rooms from: €160* ✉ *Belfort Straße 21, Prenzlauer Berg* ☎ *030/4433-76 33* ⊕ *www.ackselhaus.de/* ⇱ *35 rooms* ⓘⓞⓘ *Breakfast* Ⓜ *Senefelderplatz (U-bahn)* ✛ *1:D1.*

"I stayed in Prenzlauer Berg last fall and loved it for the cafes and restaurants nearby and only a couple of stops away on the U-Bahn to Museum Island, etc. Some really great restaurants there!" —amyb

WORD OF MOUTH

$$$ ▦ **Soho House.** The Berlin branch of this luxury hotel–club brings the
HOTEL chic atmosphere of London and New York's Soho to the German capi-
Fodor's Choice tal. **Pros:** great staff; perfect location for club- and bar-hopping; rooftop
★ pool. **Cons:** may seem too clubby. $ *Rooms from: €180* ✉ *Torstr. 1, Mitte: Scheunenviertel* ☎ *030/405–0440* ⊕ *www.sohohouseberlin.com* ⇱ *65 rooms* ⓘⓞⓘ *No meals* Ⓜ *Rosa-Luxemburg-Platz (U-bahn)* ✛ *1:D1.*

CHARLOTTENBURG

Just west of the Tiergarten, this neighborhood has a Parisian feel with its grand historic buildings, fancy five-star hotels and pensions, and the ritzy shopping street of Kurfürstendamm.

$$ ▦ **Hotel Art Nouveau.** The English-speaking owners' discerning taste in
B&B/INN antiques, color combinations, and even televisions (a few designed by Philippe Starck) makes this B&B-like pension a great place to stay. **Pros:** stylish ambience; friendly and personal service; great B&B feeling, despite being a hotel. **Cons:** front rooms can be noisy due to heavy traffic on Leibnizstrasse; few amenities for a hotel of this price category; downtown walks, yet longer walks to all major sights in the area. $ *Rooms from: €126* ✉ *Leibnizstr. 59, Charlottenburg* ☎ *030/327–7440* ⊕ *www.hotelartnouveau.de* ⇱ *16 rooms, 6 suites* ⓘⓞⓘ *Breakfast* Ⓜ *Adenauerplatz (U-bahn)* ✛ *2:C3.*

$ ▦ **Bleibtreu Berlin.** Opened in 1995, Berlin's first design hotel is relatively
HOTEL unassuming, with simple and serene rooms decorated with untreated oak, polished stone, and neutral shades. **Pros:** warm, welcoming service; top location on one of Ku'damm's most beautiful side streets; international clientele. **Cons:** design somewhat dated; rooms not overly comfortable for price; few amenities. $ *Rooms from: €92* ✉ *Bleibtreustr. 31, Charlottenburg* ☎ *030/884–740* ⊕ *www.bleibtreu.com* ⇱ *60 rooms* ⓘⓞⓘ *No meals* Ⓜ *Uhlandstrasse (U-bahn)* ✛ *2:D4.*

$$$ ▦ **Brandenburger Hof.** On a quiet residential street this turn-of-the-20th-
HOTEL century mansion feels like a hideaway even though Ku'damm is a short walk away. **Pros:** great mansion; quiet location only steps away from the Ku'damm; large rooms. **Cons:** stuffy atmosphere; extras are expensive; no pool or fitness club on-site. $ *Rooms from: €215* ✉ *Eislebenerstr. 14, Tiergarten* ☎ *030/214–050* ⊕ *www.brandenburger-hof.com* ⇱ *58 rooms, 14 suites* ⓘⓞⓘ *No meals* Ⓜ *Augsburger Strasse (U-bahn)* ✛ *2:D5.*

$ **Hotel Bogota.** Fashion photogra-
B&B/INN phy and colorful artwork remind
guests of the artists and designers
who lived in this circa 1900 apartment house on an elegant Ku'damm
side street. **Pros:** historic ambience;
on one of Ku'damm's most beautiful side streets; large, comfortable rooms. **Cons:** thin walls; some
rooms with 1950s feeling; breakfast
is included, but nothing special.
$ *Rooms from: €85 ⊠ Schlüterstr.
45, Charlottenburg ☎ 030/881–
5001 ⊕ www.bogota.de ➴114
rooms, 70 with bath ⦿ Breakfast
Ⓜ Uhlandstrasse (U-bahn) ✢ 2:D4.*

$$ **Hotel Q!.** The Q! has received several international design awards,
HOTEL and it's easy to see how the gently sloping, sweeping interior of the hotel
could charm any judge. **Pros:** beautiful design; affordable rates; great
location for exploring western downtown. **Cons:** not for families; night-
life makes hotel noisy at times. $ *Rooms from: €120 ⊠ Knesebeckstr.
67, Charlottenburg ☎ 030/810–0660 ⊕ www.loock-hotels.com ➴73
rooms, 4 suites ⦿ No meals Ⓜ Uhlandstrasse (U-bahn), Savignyplatz
(S-bahn) ✢ 2:C4.*

$$ **InterContinental Berlin.** From the heavily trafficked street, the huge
HOTEL "InterConti," the epitome of old West Berlin, evokes the Louvre with
its glass pyramid entrance. **Pros:** large rooms with great views; friendly
and impeccable service; one of Berlin's best spa areas. **Cons:** street is
not inviting; huge hotel lacks atmosphere and can feel businesslike;
room design somewhat bland. $ *Rooms from: €104 ⊠ Budapester Str.
2, Charlottenburg ☎ 030/26020 ⊕ www.berlin.intercontinental.com/
➴498 rooms, 60 suites Ⓜ Zoologsicher Garten (U-bahn and S-bahn)
✢ 2:C6.*

$$ **Propeller Island City Lodge.** At this wildly eccentric accommodation,
B&B/INN you can choose from 27 Wonderlands, each with one-of-a-kind design
by multitalented artist Lars Stroschen. **Pros:** individually designed
rooms; personal and friendly atmosphere; quiet location on Ku'damm
side street. **Cons:** designer art rooms can be overwhelming; few ame-
nities; slow service. $ *Rooms from: €130 ⊠ Albrecht-Achilles-Str. 58,
Charlottenburg ☎ 030/891–9016 8 am–noon, 0163/256–5909 noon–8
pm, general info/inquiries ⊕ www.propeller-island.de ➴25 rooms, 20
with bath; 2 suites Ⓜ Adenauerplatz (U-bahn) ✢ 2:D3.*

FRIEDENAU

This western neighborhood, directly south of Charlottenburg, is fairly
residential, with quiet tree-lined streets and a handful of cafés.

$ **Hotel Klee.** Located on a quiet residential street, this new basic hotel
HOTEL is a great option if you're looking for a reasonable price with some
extras. **Pros:** large rooms and good amenities for the price; pretty, quiet

street; near transportation with quick access to city center. **Cons:** very residential neighborhood is not within walking distance to landmarks; smallish beds; furniture a bit dated. $ *Rooms from: €99* ✉ *Bundesallee 75, Friedenau* ☎ *030/4050–8630* ⊕ *www.hotelklee.com* ⌂ *79 rooms, 3 suites* ⦿| *No meals* Ⓜ *Friedrich-Wilhelm-Platz (U-bahn)* ✛ *2:D5.*

GRUNEWALD

Grunewald is a massive forest that sits directly west of the city. There are exquisite historic mansions in the surrounding residential neighborhoods but it's less convenient to the major sights of the city.

$$$$
HOTEL
🏨 **Schlosshotel im Grunewald.** In the beautiful, verdant setting of residential Grunewald, the small but palatial hotel is full of classic style and lavish decor. **Pros:** quiet and green setting with lovely garden; large rooms in classic style; impeccable service. **Cons:** far away from any sights; sometimes stiff atmosphere; not for families. $ *Rooms from: €239* ✉ *Brahmsstr. 10, Grunewald* ☎ *030/895–840* ⊕ *www.schlosshotelberlin.com* ⌂ *43 rooms, 10 suites* ⦿| *No meals* Ⓜ *Grunewald (S-bahn)* ✛ *2:D2.*

SHOPPING

Updated by
Katherine
Sacks

Thanks to its unique mixture of old-world charm and eclectic creativity, Berlin is a shopper's paradise. The city becomes a veritable fashion capital during the exquisite fashion shows and events of the biannual Berlin Fashion Week, and trade events like Bread & Butter regularly encourage local and international designers to highlight their work in showrooms and boutiques here. From extravagant designer shopping malls and high-end fashion boutiques to artisan handcraft producers, antique markets, and vintage stores, Berlin has something for everyone.

The city's history plays an important part in its geography. Because Berlin was divided by the Berlin Wall for so many years, there is no pedestrian zone or single city center like many other European cities. Instead Berlin has many different areas to explore and pockets of retailers are spread throughout its neighborhoods.

The city's most glamorous shopping can be done near Mitte's Friedrichstrasse and in the West Berlin promenade Kurfürstendamm, known as the Shopping Mile and home to the luxurious Kaufhaus des Westens department store, as well as many designer and big name international brands. But the charming side streets nearby Mitte's Torstrasse and Hackescher Markt have become a much more popular destination for shopping in the city, with chic designers opening up ateliers and concept shops.

For the fashionable bohemian set, designer labels have less appeal here than elsewhere. You'll see many of the young and trendy wearing clothes that appear to have cost not much more than a brötchen (bread roll), and vintage and secondhand clothes are popular. The eastern neighborhoods of Kreuzberg and Neukölln are home to a growing number of vintage and secondhand shops, and the city has a wonderful collection of flea markets that operate year-round. You'll see modern influences of the Berlin's Bauhaus architecture background in many of shops, incorporated into the store displays or as part of the home decor items. Near West Berlin's charming Savignyplatz, the stilwerk interior design center and surrounding design and home stores on Kantstrasse, have become the design hub for the city. For shoppers looking for more price-conscious home furnishings, Neukölln offers several vintage furniture shops featuring Danish and Scandinavian home decor.

PLANNING

OPEN HOURS

Don't expect round-the-clock shopping in Germany; most shops are only open until 8 pm, and nearly all of the major shops, excluding restaurants, tourist retailers, and transportation operators are closed on Sunday. There are the occasional Sunday shopping days—on two Advent Sundays and near important events—when the stores open on Sunday afternoon for several hours.

CASH OR CREDIT

Visitors should keep in mind that credit card usage is not as common in Germany as it is elsewhere. Although it's becoming more widely accepted, especially in luxury fashion stores and large international chains, many stores don't accept credit cards and in smaller boutiques and shops, you should expect to pay in cash.

MARKETS

Berlin's many antique- and flea markets offer another option when looking for vintage, secondhand, and unique items. Along with brunch, flea markets are another perennial Sunday staple in Berlin, and this town has one of them to suit every disposition.

TOP SOUVENIRS

Favorite souvenirs to buy in Berlin include anything with the Brandenburger Tor or Fernsehturm motif; Buddy Bears, which come painted in a variety of colors and themes; and items decorated with the Monopolylook-alike red-and-green Ampelmännchen. And always looking to reinvent itself, the city sponsored a souvenir competition contest in 2013, encouraging creative designs to represent the city's unique spirit. For something with a bit more historical weight, look for GDR-era souvenirs from one of the few shops that still stocks items made in the former East.

MITTE

The finest shops in historic Berlin, including the French department store Galeries Lafayette and the international luxury department store Department Store Quartier 206, are along Friedrichstrasse. And near Friedrichstrasse, Unter den Linden has a few souvenir shops and a Meissen ceramic showroom, while the area surrounding the picturesque Gendarmenmarkt is home to top fashion designers and many international brands.

In Mitte, the charming side streets of the Scheunenviertel area have become the true destination for serious fashion aficionados. The area between Hackescher Markt, Weinmeister Strasse, and Rosa-Luxemburg-Platz have pricey independent designers alongside groovy secondhand shops and a string of ultrahip flagship stores by the big sports and fashion designer brands. Neue Schönhauser Strasse meets up with Rosenthaler Strasse on one end and curves into Alte Schönhauser Strasse on the other. All three streets are full of stylish and original casual wear. Galleries along Gipsstrasse and Sophienstrasse round out the mix.

BEAUTY SHOPS

Aesop. The first German branch of this Australian luxury cosmetics label opened in 2013 in Mitte to the pleasure of many Berliners. The entire line of Aesop's natural skin, hair, and body care products are sold here, in a lovely shop decorated with handmade jade green tiles and a vintage 1950s farmhouse sink. ✉ *Alte Schönhauserstr. 48, Mitte: Scheunenviertel* ☎ *030/2809–6560* ⊕ *www.aesop.com.*

Wheadon's Beauty Shop. This cool beauty shop offers an assortment of goods, from lovely scented candles to lotions and body products to make-up and cosmetics, with popular brands like Dr. Bronner, Börlind, and Susanne Kaufmann. But the real gem is the basement level men's barbershop and spa area, where a 20-minute "Jet O2 peeling" facial is available. ✉ *Steinstrasse 17, Mitte: Scheunenviertel* ☎ *017/6361–44509* ⊕ *www.wheadon.de/* ☯ *Tue.–Sat. 12-7.*

BOOK STORES

Fodor's Choice
★

Do You Read Me? Whether you're looking for something to read on the plane or a special present, this charming bookstore is guaranteed to have something to pique your literary interests. The wide selection of magazines and literature—many of the titles are in English—comes from around the world and spans fashion, photography, architecture, interior design, and cultural topics. ✉ *Auguststr. 28, Mitte: Scheunenviertel* ☎ *030/6954–9695* ⊕ *www.doyoureadme.de* ☯ *Closed Sun.*

Dussmann das KulturKaufhaus. Berlin's largest general bookstore, this five-story emporium has two levels of English language titles, including unusual books, new releases, and classics. The store is open until midnight on weekdays, and until 11:30 on Saturday. ✉ *Friedrichstraße 90, Mitte: Unter den Linden* ☎ *030/2025–1111* ⊕ *www.kulturkaufhaus. de* ☯ *Closed Sun.*

CLOTHING

14 oz. Inside a beautiful old building in the heart of Mitte's Hackescher Markt shopping district, 14 oz. sells high-end denim (Citizens of Humanity, Dondup, 3x1 Denim), along with sneakers, accessories, knitwear, and outerwear. For true VIP treatment, a private shopping area is available on the second floor. ✉ *Neue Schönhauserstr. 13, Mitte: Scheunenviertel* ⊕ *www.14oz-berlin.com/berlin* ☯ *Closed Sun.*

Annette Görtz. This Gendarmenmarkt showroom is German fashion icon Annette Görtz's Berlin flagship. Her collection of women's clothing is known for the clean lines, dark colors, and a combination of comfort and refined tailoring and elegance. ✉ *Markgrafenstr. 42, Mitte: Unter den Linden* ☎ *030/20074–613* ⊕ *www.annettegoertz.de.*

Apartment. Don't be deterred when you arrive at this seemingly empty storefront: the real treasure lies at the bottom of the black spiral staircase. On the basement level you'll find one of Berlin's favorite shops for local designs and wardrobe staples for both men and women. Think distressed tops, shoes, leather jackets, and skinny jeans. ⊠ *Memhardstr. 8, Mitte: Scheunenviertel* ☎ *030/2804–2251* ⊕ *www.apartmentberlin. de* ⊘ *Closed Sun.*

Baerck. Baerck artfully displays its mix of European and Berlin men's and women's wear on wheeled structures, allowing them to be rearranged in the store whenever necessary. Along with designers like Stine Goya, Henrik Vibskov, and Hope, you'll find the store's own labels NIA and llot llov. Lifestyle and interior decor items are on the basement level. ⊠ *Mulackstr. 12, Mitte: Scheunenviertel* ☎ *030/2404–8994* ⊕ *www.baerck.net* ⊘ *Closed Sun.*

Fodor'sChoice
★
C'est Tout. Formerly the head of style for MTV networks, Katja Will opened this boutique in 2007 to share her love of French style and bring a Parisian look to the German capital. Layering the neutral pieces here with a touch of sparkle creates a defininte *ooh-la-la* effect. ⊠ *Mulackstr. 26, Mitte: Scheunenviertel* ☎ *030/2759–5530* ⊕ *www.cesttout.de* ⊘ *Closed Sun.*

Claudia Skoda. Claudia Skoda is one of Berlin's top avant-garde designers. Her creations are mostly for women, but there's also a selection of men's knitwear. ⊠ *Mulackstr. 8, Mitte: Scheunenviertel* ☎ *030/4004– 1884* ⊕ *www.claudiaskoda.com* ⊘ *Closed Sun.*

The Corner Berlin. In the heart of the stunning Gendarmarkt, this luxury concept store sells a contemporary collection of new and vintage clothing from high-end designers like Yves Saint Laurent and Chloé, as well as cosmetics, home furnishings, and art books. The shop is also a popular venue for exclusive fashion events and is home to a gallery and café. ⊠ *Franzoesischestr. 40, Mitte: Unter den Linden* ☎ *030/2067–0940* ⊕ *www.thecornerberlin.de* ⊘ *Closed Sun.*

Fodor'sChoice
★
Das Neue Schwarz. Whether you want a new little black dress or a cool vintage bag to carry around this season, a peek into the lovely Das Neue Schwarz (The New Black) is guaranteed to result in some special finds. In the midst of Mitte's fashionista neighborhood of avant-garde designers and exclusive boutiques, this shop holds its own with a collection of secondhand items, many never worn, from big name designers including Vivienne Westwood, Helmut Lang, and Yves Saint Laurent. ⊠ *Mulackstr. 38, Mitte: Scheunenviertel* ☎ *030/2787–4467* ⊕ *www. dasneueschwarz.de* ⊘ *Closed Sun.*

Fodor'sChoice
★
Lala Berlin. Former MTV editor Lelya Piedayesh is one of Berlin's top young design talents and she has a contemporary boutique on Mulackstrasse. It's pricey, but the scarves are to die for; clothes have bold prints on high-quality fabric. ⊠ *Mulackstr. 7, Mitte: Scheunenviertel* ☎ *030/2576–2924* ⊕ *www.lalaberlin.com* ⊘ *Closed Sun.*

Made in Berlin. One of the more established secondhand shops in Berlin, this outpost has two popular locations that crowd with trend-setting locals and discerning visitors looking for hidden gems. The selection is more curated thrift looks than high-end designs, and includes an extensive range of 1980s wear as well as a broad selection of shoes. ■ TIP→ Make sure to pop in for the shops' happy hours, where you'll get 20 percent off on purchases (Tues. 12-3 at Neue Schönhauser Str.; Wed 10-3 at Friedrichstr.). ⊠ *Neue Schönhauser Strasse 19, Mitte: Scheunenviertel* ☎ *030/2404–8900* ⊕ *https://www.facebook.com/MadeinBerlinVintage* ☉ *Mon.–Sat. 12-8.*

Oukan. This demure boutique originally began as a fundraising project during Berlin's Fashion Week in response to the 2011 Japanese tsunami. Along with two floors of avant garde Japanese designs, lifestyle products, and interior décor, the space is also home to Avan, an in-house tea house serving a variety of Asian-fusion dishes like banh mi sandwiches, dumplings, and curries. ⊠ *Kronenstrasse 71, Mitte: Unter den Linden* ☎ *030/2062–6700* ⊕ *www.oukan.de/* ☉ *Mon.–Sat. 12–7.*

Wald. Run by model Joyce Binnebose and stylist Dana Roski, this brightly colored boutique offers Mitte's discerning shoppers a carefully curated mix of international designers such as Don't Shoot the Messengers and Stefanel. ⊠ *Alte Schönhauserstr. 32c, Mitte: Scheunenviertel* ☎ *030/6005–1164* ⊕ *www.wald-berlin.de* ☉ *Closed Sun.*

Wunderkind. Potsdam's hometown hero, fashion designer Wolfgang Joop brings his vibrant designs to Berlin at this Mitte atelier. ⊠ *Tucholskystrasse 36, Mitte: Scheunenviertel* ☎ *030/280–41817* ⊕ *wunderkind. com/* ☉ *Mon.–Sat. 11-7.*

XVII. This Mitte vintage closet, pronounced dix-sept, carries a beautiful collection of vintage items, from high-end designer pieces to carefully selected off brands. Styles range from 1960s printed dresses to leather jackets from the 90s, as well as shoes, bags, and jewelry. ⊠ *Steinstr. 17, Mitte: Scheunenviertel* ☎ *030/544–82882* ⊕ *www.xvii-store.com/* ☉ *Mon.-Fri. 12-7; Sat. 12-5.*

CLOTHING: MEN'S

A.D. Deertz. This tiny shop on Torstrasse is the flagship outlet for designer Wibke Deertz, who uses fabrics and inspirations from her travels around the world to create a collection of handmade, limited-edition pieces, including pants, shirts, jackets, and accessories. ⊠ *Torstr. 106, Mitte: Scheunenviertel* ☎ *030/9120–6630* ⊕ *www.addeertz.com/* ☉ *Closed Sun.*

Fodor's Choice
★
Atelier Akeef. This Mitte store combines men's luxury style with a holistic, eco-conscious shopping approach. The upcycled wood-paneled store was constructed using nontoxic colorants, sustainable clay, and energy-saving lightening, and each garment comes with a tag outlining the specifics of its eco-production. ⊠ *Max-Beer-Str. 31, Mitte: Scheunenviertel* ☎ *030/2198–2645* ⊕ *www.atelierakeef.com.*

Fodor's Choice
★
SOTO. SOTO is the name of the hip, fashion-forward area of Mitte, south of Torstraße, filled with charming side streets and numerous fashion boutiques. At the SOTO boutique you'll find a mix of timeless and trendsetting menswear including the house label, Le Berlinois, along with brands like Band of Outsiders, Norse Projects, and Our Legacy, grooming products, and accessories ranging from cameras to lanyards.

✉ *Torstraße 72, Mitte: Scheunenviertel* ☎ *030/257–62070* ⊕ *www. sotostore.com* ☾ *Closed Sun.*

DEPARTMENT STORES

Fodor's Choice ★ **DepartmentStore Quartier 206.** The smallest, and often considered the most luxurious, department store in town, DepartmentStore Quartier 206 has a wide range of women's and men's international designers from the likes of Prada, Givenchy, and Tom Ford. Much of the store's inventory is handpicked by founder Anne Maria Jagdfeld on travels around the world, and the store also carries a variety of cosmetics, perfumes, home accessories, art, and books. ✉ *Friedrichstr. 71, Mitte: Unter den Linden* ☎ *030/2094–6500* ⊕ *www.dsq206.com* ☾ *Closed Sun.*

Galeria Kaufhof. Anchoring Alexanderplatz, Galeria Kaufhof is the most successful branch of the German department store chain, with six floors offering more than 600 brands, though the wares are fairly basic. ✉ *Alexanderpl. 9, Mitte: Alexanderplatz* ☎ *030/247–430* ⊕ *www.kaufhof. de* ☾ *Closed Sun.*

Fodor's Choice ★ **Galeries Lafayette.** At the corner of Französische Strasse (it means "French Street" and is named for the nearby French Huguenot cathedral) is the French department store Galeries Lafayette. French architect Jean Nouvel included an impressive steel-and-glass funnel at the center of the building, and it's surrounded by four floors of expensive clothing and luxuries as well as an excellent food department with counters offering French cuisine, and a market with some of the best produce in the area. Intimate and elegant, Galeries Lafayette carries almost exclusively French products. ✉ *Friedrichstr. 76–78, Mitte: Unter den Linden* ☎ *030/209–480* ⊕ *www.galerieslafayette.de* ☾ *Closed Sun.*

Hackesche Höfe. Tucked behind the tourist heavy streets of Hackesche Markt, this labyrinth of small galleries, boutiques, and shops offers a wide range of fashion. The outdoor shopping mall links Rosenthaler and Sophienstraße with big brands like H&M and Mac Cosmetics, as well as independent boutiques and small gift shops. ✉ *Rosenthaler Straße 40-41, Mitte: Scheunenviertel* ☎ *030/280–98010* ⊕ *www. hackesche-hoefe.com.*

GIFT IDEAS

Absinthe Depot Berlin. This old-fashioned-style liquor store harkens back to the age of the green fairy—complete with antique wooden cabinets and vintage absinthe fountains—although the primary ingredient, thujone, is now strictly regulated in countries around the world. A friendly proprietor is on hand to help you choose which of the more than 100 different varieties you'd like to carry home. ✉ *Weinmeisterst. 4, Mitte: Scheunenviertel* ☎ *030/281–6789* ⊕ *www.erstesabsinthdepotberlin.de* ☾ *Closed Sun.*

Ampelmann. This gallery shop opened in the mall-like Hackesche Höfe shopping area in 2001, promoting the red and green Ampelmännnchen, the charming symbol used on the former East traffic lights. The brand now operates six shops in Berlin, and you can find the logo on everything from T-shirts and umbrellas to ice cube trays and candy. Perfect for souvenirs. ⊠ *Hackesche Höfe, Hof 5, Rosenthalerstr. 40–41, Mitte: Scheunenviertel* ☎ *030/4472–6515* ⊕ *ampelmann.de/* ⊙ *Mon.–Sat. 9:30–10, Sun. 10–7.*

ausberlin. This small shop near Alexanderplatz provides a wide range of Berlin memories, all designed and manufactured in the city. There is everything from Berlin-themed emergency candy bars and tote bags with city landmark designs to Berlin produced liquors. ⊠ *Karl-Liebknechtstr. 17, Mitte: Alexanderplatz* ☎ *030/4199–7896* ⊕ *www. ausberlin.de* ⊙ *Closed Sun.*

Berlin Story. More than 5,000 different books, maps, and souvenirs about the city of Berlin can be found at this shop, which is, unlike many, open on Sunday. The company also runs a translation and publishing house and a small museum, as well as a webshop for those still looking for souvenirs after the trip is over. ⊠ *Unter den Linden 40, Mitte: Unter den Linden* ☎ *030/2045–3842* ⊕ *www.berlinstory.de.*

Fodor's Choice ★ **Bonbonmacherei.** Tucked into a small courtyard near the New Synagogue, this charming candy store has been making and selling hand-made sweets for the past 100 years. The brightly colored sugar bonbons are pressed on vintage molds into leaf, raspberry, and diamond shapes, and more than 30 different varieties are available. For a real insider's peek at candy production, join one of the store's daily tours, which walk customers step-by-step through the candy production. Note that the store is only open Wednesday and Thursday. ⊠ *Oranienburgerstr. 32, Mitte: Scheunenviertel* ☎ *030/4405–5243* ⊕ *www.bonbonmacherei. de* ⊙ *Closed July and Aug., and Sun.–Tues.*

Jünemann's Pantoffeleck. The Jünemann family has owned this basement shop on Torstrasse for over 100 years, producing their quality handmade felt *hausschuhe*, or slippers, for four generations. The shoes come in a variety of colors and two simple styles, a classic backless version or the full slipper. Either is the perfect way to bring a piece of German tradition back home. ⊠ *Torstrasse 39, Mitte: Scheunenviertel* ☎ *030/4425337* ⊕ *www.pantoffeleck.de/* ⊙ *Mon.–Fri. 9-6.*

Ostpaket. Step back in time with a trip to this shop, which specializes in the products from the former East, many still stamped "Made in the GDR." The largest of Berlin's shops catering to ostalgie, or a fond remembrance for some aspects of life in the former East, the supermarket's selection includes everything from chocolate and sodas to toiletries. ⊠ *Spandauer Str. 2, Mitte: Alexanderplatz* ☎ *030/2888–4518* ⊕ *www.ostpaket-berlin.de/* ⊙ *Mon.-Fri. 9-7; Sat. 9-6.*

Puppenstube im Nikolaiviertel. This is the ultimate shop for any kind of (mostly handmade) dolls, including designer models as well as old-fashioned German dolls. It's for collectors, not kids. ⊠ *Propststr. 4, Mitte: Nikolaiviertel* ☎ *030/242–3967* ⊕ *www.puppen1.de* ⊙ *Mon.– Sat. 10–6:30, Sun. 11–6.*

R.S.V.P. This tiny store is a Berlin go-to place when looking for beautiful paper, notebooks, and other stationary needs. Along with designer parchment, high-end writing tools, and notebooks from Moleskin and others, the store carries international stationary brands, calendars, and other desk accessories. ⊠ *Mulackstr. 14, Mitte: Scheunenviertel* ☎ *030/28094644* ⊕ *https://rsvp-berlin.de/en/online-shop* ⊗ *Mon.–Thu. 12–7; Fri–Sat 12–8.*

s.wert. Products here are inspired by Berlin's facades (pillows), grafitti (scratched glasses), and civic symbols (on polo shirts). ⊠ *Brunnenstr. 191, Mitte: Scheunenviertel* ☎ *030/4005–66555* ⊕ *www.s-wert-design. de* ⊗ *Mon.–Fri., 11–7, Sat 11–6.*

JEWELRY

Fodor's Choice ★ **Hecking.** Designer Luisa Hecking opened this accessories boutique in 2007 as a showcase for her timeless collection of HeckingHandermann bags and sunglasses. It's one of the best place for scarves in the city, with a wide selection of designs, at a variety of price points. ⊠ *Gormannstr. 8–9, entrance Mulackstr., Mitte: Scheunenviertel* ☎ *030/2804–7528* ⊕ *www.hecking-shop.com* ⊗ *Closed Tues., Sun.*

Fodor's Choice ★ **Sabrina Dehoff.** The flagship store of German jewelry designer Sabrina Dehoff balances bling and minimalism—bright crystals are paired with chunky metals. ⊠ *Torstr. 175, Mitte: Scheunenviertel* ☎ *030/9362–4680* ⊕ *www.sabrinadehoff.com* ⊗ *Closed Sun.*

POTSDAMER PLATZ

On the border between the city's former east and west regions, this touristy area is popular thanks to the towering Sony Center, which has an English-language movie theater as well as restaurants and bars. The main shopping arcade here, also named Potsdamer Platz, offers a wide selection of chain shops, but there are a few original shops tucked on the side streets.

CLOTHING

Andreas Murkudis. Andreas Murkudis moved his successful concept shop from Mitte to the former Taggespiegel newspaper office space near Potsdamer Platz in 2011. Inside the stark white room you'll find hand-picked mens, women's, and children's clothing, including designs by brother Kostas Murkudis, Dries van Noten, and Christian Haas, as well as accessories, and contemporary homeware. ⊠ *Potsdamer Str. 81e, Potsdamer Platz* ☎ *030/6807–98306* ⊕ *www.andreasmurkudis. com* ⊗ *Closed Sun.*

F95. This designer showroom is the permanent space for the biannual international fashion trade fair Premium. The rest of the time, the space showcases established brands like T by Alexander Wang and Diane von Furstenberg, alongside up-and-coming designers. Expect a combination of offbeat looks, trendsetting pieces, and classic wardrobe staples. ⊠ *Luckenwalderstr. 4–6, Potsdamer Platz* ☎ *030/4208–3358* ⊕ *www. f95store.com* ⊗ *Closed Sun.*

GIFT IDEAS

Fodor's Choice ★ **Frau Tonis Parfum.** This elegant perfumery will help you create a completely personal scent; choose from vials filled with perfumes like acacia, linden tree blossoms, cedar wood, or pink peppercorns. All the perfumes are produced locally in Berlin, creating a really one-of-a kind gift. ✉ *Zimmerstr. 13, Potsdamer Platz* ☎ *030/2021–5310* ⊕ *www.frautonis-parfum.com* ⊙ *Closed Sun.*

FRIEDRICHSHAIN

The cobblestone streets and densely packed neighborhoods of cafés, shops, and boutiques make the area between Frankfurter Allee and Warschauer Strasse an ideal shopping stretch. Both Boxhagener Platz and Simon-Dach Strasse are home to fashionable shops, and the neighborhood holds shopping nights on select Saturdays.

CLOTHING

Latte Wie Hose. This shop understands the importance of keeping energized during shopping sprees, and dishes out illy coffee specialties alongside their high-end jeans. Denim labels include Dr. Denim, Patrick Mohr, and Friis & Company, and the store also stocks shoes, bags, and other accessories. ✉ *Kopernikusstr. 13, Friedrichshain* ☎ *030/6174–0817* ⊕ *www.lattewiehose.com/* ⊙ *Mon.–Sat. 11–8.*

Prachtmädchen. Nearby Boxhagener Platz, this is a great shop to find a piece of Berlin's young, hip style. Prachtmädchen specializes in trendy T-shirts, fashion forward coats, sustainable pieces from Scandinavian and Japanese brands, and accessories from their own line. There is also a small inventory of menswear. ✉ *Wühlischst. 28, Friedrichshain* ☎ *030/9700–2780* ⊕ *www.prachtmaedchen.de/* ⊙ *Mon.–Fri. 11–8; Sat. 11–4.*

Something Coloured. This Friedrichshain boutique looks like a trendy concept shop at first glance, but inside you'll find a selection of stylish secondhand pieces. Among their advertised "1,000 pieces paired with rationality," expect to find jeans from Paige and J brand, bags from Chanel, and pieces from COS, Comptoir des Cotonniers, and Zoe Karssen. ✉ *Grünberger Str. 90, Friedrichshain* ☎ *030/2935–2075* ⊕ *www.facebook.com/sometimescoloured* ⊙ *Tue.–Fri. 12–8; Sat. 11–7.*

CLOTHING: MEN'S

Van Liebling. For a peice of Berlin's street-style cool, head to this Friedrichshain shop, where you'll find essentials like caps from The Decades, Herschel bags, and sunglasses from R.T.C.O. The store also stocks a small collection of women's accessories and clothes. ✉ *Kopernikusstr. 8, Friedrichshain* ☎ *030/9900–2292* ⊕ *www.vanliebling.com/.*

Stereoki. This hip store mixes pieces from Germany, the US, France, and Switzerland, including major brands like New Balance and Sperry Topsider and lower key designs including Oregon-based Shwood, organic cotton Nudie Jeans, and Six Pack France. ✉ *Gabriel-Max-Strassse 18, Friedrichshain* ☎ *030/5379–4667* ⊕ *www.stereoki.com* ⊙ *Mon.–Sat. 11–8.*

KREUZBERG

Locals love Kreuzberg for its somewhat gritty but hip landscape, and the fashion style here is more urban as well. The lively Bergmannstrasse is home to several worthy boutiques, as is Mehringdamm. This, along with neighboring Neukölln, is the place to score a unique Berlin find.

CLOTHING

Fodor's Choice ★ **Voo.** This "super boutique" in former locksmith's workship is a Berlin favorite for women's and men's separates, shoes, accessories, and outwear, often from rare collections around the world. It's also home to Companion Coffee, for when you need a shopping pick-me-up. ⊠ *Oranienstr. 24, Kreuzberg* ☎ *030/6165–1119* ⊕ *www.vooberlin.com* ⊗ *Closed Sun.*

WORD OF MOUTH

"For a real neighborhoody shopping stroll, with nice old-Berlin style food imbiss-style in the old market hall, somebody recommended Bergmannstrasse to me (the area closer to Mehringdamm, not Suedstern to the east) and it really was a refreshing change of pace. Lots and lots of stores and restaurants, and if there were any tourists there, it was probably me."
—dfourh

CLOTHING: MEN'S

Simon & Me. This new shop offers fashion and lifestyle products for the discerning man. Along with namesake label Simon & Me, the store hand-picks products that deserve their Made in Berlin stamp—denoting high quality and fair working conditions—including Our/Berlin vodka and accessories from Happy Socks and A Kind of Guise. ⊠ *Fidicinstr. 17, Kreuzberg* ☎ *030/6396–0563* ⊕ *simonandme.com/* ⊗ *Sat. 12–6.*

GIFT IDEAS

Hardwax. This iconic record store is run by music veteran Mark Ernestus, who handpicks all the vinyl and CDs with a heavy focus on techno, electronic, and dubstep. On the third floor of a heavily graffitied building, it's the true essence of Berlin grunge and totally worth a visit for music lovers. ⊠ *Paul-Lincke-Ufer 44a, Kreuzberg* ☎ *030/6113–0111* ⊕ *www.hardwax.com* ⊗ *Closed Sun.*

Süper Store. Located in the charming neighborhood of Kreuzberg known as the Graefekiez, this cute little shop supplies a variety of lovely odds and ends, sourced from all over the world, including Turkey, Italy, and Switzerland, as well as locally produced items. Inside you'll find linens, housewares, pantry items, and jewelry. ⊠ *Dieffenbachstr. 12, Kreuzberg* ☎ *030/9832–7944* ⊕ *www.sueper-store.de/* ⊗ *Tue.–Fri. 11–7; Sat. 11-4.*

MARKETS

Grosser Antikmarkt am Ostbahnhof (*Antique Market at East Station*). The Sunday Grosser Antikmarkt am Ostbahnhof market is made up almost entirely of antiques and vintage treasures, so it takes little effort but a bit of money to find something truly special to take home. Preedited selections of antiquarian books, gramophones, jewelry, and kitschy East German items can be found here. ⊠ *Erich-Steinfurth-Str. 1, Kreuzberg* ☎ *030/2900–2010* ⊗ *Sun. 9–5.*

Hallentrödelmarkt Treptow. Most of Berlin's flea markets operate year-round, regardless of the freezing winter temperatures, but this indoor hall offers some shelter inside an old warehouse near the Arena/Badeschiff complex on the Spree River. The weekend market features tables of kitchenware and rows of old bikes and mechanical parts, which can obscure the real treasures, so be prepared to spend some time digging. ✉ *Treptow Art Center, Eichenstr. 4, Kreuzberg* ☎ *172/303–5775* ⊕ *www.xn–hallentrdelmarkt-berlin-treptow-edd.de* ⊗ *Open weekends 10–4.*

NEUKÖLLN

Just over the canal from Kreuzberg, the neighborhood of Neukölln is home to a large Turkish population, and brims with Turkish shops, cafés, and restaurants, as well as a lovely weekly market. More and more of the city's young creative types are moving into this area, and it caters to their bohemian lifestyle with a number of secondhand and vintage shops.

CLOTHING

Let Them Eat Cake. A favorite of the vintage shoppers in Nuekölln, this delightful shop offers a mixture of handmade pieces and high quality second hand. ✉ *Weserstr. 164, Neukölln* ☎ *030/6096–5095* ⊕ *letthemeatcake-berlin.tumblr.com/* ⊗ *Tue.-Sat. 1-7.*

Shio. This shop not only stocks a variety of redesigned secondhand and vintage wear, as well as new-label sustainable lines, but also offers dressmaking and alteration services, and encourages customers to bring in their own pieces for trendy modifications. ✉ *Weichselstr. 59, Neukölln* ⊕ *shiostore.com/* ⊗ *Mon.–Sat. 12–8.*

Sing Blackbird. This Kreuzkölln shop, located on the border between Kreuzberg and Neukölln, has become popular for its carefully edited collection of vintage finds, dating back to the 1960s and 70s. The shop also holds a monthly flea market, as well as occasional movie nights, and is also home to a popular café, where a menu of homemade cakes and weekend vegan brunch is served on mismatched vintage china. ✉ *Sanderstr. 11, Neukölln* ☎ *030/5484–5051* ⊕ *www.facebook.com/ singblackbir* ⊗ *Mon.-Sun. 12-7.*

Vintage Galore. Imagine bringing the midcentury European look home with a walk through this shop, which features a collection of Scandinavian furniture and lamps. The shop also has a limited selection of clothing, bags and accessories, as well as small housewares like teapots and ceramics, which should all fit more comfortably inside a suitcase. ✉ *Sanderstr. 12, Neukölln* ☎ *030/6396–3338* ⊕ *www.vintagegalore.de/* ⊗ *Tues.–Fri. 2–8; Sat. 12–6.*

MARKETS

Nowkoelln Flowmarkt. Pulling on the vibrant spirit of Berlin's young, hip inhabitants, this newish addition to the city's flea market offerings places an emphasis on the "now," with a trendy selection of vintage clothing, home goods, music, and original handmade pieces. The canal side location, tempting food stalls, and live performances provide even more reason to visit the bi-monthly Sunday event. ✉ *Maybachufer 39-50, Neukölln* ⊕ *www.nowkoelln.de/* ⊗ *bi monthly, Sun. 10–6.*

Türkischer Markt. On the edge of the Kreuzberg-Neukölln border, this weekly market is a gathering spot for the local Turkish community, and offers many traditional products, including delicious delicacies (olives, cheese, dried fruits, hummus, and fresh breads) and a bazaar of house goods. ⊠ *Maybachufer, Kreuzberg* ☎ *030/9170–0700* ⊕ *www. tuerkenmarkt.de.*

RECORD STORES

Staalplaat. Amsterdam-based record label Staalplaat opened this eccentric sister record story in Neukölln to help satiate the city's massive music demand, with a specific focus on experimental music and obscure albums. The store also houses a gallery and bookstore where special books, handmade fanzines, and limited edition books and posters are sold. ⊠ *Kienitzer Str. 108, Neukölln* ☎ *030/4176–7355* ⊕ *staalplaat. com/* ⊗ *Mon.–Sat. 12–8.*

PRENZLAUER BERG

Stretching east of Mitte's Rosenthaler Platz, fashionable boutiques continue into Prenzlauer Berg. This area is well known for its collection of designer boutiques, secondhand shops, and original designers. The busy Kastanienallee is packed with shops and boutiques, as is the more quiet area around Hemholzpatz.

BOOK STORES

Shakespeare & Sons. This friendly bookstore is tucked on a side street near one of Prenzlauer Berg's most charming squares. Along with an impressive collection of new and used English books, there's also a small café offering a delicious assortment of freshly baked bagels. ⊠ *Raumerstr. 36, Prenzlauer Berg* ☎ *030/4000–3685* ⊕ *www.shakesbooks.de/* ⊗ *Mon.–Sat. 10–8; Sun. 12–7.*

CLOTHING

Fodor'sChoice
★
Garments. This chic store offers Prenzlauer Berg's fashion lovers an excellent selection of vintage and secondhand clothing, costume jewelry, and accessories. There is also a branch in Mitte, at Linienstraße 204–205. ⊠ *Stargarderstr. 12 A, Prenzlauer Berg* ☎ *030/7477–9919* ⊕ *www.garments-vintage.de* ⊗ *Closed Sun.*

Kauf Dich Glücklich. With an odd assortment of retro furnishings, this ice cream café and waffle shop takes over the entire corner of a Prenzlauer Berg sidewalk, especially on sunny days. Head to the second story and you'll find a shop that captures young Berliner style, with vintage pieces, bold prints, and skinny fits, as well as shoes and jewelry. The collection focuses on womenswear although there is also a small offering of men's clothing. ⊠ *Kastanien Allee 54, Prenzlauer Berg* ☎ *030/4172–5651* ⊕ *www.kaufdichgluecklich-shop.de/* ⊗ *Mon.–Sat. 10–8.*

Majaco. Just off the lovely Zionskirchplatz, this shop is home to Berlin designers Anna Franke and Janine Weber. Their collection has a whimsical, feminine style and incorporates flowing fabrics and clean cuts. The shop also carries beautiful bags and accessories from Scandinavian and German designers. ⊠ *Fehrbelliner Str. 24, Prenzlauer Berg* ☎ *303/3830400566* ⊕ *www.majaco-berlin.de* ⊗ *Mon.–Fri. 12–9; Sat. 12–8.*

Temporary Showroom. This small boutique showcases a revolving collection of select European and international designers, spanning high fashions, streetwear, and accessories. The store is rearranged every six months in collaboration with a new designer's collection. ⊠ *Kastanienallee 36a, Prenzlauer Berg* ☎ *030/6220–4563* ⊕ *www. temporaryshowroom.com/* ⊗ *Mon.–Sat. 11–7.*

Workaholic Fashion. This showroom puts Berlin's music culture front and center, with fashion inspired by the DJ and club scene. Along with a collection of shoes, bags, accessories, the store also carries records and CDs and has a separate music room with a DJ stand. ⊠ *Kastanienallee 60, Prenzlauer Berg* ☎ *030/8411–8358* ⊕ *www.workaholicfashion.net* ⊗ *Mon.—Fri. 11–8; Sat. 12–8.*

GIFT IDEAS

Goldhahn und Sampson. A food lover's paradise, this epicurean shop sells a wide range of products, from gourmet pantry ingredients and kitchen tools to an extensive collection of cookbooks and food magazines. Handmade breads, pastries, and chocolates are available to satiate your appetite, and if you want to dig in deeper, cooking classes are regularly held in the shop's back room. ⊠ *Dunckerstr. 9, Prenzlauer Berg* ⊕ *www. goldhahnundsampson.de* ⊗ *Mon.–Fri. 8–8; Sat. 10–8.*

Fodor'sChoice
★   **Dr. Kochan Schapskultur.** This small shop embodies traditional German liquor culture; there are schnapps and fruit brandies from family farms and independent distilleries for sale, among other items to pique a tippler's interest. ⊠ *Immanuelkirchstr. 4, Prenzlauer Berg* ☎ *030/3462–4076* ⊕ *www.schnapskultur.de* ⊗ *Closed Sun.*

MARKETS

Markt am Kollwitzplatz. One of the city's best farmer's markets sits on the pretty Kollwitplatz square in Prenzlauer Berg. During its smaller Thursday and bustling Saturday markets, you'll not only find a superb selection of organic produce, meats, cheeses, and pantry items, but also an array of prepared foods and sellers offering handmade home goods and gifts. ⊠ *Kollwitzplatz, Prenzlauer Berg* ⊗ *Thurs. 12–7; Sat. 9–4.*

Mauerpark Flohmarkt. The Sunday flea market at Mauer Park, a favorite among hipsters and tourists, is absolutely packed in nice weather, turning the intersection of Bernauer Strasse and Oderberger Strasse (where the unofficial market outside the market begins) into a veritable Times Square of fun- and sun-loving young people. Head out early to find the best pickings, as most of the selection here is junkyard and the occasional hand-made or re-purposed product. ⊠ *Bernauer Strasse 63-64, Prenzlauer Berg* ☎ *017/6292–5002* ⊕ *www.mauerparkmarkt. de* ⊗ *Sun. 8–6.*

Trödelmarkt Arkonplatz. This is a smaller Sunday marke tucked on a neighborhood square in Prenzlauer Berg, but one that many locals say is Berlin's best, especially for its wide selection of vintage and second hand furniture, housewares, books, and records. ⊠ *Arkonplatz, Prenzlauer Berg* ☎ *030/786–9764* ⊕ *www.troedelmarkt-arkonaplatz.de/* ⊗ *Sun. 10–4.*

SHOES

Calypso Shoes. A must visit for shoe lovers, this shop has an impressive collection of exotic and vintage footwear, including suede heels, leather-trimmed boots, embroidered flats, and men's work boots—all spanning the last six decades. Because of their diverse collection, the shop also regularly works with film and theater stylists. ⊠ *Oderbergerstr. 14, Prenzlauer Berg* ☎ *030/281–6165* ⊕ *www.facebook.com/ calypsovintageshoes* ⊗ *Closed Sun.*

CHARLOTTENBURG

Although Ku'damm is still touted as the shopping mile of Berlin, the best stretch for exclusive fashions, such as Louis Vuitton, Hermès, and Jil Sander, are the three blocks between Leibnizstrasse and Bleibtreustrasse. For home furnishings, gift items, and unusual clothing boutiques, follow this route off Ku'damm: Leibnizstrasse to Mommsenstrasse to Bleibtreustrasse, then on to the ring around Savignyplatz. Fasanenstrasse, Knesebeckstrasse, Schlüterstrasse, and Uhlandstrasse are also fun places to browse.

Ku'damm ends at Breitscheidplatz, but the door-to-door shopping continues along Tauentzienstrasse, which, in addition to international retail stores, offers continental Europe's largest department store, the upscale Kaufhaus des Westens, or KaDeWe.

BOOKSTORES

Fodor'sChoice ★ **Bucherbogen.** Peek under the rails of Charlottenburg's Savignyplatz and you'll find this much-loved bookstore. The large selection of books, many special edition or out-of-print, include numerous titles on art, design, and architecture, and the international offerings are extensive. ⊠ *Stadtbahnbogen 593, Charlottenburg* ☎ *303/186–9511* ⊕ *www. buecherbogen.com* ⊗ *Closed Sun.*

CLOTHING

Arianne. One of the city's best for designer secondhand finds, this tiny shop is tucked away near West Berlin's Savignyplatz. You'll find labels like Hermès, Versace, Chanel, and Jil Sander on the racks. ⊠ *Wielandstr. 37, Charlottenburg* ☎ *030/881–7436* ⊕ *www.ariane-secondhand. de* ⊗ *Closed Sun.*

Jil Sander. The flagship store of German designer Jil Sander carries the newest collections from this iconic, understated brand, including fashions for men. ⊠ *Kurfürstendamm 185, Charlottenburg* ☎ *030/886– 7020* ⊕ *www.jilsander.com.*

Peek & Cloppenburg. Peek & Cloppenburg, or "P & C," stocks women's, men's, and children's clothes on six floors. Don't miss the designer shop-in-shop FashionNation areas and the international, young-designer department in the basement. ⊠ *Tauentzienstr. 19, Charlottenburg* ☎ *030/212–900* ⊕ *www.peek-cloppenburg.de/* ⊗ *Mon.–Sat. 10–8.*

CLOTHING: MENS

Budapester Schuhe. Handmade, classic styles of shoes and brogues, mostly from England, Austria, and Hungary, are sold at Budapester Schuhe. There is another shop at Kurfürstendamm 199. ⊠ *Kurfürstendamm 43, Charlottenburg* ☎ *030/8862–4206* ⊕ *www.budapester.eu* ⊠ *Bleibtreustr. 24, Western Downtown* ☎ *030/8862–9500.*

Fodor'sChoice ★ **Chelsea Farmer's Club.** This living-room-like space is the go-to for sophisticated menswear with a British posh edge; you'll find everything from tuxedoes to hunting jackets on their shelves. The owners manufacture their own line of quality British-style smoking jackets, and the inventory also includes top brands and small fashion accessories. There's a small bar in the back, where you can toast your latest purchase in style. ⊠ *Schlüterstr. 50, Charlottenburg* ☎ *030/8872–7474* ⊕ *www.chelseafarmersclub.de* ⊗ *Closed Sun.*

Mientus. The trendsetting outfitter Mientus stocks Armani, Dolce & Gabbana, and Boss and has an in-house tailor. The Wilmersdorfer Strasse location is their flagship, and offers free parking for customers. ⊠ *Wilmersdorfer Str. 73, Charlottenburg* ☎ *030/323–9077* ⊕ *www.mientus.com/* ⊠ *Kurfürstendamm 52, Charlottenburg* ☎ *030/323–9077* ⊕ *www.mientus.com/.*

DEPARTMENT STORES

Fodor'sChoice ★ **Kaufhaus des Westens** (*KaDeWe*). The largest department store in continental Europe, classy Kaufhaus des Westens (KaDeWe) has a grand selection of goods, spread over seven floors, as well as food and deli counters, champagne bars, beer bars, and a beautiful art deco–style atrium café on the top floor. The wealth of services offered here includes luxury gift basket arrangements, exclusive travel guides, and an international box office. ⊠ *Tauentzienstr. 21–24, Charlottenburg* ☎ *030/21210* ⊕ *www.kadewe.de* ⊗ *Closed Sun.*

Stilwerk Berlin. The five-storey Stilwerk houses a variety of upscale shops that all specialize in home furnishings and accessories. The location has helped turn the surrounding neighborhood into Berlin's Design Mile, with numerous interior design and furnishing stores on Kantstrasse and nearby. ⊠ *Kantstr. 17, Charlottenburg* ☎ *030/315–150* ⊕ *www.stilwerk.de/berlin.*

GIFTS AND SOUVENIRS

Harry Lehmann. If you want a taste—or rather, a smell—of old Berlin, head to Harry Lehmann on Kantstrasse in Charlottenburg. The shopkeeper will greet you in a white lab coat, helpfully explaining the origin and inspiration of the expertly mixed perfumes, which fill large apothecary jars along a mirrored wall. This is definitely old school—the shop has been open since 1926. Scents are fresh, simple, and clean, and a 30ml bottle (€15.50) makes for a reasonably priced gift or souvenir. ⊠ *Kantstr. 106, Charlottenburg* ☎ *030/324–3582* ⊕ *www.parfum-individual.de* ⊗ *Closed Sun.*

Königliche Porzellan Manufaktur. Fine porcelain is still produced by Königliche Porzellan Manufaktur, the former Royal Porcelain Manufactory for the Prussians, also called KPM. You can buy this delicate handmade, hand-painted china at KPM's two stores, but it may be more fun to visit the factory salesroom, which also sells seconds at reduced prices. ⊠ *Wegelystr. 1, Tiergarten* ☎ *030/390–09215* ⊕ *www.de-de.kpm-berlin.com/* ⊠ *Kurfürstendamm 27, Charlottenburg* ☎ *030/8862–7961* .

Fodor's Choice ★ **Paper & Tea.** Enter this serene shop just off Kantstrasse and you'll be stepping into a world of high-quality, loose leaf teas. Rather than bulk up on inventory, the store has a restrained selection of 70 teas, all displayed in museumlike cases, where you can smell the wares. There are two tasting areas, where expert attendants brew and explain the teas. ⊠ *Bleibtreust. 4, Charlottenburg* ☎ *030/9561–5468* ⊕ *www.paperandtea.com* ⊗ *Closed Sun.*

Scenario. Tucked under the elevated train tracks, Scenario sells stationery articles, gifts of any kind, and a lot of leather wares and jewelry. The designs here are modern. ⊠ *Savignypl. 1, Charlottenburg* ☎ *030/312–9199* ⊗ *Mon.–Fri. 1–7; Sat. 11–4.*

Fodor's Choice ★ **Wald Königsberger Marzipan.** This third-generation artisan shop offers a taste of the old-world treat marzipan, using a family recipe that dates back to the turn of the 20th century. The vintage-style shop features candy-striped wall paper, vintage tools, and rows of handmade marzipan, all wrapped in delicate packaging. ⊠ *Pestalozzistr. 54 a, Charlottenburg* ☎ *030/323–8254* ⊕ *www.wald-koenigsberger-marzipan.de* ⊗ *Closed Sun.*

Wohnart Berlin. In the homey setting of Wohnart Berlin you can imagine how the stylish European furnishings, lamps, house wares, or stationery items might suit your own pad. ⊠ *Uhlandstr. 179–180, Charlottenburg* ☎ *030/882–5252* ⊕ *www.wohnart-berlin.de/* ⊗ *Mon.–Fri. 10–7, Sat. 11–5.*

JEWELRY

Bucherer. Fine handcrafted jewelry, watches, and other stylish designer accessories can be found at Bucherer. ⊠ *Kurfürstendamm 45, Charlottenburg* ☎ *030/880–4030* ⊕ *www.bucherer.com* ⊗ *Closed Sun.*

Oliver Hofmann. German designers featured at Oliver Hofmann share a philosophy of sleek minimalism. Rubber and diamond rings and matte platinum and diamond pieces are conscious understatements at this jewelry showroom. ⊠ *Kurfürstendamm 197, Charlottenburg* ☎ *030/8847–1790* ⊕ *www.schmuckraeume-berlin.de/* ⊗ *Weekdays 10–7, Sat. 10–6.*

MARKETS

Berliner Trödelmarkt und Kunstmarkt (*Berlin Flea and Art Market*). While markets in former East Berlin districts are perfect for unearthing both trash and treasures, the antique market on Strasse des 17. Juni is at the high end of the spectrum. Open on weekends, the Berliner Trödelmarkt und Kunstmarkt is home to one of the city's more curated selections, with vintage and high-end secondhand jewelry, housewares, silverware, books, and toys. The flea market stands are nearer the Tiergarten S-bahn station, while handicrafts begin past the Charlottenburg gates. ⊠ *Strasse des 17. Juni, Charlottenburg* ⊕ *www.berliner-troedelmarkt. de* ☉ *Open weekends 10–5.*

NIGHTLIFE

Updated by
Giulia Pines

Nearly a century after Weimar-era Berlin redefined the meanings of decadence and excess, the city is still pulsing at pretty much all hours of the night. Berlin nightlife still pushes boundaries and takes risks. In fact, to non-Berliners who aren't used to it, some of the clubs and bars here can appear to be operating far out of the boundaries of decency—or even the law.

Many Berlin bars will often open as cafés in the afternoon, slowly getting darker and smokier as the hours wear on and the coffee and tea turns into beer and wine. In Germany the term *Kneipen* is used for down-to-earth bars that are comparable to English pubs. These places are pretty simple and laid-back; you probably shouldn't try to order a three-ingredient cocktail at one unless you spot a lengthy drink menu. If you're looking for something more upscale, elegant bars and lounges can be found in Mitte's Scheunenviertel, in Charlottenburg, and in Berlin's five-star hotels, and new cocktail bars are cropping up in unexpected places, like Kreuzberg and Schöneberg.

The best and most notorious clubs in Berlin occupy old industrial buildings in formerly shabby, alternative neighborhoods like Friedrichshain and Kreuzberg. As with bars, the snazziest clubs and lounges can be found near high-end hotels in Mitte around Unter den Linden and Gendarmenmarkt, or in Charlottenburg. Clubs are notorious for getting a shockingly late (or should we say early?) start: many don't open until midnight, and aren't worth visiting before 2 or 3 in the morning. Happily, the club scene is far less snooty and self-absorbed than in other major cities: for the most part, you'll encounter lax door policies and casually dressed revelers. Since the fall of the Wall, Berlin has become a mecca for electronica, and that means club-goers take dancing as seriously as partying. Prepare to be swept up in waves of endless, exuberant movement, much of it—especially in the case of Berlin's most popular techno club Berghain—fueled by drug use. If that's not your thing, though, don't worry: there's something for everyone in the city these days, especially now that the landscape has gone a bit more upscale. Note that clubs often switch the music they play nightly so the crowds and popularity can vary widely. Though club nights are driven by the DJ name, the music genres are written in English in listing magazines.

Berlin is unmistakably Germany's gay capital, and many Europeans come to partake in the diverse scene, which concentrates on Schöneberg (around Nollendorfplatz) and Kreuzberg. Check out the magazines *Siegessäule, (030),* and *blu.*

You might not know to look at it, but Berlin is a veritable jazz destination. Home to one of Germany's earliest programs of jazz study (at the Üniversitat der Kunste or University of the Arts) Berlin attracts serious jazz musicians from around the world, and nurtures its own homegrown talents. Aside from the large, long-running clubs focusing on international acts, smaller, cozier jazz clubs, barely larger than living rooms, are sprinkled throughout the city. The Berlin Jazz Festival takes place every November, uniting many of them.

PLANNING

LATE-NIGHT TRANSPORTATION

If you plan on staying out late, just know that after 1 am on a week-night (Sunday–Thursday), Berlin's U-bahn and S-bahn trains shut down. To get back to where you're staying, you'll have to catch a night bus (designated by "N" before the number, which often corresponds to the subway line it replaces). These buses come infrequently (every 30 minutes) and often don't stop directly at a station entrance, so be prepared to do some searching. On Friday and Saturday nights all subway lines (except U4) run every 15 to 20 minutes throughout the night.

GETTING INFORMATION

For the latest information on Berlin's house, electro, and hip-hop club scene, pick up *(030)*, a free weekly. For more general information on performing arts and nightlife, the weekly Berlin magazines *Zitty* and *Tip* are good resources.

MITTE

BARS

Bar Tausend. In the grand tradition of upscale clubs, Bar Tausend is well-hidden behind a steel door under the Friedrichstrasse S-bahn tracks and guarded by a discerning doorman. The futuristic main bar area, basically a long tunnel with circular lights at either end and mirrors above, looks like something out of the classic German film *Metropolis*. It would feel a bit claustrophobic if not for the excellent cocktails and stylish clientele. ■ TIP➔ **Hidden behind the bar is an even harder-to-get-into restaurant, whispered about by Berlin foodies—the so-called Tausend Cantina. For an unforgettable meal, call in advance for reservations.** ⊠ *Schiffbauerdamm 11, under S-bahn tracks, Mitte* ☎ *030/2758–2070* ⊕ *www.tausendberlin.com.*

Bebel Bar. Just off the luxurious Hotel de Rome's main reception area, this sumptuous bar and lounge, one of the city's most upscale evening spots, has deep leather sofas, high ceilings, and an impressive collection of spirits. Cocktails range from the classic to the inventive, with ingredients like arugula, oregano, balsamic vinegar, and rose syrup. Prices are high for Berlin but worth every penny. ■ TIP➔ **In warm weather, the bar**

6

opens up on the hotel's roof terrace, which offers one of the only great city views you can enjoy without waiting in line or paying admission. ✉ *Behren-str. 37, Mitte* ☎ *030/460–6090* ⊕ *www.hotelderome.com.*

Newton Bar. This posh bar in Mitte has been around for ages. Helmut Newton's larger-than-life photos of nude women decorate the walls. ✉ *Charlottenstr. 57, Mitte* ☎ *030/2029–5421* ⊕ *www.newton-bar.de.*

Neue Odessa Bar. Many patrons of this cocktail bar come to see and be seen; there are also a number of first-time visitors who stumble in from nearby Rosenthaler Platz, a central party destination in Mitte. Given this crowd, it's easy to forget just how good the drinks are here. While other cocktail bars in Berlin are content to regenerate the classics, Neue Odessa takes it a step further, with delicious, original concoctions using ingredients like lavender, lychee, and ginger. ✉ *Torstr. 89, Mitte* ⊕ *www. neueodessabar.de/.*

Redwood. Run by a California native, this simple, solid cocktail bar serves near-perfect concoctions that belie the bare wood surroundings. If loud crowds and smoky rooms aren't your thing, this is the place for you— the cocktails are excellent and you'll be able to carry on a conversation in a normal voice. The menu is helpfully arranged according to "dry" or "sweet and sour" but if you're still unsure whether to go for a Dark and Stormy or a Blood and Sand, ask the friendly young bartenders— everyone speaks English here. ✉ *Bergstr. 25, Mitte* ☎ *030/7024–8813* ⊕ *www.redwoodbar.de* ☉ *Closed Sun.–Mon.* Ⓜ *Nordbahhof (S-bahn).*

CLUBS

Fodor'sChoice
★
Clärchen's Ballhaus. A night out at Clärchen's Ballhaus (Little Clara's Ballroom) is like a trip back in time. Opened in 1913, the club is an impressive sight on Mitte's now-upscale Auguststrasse. On summer nights, lines often stretch out the door, while the front courtyard comes alive with patrons dining alfresco on brick-oven pizzas. The main ball-room features a different style of music every night and there are often dance lessons before the party starts. One of the best things about this place, though, is the variety of people of different ages, nationalities, and social backgrounds that mix. The upstairs Spiegelsaal ("mirror hall") has intimate, salon-type concerts on Sunday. ✉ *Auguststr. 24, Mitte* ☎ *030/282–9295* ⊕ *www.ballhaus.de* ☉ *Lunch and dinner daily.*

Felix. The over-the-top Felix greatly benefits from its location behind the famous Adlon Kempinski Hotel—Hollywood stars drop by when they're in town, or during the frenzied weeks of the Berlinale. The door policy can be tough, but dress in your finest and hope for the best. ✉ *Beh-renstr. 72, Mitte* ☎ *030/301–117–152* ⊕ *www.felix-clubrestaurant.de/.*

Kaffee Burger. More of a neighborhood clubhouse than a bar, there's always something going on at Kaffee Burger. The original home of writer Wladimir Kaminer's popular Russendisko ("Russian disco") nights, this spot has a cozy dance floor and a separate smoking room. On any given night, you might encounter electro, rock, funk, swing, or Balkan beats; live bands play frequently. ✉ *Torstr. 58/60, Mitte* ☎ *030/2804–6495* ⊕ *www.kaffeeburger.de.*

Sage Club. House and techno music make this a popular venue for a younger crowd. On some nights it can be tough getting past the man

CLOSE UP

Berlin's Hot Spots, Day and Night

Here's a quick list of the city's best streets and squares.

■ Savignyplatz in Charlottenburg: Great restaurants and shopping.

■ Ludwigkirchplatz in Wilmersdorf: Charming cafés surrounding a beautiful church.

■ Nollendorfplatz and Winterfeldplatz in Schöneberg: The cultural centers of Schöneberg; the latter hosts a fab weekly market.

■ Oranienstrasse and Wiener Strasse as well as both riverbanks of the Spree in Kreuzberg and Friedrichshain to Treptow: The former is the lively center of Turkish Kreuzberg; the banks of the Spree have a number of large clubs in industrial spaces.

■ Hackescher Markt and Oranien-burgerstrasse as well as surrounding side streets in Mitte-Scheunenviertel: The center of historical and cultural Berlin, with the most mainstream and popular nightlife.

■ Kastanienallee and Helmholzplatz in Prenzlauer Berg: A widely trafficked street and square in Berlin, full of both young expats and local families.

■ Boxhagenerplatz and Boxhagener Strasse in Friedrichshain: Home to a weekly flea market, a busy area both day and night with cafés, bars, and restaurants.

■ Hermannplatz in Neukölln: The jumping off point for a night out in one of Berlin's newly hip districts.

with the "by invitation only" list. Expect a line out the door, and very different partiers depending on the night of the week (check the program on the website). ⊠ *Köpenicker Str. 76, Mitte* ☎ *030/278–9830* ⊕ *www.sage-club.de.*

JAZZ CLUBS

b-flat. Young German artists perform most nights at b-flat. The club has some of the best sight lines in town, as well as a magnificent floor-to-ceiling front window that captures the attention of passersby. The well-known and well-attended Wednesday jam sessions focus on free and experimental jazz, and once a month on Thursday the Berlin Big Band takes over the small stage with up to 17 players. Snacks are available. ⊠ *Rosenthalerstr. 13, Mitte* ☎ *030/283–3123* ⊕ *www.b-flat-berlin.de.*

Kunstfabrik Schlot. Schlot hosts Berlin jazz scenesters, aspiring musicians playing Monday night free jazz sessions, and local heavy-hitters. It's a bit hard to find—it's in the cellar of the Edison Höfe—but enter the courtyard via Schlegelstrasse and follow the music. ⊠ *Invalidenstr. 117, entrance at Schlegelstr. 26, Mitte* ☎ *030/448–2160* Ⓜ *Nordbahnhof (S-bahn), Naturkundemuseum (U-bahn).*

TIERGARTEN

BARS

Brewbaker. Moabit isn't quite known for its restaurants and nightlife, but this small brewery, open since 2005, is a beer-lover's destination. After operating a short-lived but beloved restaurant under the S-bahn tracks nearby, Brewbaker moved its operation to the newly renovated redbrick Arminiushalle market hall. Expect a pale ale on tap as well as their very own pilsner, and look forward to seasonal variations like pumpkin lager in fall or ginger beer in winter. They also offer frequent brewing courses and beer seminars to inspire the next generation of small brewers. ⊠ *Arminiusstr. 2–4, inside Arminiushalle, Tiergarten* ☎ *0177/694–0961* ⊕ *www.brewbaker.de/.*

POTSDAMER PLATZ

BARS

Victoria Bar. The elegant Victoria Bar is a stylish homage to 1960s and '70s jet-setters, and the cocktails are mixed with care. It usually attracts a middle-age, affluent, and artsy crowd. ⊠ *Potsdamerstr. 102, Tiergarten* ☎ *030/2575–9977* ⊕ *www.victoriabar.de.*

FRIEDRICHSHAIN

BARS

Sisyphos. This sprawling adults' playground, located Spree-side in an old dog biscuit factory in a former no-go neighborhood, has a cobbled together feel: you'll find a sandy beach, a man-made pond with a raft in the middle, a camper van, and a number of wooden huts. The club is truly a late-night spot; don't expect much to be happening here before 3 am. ⊠ *Hauptstr. 15, Friedrichshain* ☎ *030/9836–6839* ⊕ *www.sisyphos-berlin.net/.*

GAY AND LESBIAN NIGHTLIFE

Fodor's Choice
★

Berghain. In an imposing power station in a barren stretch of land between Kreuzberg and Friedrichshain (the name borrows from both neighborhoods), Berghain has achieved international fame as the hedonistic heart of techno music—it was originally a '90s techno club called Ostgut. Although it's also a well-respected center of gay nightlife in Berlin, the club welcomes both genders. It's only open on weekends (for 48 hours straight, from midnight on Friday to midnight on Sunday), and it has become something of a local tradition to arrive on Sunday morning and dance until closing. Upstairs, the slightly smaller (but by no means intimate) Panorama Bar offers different beats and a place to go on Friday before the main club opens at midnight. ⊠ *Am Wriezener Bahnhof, Friedrichshain* ⊹ *Exit north from Ostbahnhof and follow Strasse der Pariser Kommune, then make a right on badly marked Am Wriezener Bahnhof and look for a line* ☎ *030/2936–0210* Ⓜ *Ostbahnhof (S-bahn).*

KREUZBERG

BARS

Bellmann Bar. The candle-lit, rough wood tables, water-stained walls, and frequent appearances by local musicians just dropping by for a few tunes gives this cozy cocktail bar an artsty old-world feel. Lovingly nicknamed "the gramophone bar" for the old gramophone that sits in its window, Bellmann is a place to linger and chat over a glass of wine or a whiskey from the outstanding collection. ✉ *Reichenbergerstr. 103, Kreuzberg* ☎ *030/3117–3162.*

Freischwimmer. When it's warm out, the canal-side deck chairs at Freischwimmer are the perfect place to be, though heat lamps and an enclosed area make this a cozy setting for cool nights, too. To get here, walk five minutes east of the elevated Schlesisches Tor U-bahn station and turn left down a path after the 1920s Aral gas station, the oldest in Berlin. ✉ *Vor dem Schlesischen Tor 2a, Kreuzberg* ☎ *030/6107–4309* ⊕ *www.freischwimmer-berlin.com.*

Heidenpeters. Named after owner and head brewer Johannes Heidenpeter, this brewery has transformed its little corner of the bustling Markthalle IX market hall into a pleasant taproom (the brewing happens just below, in the basement). Enjoy the three beers on tap here, or take them with you in hand-labeled bottles; choices typically include an IPA and a couple seasonal ales. Open Thursday–Saturday only. ✉ *Eisenbahnstr. 42–43, in Markthalle IX, Kreuzberg* ⊕ *www.heidenpeters.de/.*

KaterHolzig. Despite its attempt to be as decadent as the legendary, anything-goes Bar 25, KaterHolzig comes across as the grown-up version of its predecessor: more put together, a bit less gritty and scrappy, and with a more upscale restaurant. Yet it attracts a similar crowd of crazy dreamers, artists, musicians, and partiers. ✉ *Michaelkirchstr. 23, Kreuzberg* ⊕ *www.katerholzig.de/.*

Soju Bar. This cavernous space does not feel like part of Berlin; its high ceilings and neon signs might make you think you're still outside—perhaps on the busy streets of Seoul at night. The bar is a great postdinner hangout, near two other popular Korean joints under the same ownership (to get to the bar, you'll walk through the Angry Chicken). True to its name, the bar specializes in cocktails made with the Korean spirit soju. Both DJs and live music make this a great dance spot, while so-called toilet karaoke sessions (exactly what they sound like) add some grungy fun to the mix. ✉ *Skalitzerstr. 34, Kreuzberg* ☎ *0163/458–0203* ⊕ *www.soju-bar.com/.*

Würgeengel. Named after a 1962 surrealist film by Luis Buñuel (it's "The Exterminating Angel" in English), this classy joint has offered an elaborate cocktail menu in a well-designed space off Kottbusser Tor since 1992—long before this part of Kreuzberg was hip, or even safe. Today, the bar's loyal fans spill out onto the streets on busy nights, and an evening tapas menu comes from the neighboring restaurant **Gorgonzola Club.** The team behind the restaurant **Renger-Patzsch** run Würgeengel and the Gorgonzola Club. ✉ *Dresdenerstr. 122, Kreuzberg* ✛ *Dresdener Str. is reachable through passageway under buildings at Kottbusser Tor, next to Adalbertstr.* ☎ *030/615–5560* ⊕ *www.wuergeengel.de* ☺ *Open 7–late.*

CLUBS

Prince Charles. This club, located under the multipurpose art space Planet Modulor Aufbau Haus, has become a neighborhood hang-out spot. DJs, live bands, flea markets, and even food events have all found a home in here. ■TIP➔ **The club is a bit hard to find—look for the ramp leading down to what seems like a parking garage off Prinzenstrasse.**

Gay Berlin

The area around Nollendorfplatz is the heart and soul of gay Berlin, even though areas like Schönhauser Allee in Prenzlauer Berg, Schlesische Strasse in Kreuzberg, and various clubs in the Mitte-Scheunenviertel area are more popular with a younger crowd. In a city that historically has been a center of gay culture and one that has an openly gay mayor, Klaus Wowereit, the gay scene is not limited to these areas. Typical for Berlin is the integration of homosexuals of all walks of life throughout the city—from the politician and manager to the bus driver and waiter. The general attitude of most Berliners toward gays is tolerant and open-minded, but, openly gay couples should still avoid outer areas such as Lichtenberg and Marzahn or some towns in Brandenburg, the region surrounding Berlin. These areas are exceptions in a city that has an estimated 300,000 gays and lesbians in residence.

Large festivals such as the annual Christopher Street Day bring together hundreds of thousands of gays and lesbians each summer. Gay travelers are embraced by the city's tourist office: up-to-date information is provided in special brochures, such as "Out in Berlin" at tourist info stores.

Mann-o-Meter. Detailed information on gay-friendly hotels and the clubbing and bar scene are provided by the city's largest gay community center, the Mann-o-Meter. Talks are sometimes held in the café, which has a variety of books and magazines. It's open Tues.–Fri 5–10, and Sat.–Sun 4–8. ⊠ *Bülowstr. 106, Schöneberg* ☎ *030/216–8008* ⊕ *www.mann-o-meter.de.*

⊠ *Prinzenstr. 85F, underneath Planet Modulor, Kreuzberg* ⊕ *www.princecharlesberlin.com/.*

Ritter Butzke. This club may not enjoy the breathless hype of some of its brethren, but it has consistency, and perhaps staying power (it's been open since 2007—a lifetime in Berlin). Only the determined will find the place: it's in an old factory that you reach via a courtyard off a quiet street. Three dance floors with different kinds of music allow you to pick and choose, and the club's decor includes some Alice-in-Wonderland-like objects like a giant teapot, strangely illuminated stacked cubes, and a ceiling made of umbrellas. ⊠ *Ritterstr. 24, Kreuzberg* ⊕ *www.ritterbutzke.de/.*

Watergate. The elegant Watergate is a club for people who usually don't like clubbing. It sits languidly at the base of the Oberbaumbrücke, on the Kreuzberg side, and has two dance floors with bars. The terrace extending over the River Spree is one of the city's best chill-out spaces. In addition to hosting internationally renowned DJs, the club is a beautiful and intimate setting for infrequent but popular classical music nights. ⊠ *Falckensteinstr. 49, Kreuzberg* ☎ *030/6128–0396* ⊕ *www.water-gate.de* Ⓜ *Schlesisches Tor (U-bahn); Warschauer Strasse (U-bahn and S-bahn).*

GAY AND LESBIAN NIGHTLIFE

Roses. If you don't find any eye candy at tiny Roses there are always the furry red walls and kitschy paraphernalia to admire. It opens at 10 pm. ✉ *Oranienstr. 187, Kreuzberg* ☎ *030/615–6570.*

SchwuZ. SchwuZ moved to the newly hip Neukölln neighborhood from its original location on Mehringdamm, in Kreuzberg, and the new digs in the old Kindl brewery should serve it well: in addition to 1980s music and house dance nights, expect more varied offerings like exhibitions, as well as a new stage and lounge room. ✉ *Rollbergstr. 26, Neukölln* ☎ *030/629–0880* ⊕ *www.schwuz.de.*

JAZZ CLUBS

Yorckschlösschen. A bit rougher around the edges than most Berlin jazz clubs, Yorckschlösschen ("little York castle") has become the unofficial living room of the area's musicians and jazz aficianados. The club is plastered with posters and decorated with old instruments, and the stage isn't much more than a slightly raised platform—but some of the area's best play here. The Thursday night jam session is free; other nights, a music charge will be added to your bill. ✉ *Yorckstr. 15, Kreuzberg* ☎ *030/215–8070* ⊕ *www.yorckschloesschen.de.*

SCHÖNEBERG

BARS

Green Door. A grown-up crowd focused on conversation and appreciating outstanding cocktails heads to Green Door, a Schöneberg classic. The decor is 1960s retro style, with gingham walls and stand-alone lamps. ■ TIP➔ **Although the expertly crafted drinks are not cheap by Berlin standards, happy hour (6–8) means you can order them at nearly half price.** ✉ *Winterfeldstr. 50, Schöneberg* ☎ *030/215–2515* ⊕ *www.greendoor.de.*

Lebensstern. A drinking spot for people who love cigars, or a smoking room for people who love top-shelf alcohol, Lebensstern consistently wins awards, in and out of Germany, as one of the best bars in the world. If the floor-to-ceiling cases full of bottles make you dizzy, ask the bartenders for a recommendation: all are well-versed in the relative merits of rums and whiskeys. ✉ *Kurfürstenstr. 58, upstairs from Café Einstein Stammhaus, Schoeneberg* ☎ *030/2639–1922* ⊕ *www.lebensstern.de.*

CLUBS

Havanna Club. Berlin's multiculti crowd frequents the Havanna Club, where you can dance to soul, R&B, or hip-hop on four different dance floors. The week's highlights are the wild salsa and merengue nights (Wednesday at 9 pm, Friday and Saturday at 10 pm). If your Latin steps are weak, come an hour early for a lesson. ■ TIP➔ **Friday and Saturday are "ladies free" nights until 11.** ✉ *Hauptstr. 30, Schöneberg* ☎ *030/784–8565* ⊕ *www.havanna-berlin.de.*

GAY AND LESBIAN NIGHTLIFE

Connection Club. Just south of Wittenbergplatz, the dance club Connection is known for heavy house music and lots of dark corners. ✉ *Fuggerstr. 33, Schöneberg* ☎ *030/218–1432* ⊕ *www.connection-berlin.de.*

Hafen. The decor and the energetic crowd at Hafen make it a popular singles hangout. ⊠ *Motzstr. 19, Schöneberg* ☎ *030/211–4118* ⊕ *www. hafen-berlin.de.*

NEUKÖLLN

BARS

Sameheads. This bar, club, and performance venue has anchored the district's nightlife scene ever since it was founded by three visionary British brothers in 2006. The upstairs is a straightforward bar, cozy and local, while the cavelike cellar hosts live bands and a range of shows including comedy, open-mike, and burlesque. ■ TIP→ While the upstairs is one of the smokiest bars in the city, smoking is prohibited downstairs. ⊠ *Richardstr. 10, Neukölln* ☎ *030/7012–1060* ⊕ *www.sameheads.com.*

TREPTOW

CLUBS

Fodor's Choice
★

Club der Visionaere. It may not be much more than a series of wooden rafts and a few shoddily constructed shacks, but this club is one of the most beloved outdoor venues in town. The place is packed at all hours, either with clubbers on their last stop of the evening, or with students soaking up the sunshine on a Sunday morning. Since it shares a narrow canal with Freischwimmer, which hosts a massive brunch on Sunday, an easy hop across the water (by bridge, of course) will get you coffee and breakfast at dawn. ⊠ *Am Flutgraben 1, Treptow* ⊹ *Follow Schlesische Strasse east from the U-bahn station until you cross two small canals. After the second bridge, look left.* ☎ *030/6951–8942* ⊗ *Weekdays 2 pm–late, weekends noon–late* Ⓜ *Schlesisches Tor (U-bahn).*

PRENZLAUER BERG

BARS

Becketts Kopf. A bar for those who like to enjoy a drink in relative calmness (and a big armchair), Becketts Kopf resembles a gentleman's club—though it's coed, of course. The only indication anything exists behind its curtained facade is a glowing photograph of the head of Samuel Beckett in the window (the bar's name simply means "Beckett's head"). Their old-world drinks seem designed to be enjoyed slowly (and with higher prices than you'll find in most Berlin bars, you're unlikely to order in bulk). If names like Lusitanian, Aviation, and El Presidente don't stoke your thirst, try a classic martini—one of the best in town. ⊠ *Pappellallee 64, Prenzlauer Berg* ☎ *0162/237–9418* ⊕ *www. becketts-kopf.de.*

Le Croco Bleu. Legendary Rum Trader barkeeper Gregor Scholl has opened this new stunner across town, in the machine room of the magnificent Bötzow Brauerei just next to the restaurant La Soupe Populaire. With old industrial remnants and sky-high ceilings, this bar feels a bit like the bowels of a great oceanliner. The extensive menu—including some favorites inspired by Rum Trader—are inventive and unexpected, employing ingredients like tamarind, thyme, or yuzu to tease the palate.

When you're making plans, remember that Le Croco Bleu is only open Thursday to Saturday. ⊠ *Prezlauer Allee 242, in Bötzow Brauerei, Prenzlauer Berg* ☎ *0177/443-2359* ⊕ *www.lecrocobleu.com.*

Visite Ma Tente. A sweet little French-owned bar with a slightly naughty name, this spot has been a local favorite for several years now—simple and comfortable yet *tres* chic. Come here when you're tired of Berlin's beer-dominated bar culture, and order a kir royal or a glass of excellent French wine, paired with a meat-and-cheese platter. In good weather, nab a rickety sidewalk table; the bar's corner location is great for people-watching. ⊠ *Christinenstr. 24, Prenzlauer Berg* ☎ *030/2936–9463.*

Weinerei. It sounds like a recipe for disaster: pay 2 euros for an empty glass, fill it with your choice of wine from a number of bottles, and when you're ready to leave, pay whatever you think you owe. But this pay-as-you-wish bar has survived for more than 15 years; in fact, Weinerei is one of three such "communist wine bars," all on the border between Mitte and Prenzlauer Berg. Although the wines aren't extraordinary, the charming concept has attracted cash-strapped Berliners steadily over the years. ⊠ *Fehrbellinerstr. 57, Prenzlauer Berg* ☎ *030/440–6983* ⊕ *www. weinerei.com.*

BEER GARDENS

Fodor's Choice ★

Prater. This sprawling biergarten, one of this city's beloved institutions, is where Berliners go when the urge for a hefeweizen and pretzel strikes. Grab a beer and a snack (a bratwurst is the classic choice, but they serve a few other meat and veggie options), squeeze in at one of the long community tables, and get ready for some marathon drinking—at least as bystander, if not a participant. If the outdoor boisterousness is too much, opt for an indoor table at the slightly more upscale restaurant, which serves an expanded menu of German classics like wiener schnitzel. ⊠ *Kastanienallee 7–9, Prenzlauer Berg* ☎ *030/448–5688* ⊕ *www.pratergarten.de.*

WEDDING

BARS

Beer4Wedding. Born out of the brewery and drink technology program (yes, it exists) at Berlin's Technical University, this Wedding-based craft brewery has been putting northern Berlin on the map. A truly local outfit, they not only brew from Wedding, but also grow the hops for their IPA, Wedding Pale Ale, on a Wedding rooftop. Other unusual but delicious concoctions include an oyster stout, brewed with notes of oat, coffee, and chocolate. ■ TIP→ **Unlike other brewers in Berlin, this one doesn't have a public tap room or bar. Instead, check the list of distributors on their website.** ⊠ *Wedding* ⊕ *www.beer4wedding.de/.*

Eschenbräu. This Wedding brewery has major bragging rights within Berlin's craft beer scene. Not only has it been around for more than a decade (since 2001), it also offers something the newcomers don't: a beer garden. The brewery's taproom is hidden away on the ground floor of an undistinguished apartment complex; finding it is like discovering buried treasure. The brewery usually has three concoctions on tap, which can include anything from the typical pilsner or hefeweizen to the unusual smoky Rauchbier to drinks with playful names like the Weddinator or the Black Mamba. There's also a small distillery on the premises, where ambitious and talented owner Martin Eschenbrenner tries his hand at schnapps and whiskey. ⊠ *Triftstr. 67, Wedding* ☏ *030/462–6837* ⊕ *www.eschenbraeu.de.*

Vagabund. This scrappy little bar and brewery opened in summer 2013 after a successful Kickstarter campaign and has already become a local favorite for all ages. The three friendly American proprietors are beer aficianados who began brewing for fun, but soon realized there was a market for their small-batch craft products. On any given night, they'll have a selection of local beers on tap, including brews from Wedding compatriots Beer4Wedding or Kreuzberg favorites Heidenpeters, as well as an impressive selection of imported bottles. ⊠ *Antwerpenerstr. 3, Wedding* ⊕ *www.vagabundbrauerei.com.*

CLUBS

Humboldthain. This club is in an old brick building bordering one of Wedding's most beloved green spaces, Volkspark Humboldthain; its sprawling outdoor area gives it a feeling of woodsy openness quite different from other Berlin clubs. During the day in warm weather, the courtyard functions as a beer garden, complete with ping-pong table and bocce ball. At night, the club's two dance floors draw revelers from all over the city with an excellent DJ lineup—even on weekdays. It's a welcome addition to the Wedding nightlife scene. ⊠ *Hochstr. 46, Wedding* ☏ *030/4690–5365* ⊕ *www.humboldthain.com/.*

CHARLOTTENBURG

BARS

Rum Trader. This cocktail bar, which bills itself as the oldest in Berlin (it opened in 1975), may have the right to be a bit snooty: there's only 30 seats, and if they're full you'll be waiting outside in the cold. But inside, the bar is classic and cozy, with built-in shelves for spirits, and every patron has a front-row seat to the bartenders' show. The drinks, too, are worth the wait—just don't let the bartender catch you showing ignorance about alcohol or, God forbid, treating your cocktail as anything less than a work of art. ⊠ *Fasanenstr. 40, Wilmersdorf* ☏ *030/881–1428.*

JAZZ CLUBS

A-Trane. A-Trane in West Berlin has hosted countless greats throughout the years, including Herbie Hancock and Wynton Marsalis. Weekly free jam nights on Saturday and numerous other free events make it a good place to see jazz on a budget. ⊠ *Bleibtreustr. 1, Charlottenburg* ☏ *030/313–2550* ⊕ *www.a-trane.de* Ⓜ *Savignypl. (S-bahn).*

Quasimodo. To get to Quasimodo, the most established and popular jazz venue in the city, you'll need to descend a small staircase to the basement of the Theater des Westens. Despite its college-town pub feel, the club has hosted many Berlin and international greats. Seats are few, but there's plenty of standing room in the front. ⊠ *Kantstr. 12a, Charlottenburg* ☏ *030/312–8086* ⊕ *www.quasimodo.de.*

THE ARTS

Updated by
Giulia Pines

Berlin has been an extremely creative capital ever since the 1920s when the liberal spirit of the Weimar Republic allowed it to give birth to more literary masterpieces, plays, musical performances, and even films (at the film studio in neighboring Babelsberg) than at perhaps any other time in German history.

The creative spirits have continued to flourish and, thanks to Berlin's relatively cheap standard of living and high government subsidies for the arts, the city still offers an atmosphere like no other for those looking to be creative—and for those looking to enjoy their creations.

With four opera houses, an endless number of theaters, and cinemas both big and small, Berlin has something to offer the performing arts aficionado almost every day of the week. It's just a matter of knowing where to find what interests you.

PLANNING

INFORMATION

Detailed information about events is covered in the *Berlin Programm,* a monthly tourist guide to Berlin arts, museums, and theaters. The magazines *Tip* and *Zitty,* which appear every two weeks, provide full arts listings (in German), although the free weekly *(030)* is the best source for club and music events. For listings in English, consult the monthly *ExBerliner,* or their website (⊕ *www.exberliner.com*), which is updated regularly.

WHERE TO GET TICKETS

Hekticket offices. The Hekticket offices offers discounted and last-minute tickets, including half-price, same-day tickets daily at 2pm. ⊠ *Karl-Liebknecht-Str. 13, off Alexanderpl., Mitte: Alexanderplatz.*

Showtime Konzert und Theaterkassen. If your hotel can't book a seat for you or you can't make it to a box office directly, go to a ticket agency. Surcharges are 18%–23% of the ticket price. Showtime Konzert und Theaterkassen has offices within the major department stores, including KaDeWe and Karstadt. ⊠ *KaDeWe, Tauentzienstr. 21, Charlottenburg* ☎ *030/8060–2929* ⊕ *www.showtimetickets.de.*

BERLIN FESTIVAL WEEKS

Berliner Festspiele. This annual Berlin festival, held from late August through September or early October, unites all the major performance halls as well as some smaller venues for concerts, opera, ballet, theater, and art exhibitions. It also sponsors some smaller-scale events throughout the year. ⊠ *Ticket office, Schaperstr. 24* ☎ *030/2548–9100* ⊕ *www. berlinerfestspiele.de.*

CLASSICAL MUSIC

Konzerthaus Berlin. The beautifully restored hall at Konzerthaus Berlin is a prime venue for classical music concerts. The box office is open from noon to curtain time. ⊠ *Gendarmenmarkt, Mitte: Unter den Linden* ☎ *030/2030–92101* ⊕ *www.konzerthaus.de.*

Berliner Philharmonie. The Berlin Philharmonic Orchestra is one of the world's best and their resident venue is the Philharmonie, comprising the Grosser Saal or large main hall, and the smaller Kammermusiksaal, dedicated to chamber music. Tickets sell out in advance for the nights when Sir Simon Rattle or other star maestros conduct, but other orchestras and artists appear here as well. ■ TIP→ **Tuesday's free Lunchtime Concerts fill the foyer with eager listeners of all ages at 1 pm. Daily guided tours (€3) also take place at 1 pm.** ⊠ *Herbert-von-Karajan-Str. 1, Tiergarten* ☎ *030/254–880* ⊕ *www.berliner-philharmoniker.de.*

DANCE

Vladimir Malakhov, a principal guest dancer with New York's American Ballet Theatre, is a principal in the Staatsballett Berlin as well as its director. The company performs its classic and modern productions between the Deutsche Oper and the Staatsoper.

Tanzfabrik. The Tanzfabrik is Berlin's best venue to see young dance talent and the latest from Europe's avant-garde. ⊠ *Möckernstr. 68, Kreuzberg* ☎ *030/786–5861* ⊕ *www.tanzfabrik-berlin.de.*

FILM

International and German movies are shown in the big theaters on Potsdamer Platz and around the Ku'damm. If a film isn't marked "OF" or "OV" (*Originalfassung,* or original version) or "OmU" (original with subtitles), it's dubbed. Many Berlin theaters let customers reserve seats in advance when purchasing tickets, so buy them early to nab those coveted center spots. Aside from the big theaters, there are also numerous art house cinemas, some of them in historical buildings that are themselves architecturally interesting. If you're looking to see independent film productions that are subtitled instead of dubbed, for example, Hackesche Höfe is the perfect place for this. ■ TIP→ **Previews and commercials often run for 25 minutes, so don't worry if you walk in late.**

Babylon. Partially hidden behind Kottbusser Tor, Babylon shows English-language films with German subtitles. Ticket prices vary according to the day of the week, with Monday being the cheapest at €6. ⊠ *Dresdener Str. 126, Kreuzberg* ☎ *030/6160–9693* ⊕ *www.yorck.de.*

CineStar im Sony Center. Mainstream U.S. and British movies are screened in their original versions at the CineStar im Sony Center. Tuesday is a discount evening. ⊠ *Potsdamer Str. 4, Tiergarten* ☎ *030/2606–6400.*

Freiluftkinos. When warm weather hits the city and Berliners come out of hibernation, they often head to the Freiluftkinos (open-air cinemas). These outdoor viewing areas are in just about every park in town, offer food and drinks, and screen a good balance of German

7

and international films, many of them new releases. Check the website for schedules from three of the city's best, in Volkspark Friedrichshain, Mariannenplatz Kreuzberg, and Volkspark Rehberge in Wedding. ⊕ *www.freiluftkino-berlin.de* ⌂ *€6.50.*

Hackesche Höfe Kino. Documentary films, international films in their original language, and German art-house films are shown at the Hackesche Höfe Kino, or cinema. There's no elevator to this top-floor movie house, but you can recover on the wide banquettes in the lounge. Monday and Tuesday are discount evenings. ✉ *Rosenthaler Str. 40–41, Mitte* ☎ *030/283–4603* ⊕ *www. hoefekino.de.*

Berlinale: Internationale Filmfestspiele (*Internationale Filmfestspiele*). In February, numerous cinemas band together to host the prestigious Internationale Filmfestspiele, or Berlinale, a 10-day international festival at which the Golden Bear award is bestowed on the best films, directors, and actors. Ticket counters open three days before the party begins, but individual tickets are also sold on each day of the festival, if you're willing to wait in line for what can be hours. ■TIP→ **Film buffs should purchase the season pass, or act quickly when tickets are sold online.** ⊕ *www. berlinale.de* ☉ *10 days in Feb.*

OPERA

Berlin's four opera houses—the *Deutsche Oper* (the German Opera), the *Staatsoper* (the State Opera), and the *Komische Oper* (the Comedy Opera)—also host guest productions and companies from around the world. The *Staatsoper,* on Unter den Linden, is currently undergoing renovations, set to be completed by the end of 2015.

Deutsche Oper Berlin. Of the 17 composers represented in the repertoire of Deutsche Oper Berlin, Verdi and Wagner are the most frequently presented. ✉ *Bismarckstr. 35, Charlottenburg* ☎ *030/343–8401* ⊕ *www. deutscheoperberlin.de.*

Komische Oper. Most of the operas performed here are sung in German but the lavish and at times over-the-top and kitschy staging and costumes make for a fun night even if you don't speak the language. ✉ *Behrenstr. 55–57, Mitte* ☎ *030/4799–7400* ⊕ *www.komische-oper-berlin.de.*

Neuköllner Oper. The small and alternative Neuköllner Oper puts on fun, showy performances of long-forgotten operas as well as humorous musical productions. It also is more likely than other Berlin opera houses to stage productions offering modern social commentary and individual takes on the immigrant experience—which is fitting for this international neighborhood. ✉ *Karl-Marx-Str. 131–133, Neukölln* ☎ *030/6889–0777.*

Staatsoper Unter den Linden (*State Opera*). Frederick the Great was a music lover and he made the Staatsoper Unter den Linden, on the east side of Bebelplatz, his first priority. The lavish opera house was completed in 1743 by the same architect who built Sanssouci in Potsdam, Georg Wenzeslaus von Knobelsdorff. The house is currently undergoing a complete makeover, set to be completed in 2015, when the historic interior will be replaced with a modern design. The show goes on at the Schiller Theater across town, where maestro Daniel Barenboim continues to oversee a diverse repertoire. ⊠ *Unter den Linden 7, Mitte* ⊕ *www.staatsoper-berlin.de* ۞ *Box office Mon.-Sat. 10–8, Sun. 12–8* Ⓜ *Französische Strasse (U-bahn).*

THEATER AND MUSICALS

Theater in Berlin is outstanding, but performances are usually in German. The exceptions are operettas and the (nonliterary) cabarets. Keep in mind that tourist high season is always theater low season: almost all theaters in town take a one- to two-month break in July and August.

Berliner Ensemble. The excellent Berliner Ensemble is dedicated to Brecht and works of other international playwrights. The company might be losing its lease in 2013 so check the website for updates about a new location. ⊠ *Bertolt Brecht-Pl. 1, off Friedrichstr., just north of train station, Mitte* ☎ *030/2840–8155* ⊕ *www.berliner-ensemble.de.*

Deutsches Theater. The theater most renowned for both its modern and classical productions is the Deutsches Theater. ⊠ *Schumannstr. 13a, Mitte* ☎ *030/2844–1225* ⊕ *www.deutschestheater.de.*

English Theatre Berlin. The English Theatre presents dramas and comedies in English. ⊠ *Fidicinstr. 40, Kreuzberg* ☎ *030/691–1211* ⊕ *www.etberlin.de.*

Grips Theater. For children's theater, head to the world-famous Grips Theater, whose musical hit *Linie 1*, about life in Berlin viewed through the subway, is just as appealing for adults. ⊠ *Altonaer Str. 22, Tiergarten* ☎ *030/3974–740* ⊕ *www.grips-theater.de.*

Hebbel am Ufer Theater (*HAU*). This theater consists of three houses (HAU 1, 2, 3) within a five-minute walk of one another. Fringe theater, international modern dance, and solo performers share the stages. ⊠ *Stresemannstr. 29, Kreuzberg* ☎ *030/2590–0427* ⊕ *www.hebbel-am-ufer.de.*

Schaubühne am Lehniner Platz. The rebellious actors at the Schaubühne am Lehniner Platz, once the city's most experimental stage, have mellowed somewhat but still put on great performances. Their frequent, avant-garde stagings of well-known Shakespeare plays are a wonderful opportunity to enjoy German theater, even if you don't know a word of German. (You can always brush up on the story beforehand and follow along with your own English text.) ⊠ *Kurfürstendamm 153, Wilmersdorf* ☎ *030/890–023* ⊕ *www.schaubuehne.de.*

Schiller Theater. Currently serving as interim stage for the Staatsoper, until renovations are finished in 2015, the Schiller Theater is also known for light musical and theater fare. ✉ *Bismarckstr. 110, Charlottenburg* ☎ *030/2035–4555.*

Tempodrom. The white, tentlike Tempodrom, beyond the ruined facade of Anhalter Bahnhof, showcases international music and rock stars. ✉ *Möckernstr. 10, behind Askanischer Platz, Kreuzberg* ☎ *01806/554–111* ⊕ *www.tempodrom.de.*

Theater des Westens. The late-19th-century Theater des Westens, one of Germany's oldest musical theaters, features musicals such as *Dance of the Vampires; We Will Rock You,* the over-the-top musical about the rock band Queen; and recently, the German-language version of the international sensation *War Horse.* ✉ *Kantstr. 12, Western Downtown* ☎ *030/01805–4444* ⊕ *www.stage-entertainment.de.*

WORD OF MOUTH

"Wintergarten Varieté is cozy in size. . . . The shows are usually a variety following a certain theme. You can have a pre-show dinner here right in the theater (all seats are grouped around tables) and the service of drinks also continues during the show. Chamäleon Varieté is more an 'off' theater, though it's existed for decades now. Shows are sometimes less mainstream than at Wintergartent." —Cowboy1968

Volksbühne am Rosa-Luxemburg-Platz. The Volksbühne am Rosa-Luxemburg-Platz is unsurpassed for its aggressively experimental style, and the 750 seats are often sold out. The unusual building was reconstructed in the 1950s using the original 1914 plans. It also houses two smaller performance spaces—the Roter Salon and the Grüner Salon—which host everything from retro motown nights and salsa classes for all levels to touring pop and rock acts. ✉ *Linienstr. 227, Mitte* ☎ *030/2406–5777* ⊕ *www.volksbuehne-berlin.de.*

VARIETY SHOWS, COMEDY, AND CABARET

Berlin's variety shows can include magicians, circus performers, musicians, and classic cabaret stand-ups. Be aware that in order to understand and enjoy traditional cabaret, which involves a lot of political humor, your German has to be up to snuff.

Admiralspalast. The completely restored 1920s entertainment emporium Admiralspalast draws on its glitzy Jazz Age glamour, and houses several stages and a restaurant. The main theater features everything from large-scale shows to theater, comedy, and concerts. ✉ *Friedrichstr. 101, Mitte* ☎ *030/4799–7499* ⊕ *www.admiralspalast.de.*

Bar Jeder Vernunft. The intimate Bar Jeder Vernunft is inside a glamorous tent and usually showcases intriguing solo entertainers. Note that the venue is set back from the street and is hard to find. Just to the left of Haus der Berliner Festspiele, look for a lighted path next to a parking lot and follow it until you reach the tent. ✉ *Schaperstr. 24, Wilmersdorf* ☎ *030/883–1582* ⊕ *www.bar-jeder-vernunft.de.*

BKA–Berliner Kabarett Anstalt. Social and political satire has a long tradition in cabaret theaters and the BKA–Berliner Kabarett Anstalt is known for performances by Germany's leading young comedy talents as well as chanson vocalists. ⊠ *Mehringdamm 34, Kreuzberg* ☎ *030/202–2007* ⊕ *www.bka-theater.de.*

Chamäleon Varieté. Within the Hackesche Höfe, the Chamäleon Varieté is the most affordable and offbeat variety venue in town. German isn't required to enjoy most of the productions. ⊠ *Rosenthaler Str. 40–41, Mitte* ☎ *030/4000–590* ⊕ *www.chamaeleonberlin.com.*

Grüner Salon. This is one of Berlin's hippest venues for live music, cabaret, dancing, and drinks. The programs change almost daily. ⊠ *Freie Volksbühne, Rosa-Luxemburg-Pl., Rosa-Luxemburg-Platz, side door of the Volksbühne, Mitte* ☎ *030/2859–8936* ⊕ *www.gruener-salon.de.*

Tipi am Kanzleramt (*Tipi am Kanzleramt*). Tipi is a tent venue between the Kanzleramt (Chancellor's Office) and Haus der Kulturen der Welt. Artists featured are well suited for an international audience, and you can opt to dine here before the show. Even the back-row seats are good. ⊠ *Grosse Querallee, Tiergarten* ☎ *030/3906–6550* ⊕ *www.tipi-am-kanzleramt.de.*

Wintergarten Varieté. The Wintergarten Varieté pays romantic homage to the old days of Berlin's original variety theater in the 1920s. ⊠ *Potsdamer Str. 96, Tiergarten* ☎ *030/588–433* ⊕ *www.wintergarten-variete.de.*

7

POTSDAM

Updated by
Katherine
Sacks

A trip to Berlin wouldn't be complete without paying a visit to Potsdam, known for its 18th-century baroque architecture; Sanssouci Park, the former residence of the Prussian royals; historical landmarks; and charming boutique and café-lined cobblestone streets. The bonus is that it's only a half-hour trip from Berlin.

Although Potsdam was severely damaged in bombing during World War II, much of the city has been restored to its former glory and still retains the imperial character it accrued during the many years it served as a royal residence and garrison quarters. The Alter Markt (Old Market) and Neuer Markt (New Market) show off stately Prussian architecture, and both are easily reached from the main train station or Sanssouci Park by tram. The charming Holländisches Viertel (Dutch Quarter) is home to a collection of redbrick, gable-roofed buildings, many of which are popular restaurants, boutiques, and cafés today. Just north of Sanssouci Park is Neuer Park, site of the Potsdam Conference in 1945. Both are home to manicured gardens, stunning architecture, lakes and fountains, and several palaces, galleries, and former royal buildings.

Potsdam sits on the Havel River and its small Harbor area shows off modern and vintage-style boats, a casting off point for boat tours around the area or back to Berlin.

Potsdam also plays a central role in the history of film. The world's first major movie studios opened in 1911 in Babelsberg, just south of Potsdam, developing the area into a prewar Hollywood. Fritz Lang's *Metropolis* and *The Blue Angel* with Marlene Dietrich were both filmed here, and many modern filmmakers continue to use the studios. The historic Filmmuseum Potsdam will interest film buffs.

PLANNER

TIMING
Potsdam is the state capital of Brandenburg (the state surrounding Berlin), and can be reached in a half hour from Berlin's Zoo Station or from most major Berlin S-bahn stations. An enthusiastic history buff could happily spend several days exploring the palaces and landmarks of Sanssouci Park and Neuer Garten but considering that most of the palace interiors are quite similar, and that the city is quite compact and well connected with public transport, one day is generally sufficient for a visit.

GETTING HERE AND AROUND
Potsdam is 20 km (12 miles) southwest of Berlin's center and a half-hour journey by car or bus. From Zoo Station to Potsdam's main train station, the regional train RE 1 takes 17 minutes, and the S-7 line of the S-bahn takes about 30 minutes; use an ABC zone ticket for either service. City traffic is heavy, so a train journey is recommended.

Several Berlin tour operators have Potsdam trips. Most are five to six hours, including travel time from Berlin. They leave from the landing across from Berlin's Wannsee S-bahn station between late March and early October. Depending on the various tours on offer, a round-trip ticket costs €7.50–€23.

ESSENTIALS

City Sightseeing Potsdam. If you want to see it all, consider a hop-on, hop-off bus tour. This double-decker bus has an open-deck second floor, giving great views of the city, with seven convenient stops throughout Potsdam. ☎ *0331/ 974–376* ⊕ *www.city-sightseeing.com/tours/germany/potsdam.htm* 🖃 *€14.*

Fat Tire Bike Tours ✉ *Panoramastr. 1a, base of TV tower, Mitte, Berlin* ☎ *030/2404–7991* ⊕ *www.fattirebiketoursberlin.com.*

Sandeman's New Europe: Berlin. This company offers a five-hour walking tour of Potsdam, including the Dutch Quarter, Potsdam's Brandenburg Gate, and Park Sanssouci. The day ends at Schloss Sanssouci—if you want to tour the palace as well, the guides will give you tips on how to avoid the lines and get deals on tickets. ■ TIP→ **The tour's meeting point is at Berlin's Brandenburg Gate, and you'll need to have an ABC train ticket purchased ahead of time.** ✉ *Milastr. 2, Berlin* ☎ *030/5105–0030* ⊕ *newberlintours.com* 🖃 *€14.*

Visitor Information Potsdam Tourist Office. Two-hour walking tours (€9) are led around Potsdam's historical center from this tourist information center. ✉ *Touristenzentrum Potsdam, Brandenburgerstr. 3, at Brandenburger Tor Potsdam* ☎ *0331/275–580* ⊕ *www.potsdamtourismus.de.*

EXPLORING POTSDAM

ALTER MARKT (OLD MARKET)

This "Old Market" Square is the hub of Potsdam's historical center and was, for three centuries, home to the city's baroque palace. The area was heavily damaged by Allied bombing in World War II and then destroyed by the East German regime in 1960. After reunification, Potsdam decided to rebuild its palace, and the reconstructed structure will house the state parliament. Thanks to private donors, the first element, a magnificent replica of the **Fortunaportal,** now stands proudly on the square, while the palace's main sections are currently being built with a combination of modern and historic elements. ✉ *Am Alten Markt 1.*

Altes Rathaus. A gilded figure of Atlas tops the tower of the old Rathaus, built in 1755. ✉ *Am Alten Markt 9.*

Holländisches Viertel. The center of the small Holländisches Viertel—the Dutch Quarter—is an easy walk north along Friedrich-Ebert-Strasse to Mittelstrasse. Friedrich Wilhelm I built the settlement in the 1730s to entice Dutch artisans who could support the city's rapid growth.

Potsdam

KEY

Tram & Stop
🚉 Tourist info

Schloss Cecilienhof

Neuer Garten

Belvedere auf dem Pfingstberg

Hollándisches Viertel

Nikolaikirche
Alter Markt

Potsdam Filmmuseum

Alles Rathaus

Neuer Market

Haus der Brandenburgisch-Preussischen Geschichte

POTSDAM

Brandenburger Tor

Dampfmaschinen-haus

Bildergalerie

Friedenskirche

Schloss Sanssouci

Orangerie Schloss und Turm

Chinesisches Teehaus

Römische Bäder

Schloss Charlottenhof

Sanssouci Park

Park Charlottenhof

Neues Palais

Am Neuen Palais

Babelsberger Strasse
Friedrich-List-Strasse

Potsdam Train Station

Havel

Park Babelsberg

Nuthestrasse

Berliner Strasse

Heiliger See

Ludwig-Richter-Strasse
Rubensstrasse
Mühlenweg

Neuer Garten

Am Neuen Garten

Kurfürstenstrasse

Bassinplatz

Am Kanal

Jägerallee

Hegelallee

Gutenbergstrasse

Brandenburger Strasse

Lindenstrasse

Breite Strasse

Voltaireweg

Weinbergstrasse

Feuerbachstrasse

Zeppelinstrasse

Georg-Hermann-Allee

August-Bonnes-Strasse

Pappelallee

Volkspark Potsdam

Ulrich-Mendelsohn-Allee

Alexander-Klein-Str.

Erwin-Barth-Str.

Kirschallee

Bornstedter Strasse

Maulbeerallee

Carl-von-Ossietzky-Strasse

Geschwister-Scholl-Strasse

Havel

Eichenallee

Katharinenholzstrasse

Thaelstrasse
Haebichweg

Potsdamer Strasse

Ökonomieweg

Lindenavenue

Amundsenstrasse

3,000ft

500m

Potsdam

The 134 gabled, mansard-roof brick houses make up the largest Dutch housing development outside of the Netherlands today. Antique shops, boutiques, and restaurants fill the buildings now, and the area is one of Potsdam's most visited.

Nikolaikirche. Karl Friedrich Schinkel designed the Alter Markt's domed Nikolaikirche. In front of it stands an Egyptian obelisk erected by Schloss Sanssouci architect von Knobelsdorff. ⊠ *Am Alten Markt.*

NEUER MARKT (NEW MARKET)

Opposite the Alter Markt, the Neuer Markt (New Market) features similar baroque-style architecture as well a handful of the city's most well-preserved buildings, some of which date back to the 18th century.

Brandenburger Gate. As you exit Park Sanssouci and head into the Old Market area, you'll come across Potsdam's Brandenburger Gate, a Roman triumphal arch designed by Karl von Gontard on the orders of Frederick II. ⊠ *Luisenpl., Potsdam, Germany* ⊕ *www.potsdam.de/.*

Dampfmaschinenhaus. Friedrich Wilhelm IV modeled this building after a Turkish mosque, complete with a minaret, to serve as the palace waterworks building. Sitting on the edge of the Neuer Markt, the Dampfmaschinenhaus uses a steam engine to transport water to a large fountain in the center of Sanssouci Park. ⊠ *Breitestr. 28* ☎ *0331/969–4248* ⊕ *www.spsg.de/* 🖱 *€2* ⊟ *No credit cards* ⊘ *May–Oct., weekends 10–6.*

Haus der Brandenburg-Preussischen Geschichte (*House of Brandenburg-Prussian History*). The region's history museum, the Haus der Brandenburg-Preußischen Geschichte, is in the royal stables in the square opposite the Nikolaikirche. ⊠ *Am Neuen Markt 9* ☎ *0331/620–8550* ⊕ *www.hbpg.de* 🖱 *€4.50* ⊘ *Tues.–Thurs. 10–5, Fri.–Sun. 10–6.*

Potsdam Filmmuseum. Another facet of Potsdam's illustrious history is its place in the film industry; many early silent films were produced here, including Fritz Lang's *Metropolis*, and modern day filmmakers continue to use the studios. Inside this beautiful baroque building, visitors can look into the history of film production in the area. **Note that the museum is currently undergoing renovations and can only be visited appointment until spring 2014.** ⊠ *Breitestr. 1A* ☎ *0331/271–810* ⊕ *www.filmmuseum-potsdam.de/.*

QUICK
BITES

Wiener Restaurant. Fine coffee blends and rich cakes are available at the Wiener Restaurant, an old-style European coffeehouse not far from the Grünes Gitter entrance to Sanssouci. ⊠ *Luisenpl. 4* ☎ *0331/6014–9904* ⊕ *www.wiener-potsdam.de/.*

SANSSOUCI PARK

Fodor's Choice ★ One of the main attractions for Potsdam visitors, the sprawling Sanssouci Park has been a World Heritage Site since 1990. The former summer residence of the Prussian royals, the park is home to numerous palaces, landscaped gardens, and eye-catching architecture. Many call it the Versaille of Potsdam.

Neues Palais (*New Palace*). The Neues Palais, a much larger and grander palace than Sanssouci, stands at the end of the long avenue that runs through Sanssouci Park. It was built after the Seven Years' War (1756–63), when Frederick loosened the purse strings. It's said he wanted to demonstrate that the state coffers hadn't been depleted too severely by the long conflict. Interiors that impress include the Grotto Hall with walls and columns set with shells, coral, and other aquatic decor. The royals' upper apartments have paintings by 17th-century Italian masters. You can opt to tour the palace yourself only on weekends between late April and mid-May. ⊠ *Str. am Neuen Palais, Sanssouci* ☎ *0331/969–4200* ⊕ *www.spsg.de* ⌧ *€8* ☉ *Apr.–Oct. Wed.–Mon. 10–6; Nov.–Mar., Wed.–Mon. 10–5.*

Schloss Charlottenhof. Schloss Charlottenhof is in the southern part of Sanssouci Park, an expansive, landscaped promenade with fountains, streams, manicured gardens, and wide walkways as well as some hidden paths. After Frederick the Great died in 1786, the ambitious Sanssouci building program ground to a halt, and the park fell into neglect. It was 50 years before another Prussian king, Friedrich Wilhelm IV, restored Sanssouci's earlier glory. He engaged the great Berlin architect Karl Friedrich Schinkel to build this small palace for the crown prince. Schinkel's demure interiors are preserved, and the most fanciful room is the bedroom, decorated like a Roman tent, with its walls and ceiling draped in striped canvas. Between the Sanssouci palaces are later additions to the park. ☎ *0331/969–4228* ⌧ *€4 with tour* ☉ *May–Oct., Tues.–Sun. 10–6; Nov.–Apr. closed.*

Römische Bäder (*Roman Baths*). Friedrich Wilhelm IV built the Römische Bäder (Roman Baths), also designed by Schinkel, from 1829 to 1840. Like many of the other structures in Potsdam, this one is more romantic than authentic. Half Italian villa, half Greek temple, the structure is nevertheless a charming addition to the park. ⌧ *€3 with exhibit* ☉ *May–Oct., Tues.–Sun. 10–5*

Orangerieschloss und Turm. The Orangerieschloss und Turm was completed in 1864; its two massive towers linked by a colonnade evoke an Italian Renaissance palace. Today it houses more than 50 copies of paintings by Raphael. ⌧ *Guided tour €4, tower only €2* ☉ *Apr., weekends and holidays 10–6; May–Oct., Tues.–Sun. 10–6; Nov.–Apr. closed.*

Chinesisches Teehaus (*Chinese Teahouse*). The Chinesisches Teehaus was erected in 1754 in the Chinese style that was all the rage at the time. It houses porcelain from Meissen and Asia. ⌧ *€2* ☉ *May–Oct., Tues.—Sun. 10–6; Closed Nov.-Apr.*

Friedenskirche (*Peace Church*). Completed in 1854, the Italianate Friedenskirche houses a 13th-century Byzantine mosaic taken from an island near Venice. ☎ *0331/974–009* ⌧ *Free* ☉ *Apr. 24–30, Mon.–Sat. 11–5, Sun. 12–5; May–Sept., Mon.–Sat. 10–6, Sun. 12–6; Oct. 2–16, Mon.–Sat. 11–5, Sun. 12–5; Oct. 17–Apr. 23, Sat. 11–4, Sun. 11:30–4.*

Schloss Sanssouci. Prussia's most famous king, Friedrich II—Frederick the Great—spent more time at his summer residence, Schloss Sanssouci, than in the capital of Berlin. Its name means "without a care" in French, the language Frederick cultivated in his own private circle and within the court. Some experts believe that Frederick actually named the palace "Sans, Souci," which they translate as "with and without a care," a more apt name, since its construction caused him a lot of trouble and expense, and sparked furious rows with his master builder, Georg Wenzeslaus von Knobelsdorff. His creation nevertheless became one of Germany's greatest tourist attractions. The palace lies on the edge of Park Sanssouci, which includes various buildings and palaces with separate admissions and hours. ■TIP➔ Be advised that during peak tourism times, timed tickets for Schloss Sanssouci tours can sell out before noon.

WORD OF MOUTH

"Potsdam to me was far more than Sanssouci, which even if you are not into lavish palaces still may delight you—its tiered-terraced gardens are unique and there is a sprawling, huge park that has follies dotting it (whimsical structures) as well as things Chinoiserie reflecting the 18th-century fascination with all things Chinese. Anyway Potsdam is way more than just the palace, one of the most delightful parks I have seen."   —PalenQ

Executed according to Frederick's impeccable French-influenced taste, the palace, built between 1745 and 1747, is extravagantly rococo, with scarcely a patch of wall left unadorned. Leading up to the building is an unusual formal terrace where wine grapes were once cultivated. ⊠ *Park Sanssouci* ☎ *0331/969–4200* ⊕ *www.spsg.de* ⊟ *€12* ⊙ *Apr.–Oct., Tues.–Sun. 10–6; Nov.–Mar., Tues.–Sun. 10–5.*

Neue Kammern (*New Chambers*). To the west of the palace are the Neue Kammern, which housed guests of the king's family after its beginnings as a greenhouse. ☎ *0331/969–4206* ⊟ *€4 guided tour only* ⊙ *Apr.–Oct, Tues.–Sun. 10–6; Nov.–Mar. closed.*

Bildergalerie (*Picture Gallery*). Just east of Sanssouci Palace sits the picture gallery, which displays Frederick II's collection of 17th-century Italian and Dutch paintings, including works by Caravaggio, Rubens, and Van Dyck. The main cupola contains expensive marble from Siena. ☎ *0331/969–4181* ⊟ *€6* ⊙ *May–Oct., Tues.–Sun. 10–6; Nov.–April closed.*

QUICK BITES

Drachenhaus (*Dragon House*). Halfway up the hill leading to the Belvedere, past the Orangerie, stands the curious Drachenhaus, modeled in 1770 after the Pagoda at London's Kew Gardens and named for the gargoyles ornamenting the roof corners. It now houses a popular restaurant and café. ⊠ *Maulbeerallee 4* ⊕ *www.drachenhaus.de.*

NEUER GARTEN

Just north of the city center, the Neuer Garten (New Garden) sits along the west shore of the Heiliger Lake, with beautiful views. The park is home to the Marmorpalais and Schloss Cecilienhof, the last palace built by the Prussian Hohenzollern family.

8

Belvedere auf dem Pfingstberg. On a hill near Schloss Cecilienhof, the colonnaded Belvedere auf dem Pfingstberg was a lofty observation platform for the royals. ⊠ *Am Pfingstberg* ☎ *0331/2005–7930* ⊕ *www. pfingstberg.de* ⊡ *€4*

Schloss Cecilienhof (*Cecilienhof Palace*). Resembling a rambling, Tudor manor house, Schloss Cecilienhof was built for Crown Prince Wilhelm in 1913, on a newly laid-out stretch of park called the Neuer Garten (New Garden), which borders the Heiliger See. It was in this, the last palace to be built by the Hohenzollerns, that the Allied leaders Stalin, Truman, and Churchill (later Attlee) hammered out the fate of postwar Germany at the 1945 Potsdam Conference. ■ TIP→ **From Potsdam's main train station, take a tram to Reiterweg/Alleestrasse, and then transfer to Bus 603 to Schloss Cecilienhof.** ☎ *0331/969–4200* ⊕ *www.spsg.de* ⊡ *€6 with tour (Nov.–Mar. tour is mandatory), €4 tour of royal couple's private apartments* ⊗ *Apr.–Oct., Tues.–Sun. 10–6.; Nov.–Mar. Tues.– Sun., 10–5. Tours of royal couple's private apartments at 10, 12, 2, 4; closed Mondays.*

NEED A BREAK?

Meierei im Neuen Garten. Sitting on the tip of the Neuer Garten, Meierei brewery offers classic German beers and local cuisine, with hearty dishes like schnitzel and roast pork knuckle. The outdoor terrace offers great views of the lake and boats during the warm weather, while the indoor tavern seating has rustic charm. ⊠ *Im Neuen Garten 10* ☎ *0331/704–3211* ⊕ *www.meierei-potsdam.de/.*

FARTHER AFIELD

Heilandskirche Sacrow. You'd be forgiven for wondering if you'd been transported to Italy when you first glimpse this dreamy lakeside church, complete with Campanile ("bell-tower") and mosaic-adorned colonnade, from across the Havel Lake or through the Sacrower Schlosspark near Potsdam. Actually, the church suffered a grim fate for many years, trapped in the no-man's land of the Outer Berlin Wall. From 1961 to 1989, the East German government closed the church, fearing that it would serve as a hiding place for those trying to flee. Now it is restored and in use, and makes the perfect endpoint to a scenic walk from the lakeside village of Kladow. ■ TIP→ **To reach it, take the S75 to S-bahnhof Heerstrasse, and then the X34 Bus to Alt-Kladow, then follow the Sakrower Landstrasse.** ⊠ *Fährstr.* ☎ *0331/505–2144* ⊕ *www.heilandskirche-sacrow.de* ⊗ *Mar., Apr., Sept., Oct., Tues.– Sun. 10–3:30; Jan., Feb., Nov., Dec., weekends 10–3; May–Aug., Tues.–Sun. 10–4; Sept.–Mar.,* Ⓜ *Schloss Sacrow (Bus).*

Park Babelsberg. Less well known than the gleaming Sans Souci but still impressive, this palace was once the summer palace of Wilhelm I. This expansive park surrounding the Babelsberg castle offers acres and acres of charm, with expansive views, a wraparound waterfront promenade, and, of course, enough historical buildings to entice even the most jaded traveler. Although the Schloss (castle) itself is currently under extensive renovation, there's still plenty to explore, such as the Dampfmachinenhaus, a 19th-century steam engine building right on the water, or the Kleines Schloss, which literally translates into "small castle" and today houses an elegant wood-paneled café. Climb the Flatowturm ("Flatow Tower") for a 360-degree view of the surrounding parklands and waterways, and the city of Potsdam in the distance. ☎ *0331/969–4200* ⊕ *www.spsg.de/* Ⓜ *Wannsee (S-bahn) and Schloss Babelsberg (Bus).*

WHERE TO EAT

$
CONTEMPORARY
BAR-O-meter. This small vaulted cellar lounge, whose comprehensive cocktail list offers more than 180 classics and house creations, is much loved by both locals and visitors. ⊠ *Gutenbergerstr. 103* ☎ *0331/ 270–2880.*

$
CAFÉ
Café Guam. Tucked on a small street of antiques shops and boutiques, Café Guam is a charming bakeshop that offers visitors a taste of German-style cheesecake. The daily selection includes 6 to 10 different varieties, which rotate among 30 different flavors, including poppy seed, marbled chocolate, and caramelized almond. ⊠ *Mittelstr. 38* ⊕ *www. cafe-guam.de/.*

$
EUROPEAN
✕ **Café Heider.** A few steps away from the Nauen Gate, one of Potsdam's three persevered gates, Café Heider has been serving coffee in its Viennese-style café since 1878. In warmer weather, the outdoor seating offers views of the Dutch Quarter, while the indoor dining room has large bay windows and plush seating. The comprehensive menu includes a variety of cakes, baked goods, and German specialties, as well as a lovely Sunday brunch. Ⓢ *Average main: €13* ⊠ *Friedrich-Ebert-Str. 29* ☎ *0331/270–5596* ⊕ *www.cafeheider.de/.*

$$$$
EUROPEAN
✕ **Friedrich-Wilhelm.** Tucked away in the bucolic Wildpark, this spot offers a modern taste of Prussian cuisine, thanks to chef Alexander Dressel, who also infuses the menu with Italian influences. Although the restaurant and the accompanying Hotel Bayrisches Haus are a bit far from the center of Potsdam, they offer relaxing dining and lodging, as well as scenic woodland views. Ⓢ *Average main: €40* ⊠ *Hotel Bayrisches Haus, Elisenweg 2* ☎ *0331/55050* ⊕ *www.bayrisches-haus.de/.*

$$$
BRASSERIE
✕ **Ma Cuisine.** In this charming Dutch Quarter space, chef Tim Cumming shares his love of French cuisine. Inside the traditional dining room, you'll find a brasserie-style menu including classics like goat cheese tartlets and foie gras mousse. If you are lucky, your trip will coincide with one of the restaurant's occasional whiskey tastings. Ma Cuisine also offers cooking classes. Ⓢ *Average main: €22* ⊠ *Hebbelstr. 54* ☎ *0331/243–7720* ⊕ *www.ma-cuisine.de/.*

$$
BISTRO
✕ **Maison Charlotte.** This Dutch Quarter restaurant captures the essence of old-world France, with its rustic decor and bistro classics, including

8

Breton-style fish soup and *coq au vin*. The small outdoor area is the perfect spot to people-watch and enjoy a glass of wine on a sunny afternoon. ⑤ *Average main: €20* ✉ *Mittelstr. 20* ☎ *0331/280–5450* ⊕ *www. maison-charlotte.de/.*

$$$ ✕ **Restaurant Fiore.** For a taste of Potsdam's finer side, enjoy a meal
MODERN at Hotel am Jägertor's restaurant. Chef Rene Tinz highlights regional
EUROPEAN products and local recipes while infusing creativity into dishes like rabbit liver with wasabi foam or deconstructed Waldorf salad with apple gel and walnut oil. A summer terrace offers views of the nearby Jägertor (Hunter's Gate) while the ritzy dining rooms include gilded accents and baroque decor. ⑤ *Average main: €23* ✉ *Hotel Am Jägertor, Hegelallee 11* ☎ *0331/201–1100* ⊕ *www.hotel-am-jaegertor.de/.*

$$ ✕ **Restaurant Juliette.** In a city proud of its past French influences, the
FRENCH highly praised French cuisine here is often delivered to your table by French waiters, no less. The intimate restaurant at the edge of the Dutch Quarter has old-fashioned brick walls and a fireplace. The menu offers small portions of dishes such as rack of lamb, quail with roasted chanterelles, and a starter plate of seasonal foie-gras preparations. Its wine list of 120 French vintages is unique in the Berlin area. ■TIP➔ **Company chief Ralph Junick has really cornered the market in Potsdam, with four other French restaurants, including a tasty creperie and a coffee shop. If you'll be in Potsdam for more than one meal, check Juliette's website to see what else is in town.** ⑤ *Average main: €20* ✉ *Jägerstr. 39* ☎ *0331/270–1791* ⊕ *www.restaurant-juliette.de.*

$$$ ✕ **Specker's Landaus.** Inside this Tudor-style cottage you'll find a friendly
GERMAN family restaurant with a relaxing farmhouse-style dining room. The menu includes house-made pastas, local game, and German specialties. The three-course lunch for €15 is a great deal. The restaurant also rents out three spacious guest rooms, which each accommodate up to four people, decorated in a simple, country-home style. ⑤ *Average main: €25* ✉ *Jägerallee 13* ☎ *0331/280–4311* ⊕ *www.speckers.de/.*

WHERE TO STAY

For expanded hotel reviews, visit Fodors.com.

$$ 🖼 **Hotel am Luisenplatz.** Behind a somber-looking facade, this intimate
HOTEL hotel conceals a warmth, elegance and friendly, personal service. **Pros:** great central location near pedestrian zones of downtown Potsdam; personal flair; great views. **Cons:** tour buses stop for meals and restaurant becomes crowded during these visits; sometimes-busy Luisenplatz right in front of rooms. ⑤ *Rooms from: €138* ✉ *Luisenpl. 5* ☎ *0331/971–900* ⊕ *www.hotel-luisenplatz.de* ⮐ *34 rooms, 4 suites* ⊙| *Breakfast.*

SHOPPING

Wunderkind. Fashion designer Wolfgang Joop started his internationally acclaimed label Wunderkind in Potsdam. Peruse his latest collection at this Dutch Quarter atelier. ✉ *Friedrich-Ebert-Str. 37* ⊕ *www. wunderkind.de.*

UNDERSTANDING
BERLIN

CHRONOLOGY

ca. 5000 BC   Indo-Germanic tribes settle in the Rhine and Danube valleys.

ca. 2000–800 BC   Distinctive German Bronze Age culture emerges, with settlements ranging from coastal farms to lakeside villages.

ca. 450–50 BC   Salzkammergut people, whose prosperity is based on abundant salt deposits (in the area of upper Austria), trade with Greeks and Etruscans; Salzkammerguts spread as far as Belgium and have first contact with the Romans.

9 BC–AD **9**   Roman attempts to conquer the "Germans"—the tribes of the Cibri, the Franks, the Goths, and the Vandals—are only partly successful; the Rhine becomes the northeastern border of the Roman Empire (and remains so for 300 years).

212   Roman citizenship is granted to all free inhabitants of the empire.

ca. 400   Pressed forward by Huns from Asia, such German tribes as the Franks, the Vandals, and the Lombards migrate to Gaul (France), Spain, Italy, and North Africa, scattering the empire's populace and eventually leading to the disintegration of central Roman authority.

486   The Frankish kingdom is founded by Clovis; his court is in Paris.

497   The Franks convert to Christianity.

EARLY MIDDLE AGES

776   Charlemagne becomes king of the Franks.

800   Charlemagne is declared Holy Roman Emperor; he makes Aachen capital of his realm, which stretches from the Bay of Biscay to the Adriatic and from the Mediterranean to the Baltic. Under his enlightened patronage there is an upsurge in art and architecture—the Carolingian renaissance.

843   The Treaty of Verdun divides Charlemagne's empire among his three sons: West Francia becomes France; Lotharingia becomes Lorraine (territory to be disputed by France and Germany into the 20th century); and East Francia takes on, roughly, the shape of modern Germany.

911   Five powerful German dukes (of Bavaria, Lorraine, Franconia, Saxony, and Swabia) establish the first German monarchy by electing King Conrad I; Henry I (the Fowler) succeeds Conrad in 919.

962   Otto I is crowned Holy Roman Emperor by the pope; he establishes Austria—the East Mark. The Ottonian renaissance is marked especially by the development of Romanesque architecture.

MIDDLE AGES

1024–1125 The Salian dynasty is characterized by a struggle between emperors and the Church that leaves the empire weak and disorganized; the great Romanesque cathedrals of Speyer, Trier, and Mainz are built.

1138–1254 Frederick Barbarossa leads the Hohenstaufen dynasty; there is temporary recentralization of power, underpinned by strong trade and Church relations.

1158 Munich, capital of Bavaria, is founded by Duke Henry the Lion; Henry is deposed by Emperor Barbarossa, and Munich is presented to the House of Wittelsbach, which rules it until 1918.

1241 The Hanseatic League is founded to protect trade; Bremen, Hamburg, Köln, and Lübeck are early members. Agencies are soon established in London, Antwerp, Venice, and along the Baltic and North seas; a complex banking and finance system results.

mid-1200s The Gothic style, exemplified by the grand Köln Cathedral, flourishes.

1349 The Black Death plague kills one-quarter of the German population.

RENAISSANCE AND REFORMATION

1456 Johannes Gutenberg (1400–68) prints the first book in Europe.

1471–1553 Renaissance flowers under influence of painter and engraver Albrecht Dürer (1471–1528); Dutch-born philosopher and scholar Erasmus (1466–1536); Lucas Cranach the Elder (1472–1553), who originates Protestant religious painting; portrait and historical painter Hans Holbein the Younger (1497–1543); and landscape-painting pioneer Albrecht Altdorfer (1480–1538). Increasing wealth among the merchant classes leads to strong patronage of the revived arts.

1517 The Protestant Reformation begins in Germany when Martin Luther (1483–1546) nails his 95 Theses to a church door in Wittenberg, contending that the Roman Church has forfeited divine authority through its corrupt sale of indulgences. Luther is outlawed, and his revolutionary doctrine splits the Church; much of north Germany embraces Protestantism.

1524–30 The (Catholic) Habsburgs rise to power; their empire spreads throughout Europe (and as far as North Africa, the Americas, and the Philippines). Erasmus breaks with Luther and supports reform within the Roman Catholic Church. In 1530 Charles V (a Habsburg) is crowned Holy Roman Emperor; he brutally crushes the Peasants' War, one in a series of populist uprisings in Europe.

1545 The Council of Trent marks the beginning of the Counter-Reformation. Through diplomacy and coercion, most Austrians, Bavarians, and Bohemians are won back to Catholicism, but the majority of Germans remain Lutheran; persecution of religious minorities grows.

THIRTY YEARS' WAR

1618–48 Germany is the main theater for the Thirty Years' War. The powerful Catholic Habsburgs are defeated by Protestant forces, swelled by disgruntled Habsburg subjects and the armies of King Gustav Adolphus of Sweden. The bloody conflict ends with the Peace of Westphalia (1648); Habsburg and papal authority are severely diminished.

ABSOLUTISM AND ENLIGHTENMENT

1689 Louis XIV of France invades the Rhineland Palatinate and sacks Heidelberg. At the end of the 17th century, Germany consolidates its role as a center of scientific thought.

1708 Johann Sebastian Bach (1685–1750) becomes court organist at Weimar and launches his career; he and Georg Friederic Handel (1685–1759) fortify the great tradition of German music. Baroque and, later, rococo art and architecture flourish.

1740–86 Reign of Frederick the Great of Prussia; his rule sees both the expansion of Prussia (it becomes the dominant military force in Germany) and the spread of Enlightenment thought.

ca. 1790 The great age of European orchestral music is raised to new heights with the works of Joseph Haydn (1732–1809), Wolfgang Amadeus Mozart (1756–91), and Ludwig van Beethoven (1770–1827).

early 1800s Johann Wolfgang von Goethe (1749–1832) is part of the Sturm und Drang movement, which leads to Romanticism. Painter Caspar David Friedrich (1774–1840) leads early German Romanticism. Other luminary cultural figures include writers Friedrich Schiller (1759–1805) and Heinrich von Kleist (1777–1811); and composers Robert Schumann (1810–56), Hungarian-born Franz Liszt (1811–86), Richard Wagner (1813–83), and Johannes Brahms (1833–97). In architecture, the severe lines of neoclassicism become popular.

ROAD TO NATIONHOOD

1806 Napoléon's armies invade Prussia; it briefly becomes part of the French Empire.

1807 The Prussian prime minister Baron vom und zum Stein frees the serfs, creating a new spirit of patriotism; the Prussian army is rebuilt.

1813 The Prussians defeat Napoléon at Leipzig.

1815 Britain and Prussia defeat Napoléon at Waterloo. At the Congress of Vienna the German Confederation is created as a loose union of 39 independent states, reduced from more than 300 principalities. The Bundestag (national assembly) is established at Frankfurt. Already powerful Prussia increases its territory, gaining the Rhineland, Westphalia, and most of Saxony.

1848 The "Year of the Revolutions" is marked by uprisings across the fragmented German Confederation; Prussia expands. A national parliament is elected, taking the power of the Bundestag to prepare a constitution for a united Germany.

1862 Otto von Bismarck (1815–98) becomes prime minister of Prussia; he is determined to wrest German-populated provinces from Austro-Hungarian (Habsburg) control.

1866 Austria-Hungary is defeated by the Prussians at Sadowa; Bismarck sets up the Northern German Confederation in 1867. A key figure in Bismarck's plans is Ludwig II of Bavaria. Ludwig—a political simpleton—lacks successors, making it easy for Prussia to seize his lands.

1867 Karl Marx (1818–83) publishes *Das Kapital.*

1870–71 The Franco-Prussian War: Prussia lays siege to Paris. Victorious Prussia seizes Alsace-Lorraine but eventually withdraws from all other occupied French territories.

1871 The four South German states agree to join the Northern Confederation; Wilhelm I is proclaimed first kaiser of the united empire.

MODERNISM

1882 The Triple Alliance is forged between Germany, Austria-Hungary, and Italy. Germany's industrial revolution blossoms, enabling it to catch up with the other great powers of Europe. Germany establishes colonies in Africa and the Pacific.

ca. 1885 Daimler and Benz pioneer the automobile.

1890 Kaiser Wilhelm II (rules 1888–1918) dismisses Bismarck and begins a new, more aggressive course of foreign policy; he oversees the expansion of the navy.

1890s A new school of writers, including Rainer Maria Rilke (1875–1926), emerges. Rilke's *Sonnets to Orpheus* gives German poetry new lyricism.

1905 Albert Einstein (1879–1955) announces his theory of relativity.

1906 Painter Ernst Ludwig Kirchner (1880–1938) helps organize *Die Brücke,* a group of artists who, along with *Der Blaue Reiter,* create the avant-garde art movement expressionism.

1907   Great Britain, Russia, and France form the Triple Entente, which, set against the Triple Alliance, divides Europe into two armed camps.

1914–18   Austrian archduke Franz-Ferdinand is assassinated in Sarajevo. The attempted German invasion of France sparks World War I; Italy and Russia join the Allies, and four years of pitched battle ensue. By 1918 the Central Powers are encircled and must capitulate.

WEIMAR REPUBLIC

1918   Germany is compelled by the Versailles Treaty to give up its overseas colonies and much European territory (including Alsace-Lorraine to France) and to pay huge reparations to the Allies; Kaiser Wilhelm II repudiates the throne and goes into exile in Holland. The tough terms leave the new democracy (the Weimar Republic) shaky.

1919   The Bauhaus school of art and design, the brainchild of Walter Gropius (1883–1969), is born. Thomas Mann (1875–1955) and Hermann Hesse (1877–1962) forge a new style of visionary intellectual writing.

1923   Germany suffers runaway inflation. Adolf Hitler's Beer Hall Putsch, a rightist revolt, fails; leftist revolts are frequent.

1925   Hitler publishes *Mein Kampf* (*My Struggle*)

1932   The Nazi party gains the majority in the Reichstag (parliament).

1933   Hitler becomes chancellor; the Nazi "revolution" begins. In Berlin, Nazi students stage the burning of more than 25,000 books by Jewish and other politically undesirable authors.

NAZI GERMANY

1934   President Paul von Hindenburg dies; Hitler declares himself Führer (leader) of the Third Reich. Nazification of all German social institutions begins, spreading a policy that is virulently racist and anticommunist. Germany recovers industrial might and re-arms.

1936   Germany signs anticommunist agreements with Italy and Japan, forming the Axis; Hitler reoccupies the Rhineland.

1938   The *Anschluss* (annexation): Hitler occupies Austria. Germany occupies the Sudetenland in Czechoslovakia. *Kristallnacht* (Night of Broken Glass), in November, marks the Nazis' first open and direct terrorism against German Jews. Synagogues and Jewish-owned businesses are burned, looted, and destroyed in a night of violence.

1939–40   In August Hitler signs a pact with the Soviet Union; in September he invades Poland; war is declared by the Allies. Over the next three years there are Nazi invasions of Denmark, Norway, the Low Countries, France, Yugoslavia, and Greece. Alliances form between Germany and the Baltic states.

1941–45   Hitler launches his anticommunist crusade against the Soviet Union, reaching Leningrad in the north and Stalingrad and the Caucasus in the south. In 1944 the Allies land in France; their combined might brings the Axis to its knees. In addition to the millions killed in the fighting, more than 6 million Jews and other victims die in Hitler's concentration camps. Germany is again in ruins. Hitler kills himself in April 1945. East Berlin and what becomes East Germany are occupied by the Soviet Union.

THE COLD WAR

1945   At the Yalta Conference, France, the United States, Britain, and the Soviet Union divide Germany into four zones; each country occupies a sector of Berlin. The Potsdam Agreement expresses the determination to rebuild Germany as a democracy.

1946   East Germany's Social Democratic Party merges with the Communist Party, forming the SED, which would rule East Germany for the next 40 years.

1948   The Soviet Union tears up the Potsdam Agreement and attempts, by blockade, to exclude the three other Allies from their agreed zones in Berlin. Stalin is frustrated by a massive airlift of supplies to West Berlin.

1949   The three western zones are combined to form the Federal Republic of Germany; the new West German parliament elects Konrad Adenauer as chancellor (a post he held until his retirement in 1963). Soviet-held East Germany becomes the Communist German Democratic Republic (GDR).

1950s   West Germany, aided by the financial impetus provided by the Marshall Plan, rebuilds its devastated cities and economy—the *Wirtschaftswunder* (economic miracle) gathers speed. The writers Heinrich Böll, Wolfgang Koeppen, and Günter Grass emerge.

1957   The Treaty of Rome heralds the formation of the European Economic Community (EEC); West Germany is a founding member.

1961   Communists build the Berlin Wall to stem the outward tide of refugees.

1969–74   The vigorous chancellorship of Willy Brandt pursues *Ostpolitik,* improving relations with Eastern Europe and the Soviet Union and acknowledging East Germany's sovereignty.

mid-1980s   The powerful German Green Party emerges as the leading environmentalist voice in Europe.

REUNIFICATION

1989 Discontent in East Germany leads to a flood of refugees westward and to mass demonstrations; Communist power collapses across Eastern Europe; the Berlin Wall falls.

1990 In March the first free elections in East Germany bring a center-right government to power. The Communists, faced with corruption scandals, suffer a big defeat but are represented (as Democratic Socialists) in the new, democratic parliament. The World War II victors hold talks with the two German governments, and the Soviet Union gives its support for reunification. Economic union takes place on July 1, with full political unity on October 3. In December, in the first democratic national German elections in 58 years, Chancellor Helmut Kohl's three-party coalition is reelected.

1991 Nine months of emotional debate end on June 20, when parliamentary representatives vote to move the capital from Bonn—seat of the West German government since 1949—to Berlin, the capital of Germany until the end of World War II.

1998 Helmut Kohl's record 16-year-long chancellorship of Germany ends with the election of Gerhard Schröder. Schröder's Social Democratic Party (SPD) pursues a coalition with the Greens in order to replace the three-party coalition of the Christian Democratic Union, Christian Social Union, and Free Democratic Party.

1999 The Bundestag, the German parliament, returns to the restored Reichstag in Berlin on April 19. The German federal government also leaves Bonn for Berlin, making Berlin capital of Germany again.

1999–2003 For the first time since 1945, the German army (the Bundeswehr) is deployed in combat missions in the former Yugoslavia and Afghanistan.

2005 Chancellor Schröder asks for a vote of confidence in parliament and fails. After a new election in September, Angela Merkel (CDU) becomes the new chancellor with a "grand coalition" of CDU/CSU and SPD.

2007 Angela Merkel as German chancellor and also in her role as the then President of the Council of the European Union hosts the G-8 summit in Heiligendamm, Germany.

2009 In Bundestag elections the alliance of the CDU/CSU and FDP receive an outright majority of seats, ensuring that Angela Merkel continues as chancellor.

2014 The twenty-fifth anniversary of the fall of the Berlin Wall marks a high point for the restored German capital. Decreasing unemployment and an increasingly gentrified cityscape have made Berlin more livable than ever, and expats are still flocking to the city. Berlin also continues to top lists as one of the fastest growing tourism destinations in Europe.

GERMAN VOCABULARY

	ENGLISH	GERMAN	PRONUNCIATION
BASICS			
	Yes/no	Ja/nein	yah/nine
	Please	Bitte	**bit**-uh
	Thank you (very much)	Danke (vielen Dank)	**dahn**-kuh (**fee**-lun- dahnk)
	Excuse me	Entschuldigen Sie	ent-**shool**-de-gen zee
	I'm sorry	Es tut mir leid	es toot meer lite
	Good day	Guten Tag	**goo**-ten tahk
	Good-bye	Auf Wiedersehen	auf **vee**-der-zane
	Mr./Mrs.	Herr/Frau	hair/frau
	Miss	Fräulein	**froy**-line
NUMBERS			
	1	Ein(s)	eint(s)
	2	Zwei	tsvai
	3	Drei	dry
	4	Vier	fear
	5	Fünf	funph
	6	Sechs	zex
	7	Sieben	**zee**-ben
	8	Acht	ahkt
	9	Neun	noyn
	10	Zehn	tsane
DAYS OF THE WEEK			
	Sunday	Sonntag	**zone**- tahk
	Monday	Montag	**moan**-tahk
	Tuesday	Dienstag	**deens**- tahk
	Wednesday	Mittwoch	**mit**-voah
	Thursday	Donnerstag	**doe**-ners-tahk
	Friday	Freitag	**fry**-tahk
	Saturday	Samstag/ Sonnabend	**zahm**-stakh/ **zonn**-a-bent

ENGLISH	GERMAN	PRONUNCIATION

USEFUL PHRASES

Do you speak	Sprechen Sie	**shprek**-hun zee
English?	Englisch?	**eng**-glish
I don't speak	Ich spreche kein	ich **shprek**-uh kine
German.	Deutsch.	Doych
Please speak	Bitte sprechen Sie	**bit**-uh **shprek**-en-
slowly.	langsam.	zee **lahng**-zahm
I am	Ich bin	ich bin
American/	Amerikaner(in)/	A-mer-i-**kahn**-er(in)/
British	Engländer(in)	**Eng**-glan-der(in)
My name is . . .	Ich heisse . . .	ich **hi**-suh
Where are the	Wo ist die	vo ist dee
restrooms?	Toilette?	twah-**let**-uh
Left/right	links/rechts	links/rechts
Open/closed	offen/geschlossen	O-fen/geh-**shloss**-en
Where is . . .	Wo ist . . .	**vo** ist
the train station?	der Bahnhof?	**dare bahn-hof**
the bus stop?	die Bushaltestelle?	**dee booss-hahlt-uh-shtel-uh**
the subway?	die U-bahn-	dee oo-bahn-**staht-**
station?	Station?	Sion
the airport?	der Flughafen?	dare **floog**-plats
the post office?	die Post?	dee **post**
the bank?	die Bank?	dee **banhk**
the police station?	die Polizeistation?	dee po-lee-tsai- **staht**-sion
the hospital?	das Krankenhaus?	dahs **krahnk**-en-house
the telephone?	das Telefon?	**dahs** te-le-**fone**
I'd like . . .	Ich hätte gerne . . .	ich **het**-uh gairn
a room	ein Zimmer	ein **tsim**-er

ENGLISH	GERMAN	PRONUNCIATION
the key	der Schlüssel	den **shluh**-sul
a map	eine Stadtplan	I-nuh **staht**-plahn
a ticket	eine Karte	I-nuh cart-uh
How much is it?	Wie viel kostet das?	**vee-feel cost**-et dahs
I am ill/sick.	Ich bin krank.	ich bin krahnk
I need . . .	Ich brauche . . .	ich **brow**-khuh
a doctor	einen Arzt	**I-nen** artst
the police	die Polizei	dee po-li-**tsai**
help	Hilfe	**hilf-uh**
Stop!	Halt!	Hahlt
Fire!	Feuer!	**foy**-er
Look out/ Caution!	Achtung!/Vorsicht!	**ahk**-tung/**for**-zicht

DINING OUT

A bottle of . . .	eine Flasche . . .	I-nuh **flash**-uh
A cup of . . .	eine Tasse . . .	I-nuh **tahs**-uh
A glass of . . .	ein Glas . . .	ein glahss
Ashtray	der Aschenbecher	dare **Ahsh**-en-bekh-er
Bill/check	die Rechnung	dee **rekh**-nung
Do you have . . .?	Haben Sie . . .?	**hah**-ben zee
I am a vegetarian.	Ich bin Vegetarier(in)	ich bin ve-guh-**tah**- re-er
I'd like to order . . .	Ich möchte . . . bestellen	ich **mohr**-shtuh . . . buh-**shtel**-en
Menu	die Speisekarte	dee **shpie**-zeh-car-tuh
Napkin	die Serviette	dee zair-vee-**eh**-tuh
Knife	das Messer	das mess-ah
Fork	die Gabel	dee gah-bell
Spoon	die Löffel	der luf-fell

MENU GUIDE

	ENGLISH	GERMAN

GENERAL DINING

	Side dishes	Beilagen
	Extra charge	Extraaufschlag
	When available	Falls verfügbar
	Entrées	Hauptspeisen
	(not) included	. . .(nicht) inbegriffen
	Depending on the season	je nach Saison
	Lunch menu	Mittagskarte
	Desserts	Nachspeisen
	at your choice	. . . nach Wahl
	at your request	. . . nach Wunsch
	Prices are . . .	Preise sind . . .
	Waiter/Waitress	die Bedienung
	Service included	inklusive Bedienung
	Value added tax included	inklusive Mehrwertsteuer (Mwst.)
	Specialty of the house	Spezialität des Hauses
	Soup of the day	Tagessuppe
	Appetizers	Vorspeisen
	Is served from . . . to . . .	Wird von . . . bis . . . serviert

BREAKFAST

	Bread	das Brot
	Roll(s)	die Brötchen
	Egg/Eggs	das Ei/die Eier
	Hot	Heiss
	Cold	Kalt
	Jam	die Konfitüre
	Milk	die Milch
	Orange juice	der Orangensaft
	Scrambled eggs	die Rühreier

ENGLISH	GERMAN
Bacon	der Speck
Fried eggs	die Spiegeleier
Lemon	die Zitrone
Sugar	der Zucker

SOUPS

Stew	der Eintopf
Chicken soup	die Hühnersuppe
Potato soup	die Kartoffelsuppe
Liver dumpling soup	die Leberknödelsuppe
Onion soup	die Zwiebelsuppe

METHODS OF PREPARATION

Blue (boiled in salt and vinegar)	Blau
Baked	Gebacken
Fried	Gebraten
Steamed	Gedämpft
Grilled (broiled)	Gegrillt
Boiled	Gekocht
Sautéed	In Butter geschwenkt
Breaded	Paniert
Raw	Roh

When ordering steak, the English words "rare, medium, (well) done" are used and understood in German.

GAME AND POULTRY

Duck	die Ente
Pheasant	der Fasan
Chicken	das Hähnchen (das Huhn)
Deer	der Hirsch
Rabbit	das Kaninchen

ENGLISH	GERMAN
Venison	das Rehfleisch
Pigeon	die Taube
Turkey	die Truthahn
Quail	die Wachtel

FISH AND SEAFOOD

Eel	der Aal
Oysters	die Austern
Trout	die Forelle
Flounder	die Flunder
Prawns	die Garnelen
Halibut	der Heilbutt
Herring	der Hering
Lobster	der Hummer
Scallops	die Jakobsmuscheln
Cod	der Kabeljau
Crab	die Krabbe
Salmon	der Lachs
Mackerel	die Makrele
Mussels	die Muscheln
Squid	der Tintenfisch
Tuna	der Thunfisch

MEATS

Veal	das Kalb
Lamb	das Lamm
Beef	das Rind
Pork	das Schwein

ENGLISH	GERMAN

CUTS OF MEAT

Example: For "Lammkeule" see "Lamm" (above) +
". . . keule" (below)

Breast	die . . brust
Leg	die . . . keule
Liver	die . . . leber
Tenderloin	die . . . lende
Kidney	die . . . niere
Rib	die . . . rippe
Meat patty	die Frikadelle
Meat loaf	der Hackbraten
Ham	der Schinken

VEGETABLES

Eggplant	die Aubergine
Cauliflower	der Blumenkohl
Beans	die Bohnen
Green	Grüne
White	Weisse
Peas	die Erbsen
Cucumber	die Gurke
Cabbage	der Kohl
Lettuce	der Kopfsalat
Mix of asparagus, peas, and carrots	die Leipziger Allerlei
Corn	der Mais
Carrots	die Karotte/die Mohrrüben
Peppers	der Paprika

ENGLISH	GERMAN
Mushrooms	der Pilze/der Champignon
Celery	der Sellerie
Asparagus (tips)	der Spargel(spitzen)
Tomatoes	die Tomaten
Onions	die Zwiebeln

CONDIMENTS

Vinegar	der Essig
Garlic	der Knoblauch
Horseradish	der Meerettich
Oil	das Öl
Mustard	der Senf
Artificial sweetener	der Süssstoff
Cinnamon	der Zimt
Sugar	der Zucker
Salt	das Salz

FRUITS

Apple	der Apfel
Orange	das Orange/die Apfelsine
Apricot	die Aprikose
Blueberry	die Blaubeere
Strawberry	die Erdbeere
Raspberry	die Himbeere
Cherry	die Kirsche
Grapefruit	die Pampelmuse
Raisin	die Rosine
Grape	die Weintraube
Banana	die Banane
Pear	die Birne

	ENGLISH	GERMAN

DRINKS

English	German
Water	das Wasser
With/without carbonation	mit/ohne Gas
Juice	der Saft
Beer	das Bier
White Wine/Red Wine	der Weisswein/der Rotwein
Sparkling Wine	der Sekt
Coffee	der Kaffee
Tea	der Tee
Hot Chocolate	die heisse Schokolade
with/without ice	mit/ohne Eis
with/without water	mit/ohne Wasser
straight	Pur
mulled claret	der Glühwein
caraway-flavored liquor	der Kümmel
fruit brandy	der Obstler

When ordering a martini, you have to specify "gin (vodka) and vermouth," otherwise you will be given a vermouth (Martini & Rossi).

You will often see drinks on the menu ending in *–schorle*. Typically sparkling water will be added to either white wine (Weisswein Schorle) or many types of fruit juice (for instance Apfelsaftschorle).

TRAVEL SMART
BERLIN

GETTING HERE AND AROUND

▌ AIR TRAVEL

Air Berlin and United fly direct from the United States to Berlin. Flying time to Berlin is just over 7½ hours from New York, 8½ from Chicago, and 9½ from Miami. There are many options for non-direct flights stopping first at a major European hub such as Frankfurt or London.

Western Berlin's Tegel Airport (TXL) will continue to be used until eastern Berlin's Schönefeld Airport, about 24 km (15 miles) outside the center, has been expanded into BBI "Berlin-Brandenburg International," otherwise known as "Willy Brandt"—the international airport of the capital region. Until then, Schönefeld is mostly used by charter and low-budget airlines. The two working Berlin airports share a central phone number.

GETTING INTO THE CITY

To get into Berlin from Tegel Airport, you can take the X9, 128, or 109 buses that connect to various points and subway stations. A taxi to central Berlin will cost about €25. From Schönefeld, the Airport Express and the slower S-bahn trains travel to city center. Bus 171 connects to U7 the subway line at the Rudow station. All three options require an ABC zone ticket (€3). A taxi ride from Schönefeld Airport takes about 40 minutes and will cost around €40.

Airport Information Berlin: **Berlin Brandenburg** (*BER*). ☎ 030/6091–1150 €0.14 per min ⊕ www.berlin-airport.de. **Schönefeld** (*SXF*). ☎ 030/000–186 €0.14 per min ⊕ www.berlin-airport.de. **Tegel** (*TXL*). ☎ 030/000–186 €0.14 per min ⊕ www.berlin-airport.de.

▌ BICYCLE TRAVEL

Berlin is a great city for biking. Particularly in summer, you can get just about anywhere you want by bike. An extensive network of bike paths are generally marked by red pavement or white markings on the sidewalks (when you're walking, try to avoid walking on bike paths if you don't want to have cyclists ring their bells at you). Many stores that rent or sell bikes carry the Berlin biker's atlas, and several places offer terrific bike tours of the city. Fat Tire is a well-respected company that runs bike tours in many European cities, including Berlin.

The same traffic laws apply to bicyclists as to motorists, and the police have been known to give out tickets to violators.

Bicycle Information Fahrradstation. Fahrradstation rents bikes for €15 per day (12 hours) or €35 for three days. Bring ID and call for its other locations. ⊠ Dorotheenstr. 30, Mitte ☎ 0180/510–8000 ⊕ www.fahrradstation.de.

▌ BOAT TRAVEL

Eurailpasses and German Rail Passes are honored by KD Rhine Line on the Rhine River and on the Mosel River between Trier and Koblenz. (If you use the fast hydrofoil, a supplementary fee is required.) The rail lines follow the Rhine and Mosel rivers most of their length, meaning you can go one way by ship and return by train. Cruises generally operate between April and October. If you are planning to visit Denmark or Sweden after Germany, note that Scandlines ferries offer discounts for Eurailpass owners.

The MS *Duchess of Scandinavia* carries passengers and cars three times a week for the 19½-hour run between Cuxhaven, Germany, and Harwich, England.

Information KD Rhine Line ☎ 0221/208–8318 ⊕ www.k-d.com. **MS *Duchess of Scandinavia*** ☎ 08705/333–111 DFDS Seaways in U.K., 040/389–0371 in Germany ⊕ www.dfdsseaways.co.uk. **Scandlines** ☎ 0381/54350 ⊕ www.scandlines.de.

∎ BUS TRAVEL

BerlinLinien Bus is the only intra-Germany company serving Berlin. Make reservations through ZOB-Reisebüro, or buy your ticket at its office at the central bus terminal, the Omnibusbahnhof. Public buses are the best way to reach the bus terminal, served by the lines X34, X49, 104, 139, 218, and 349. A more central place to buy bus tickets is Mitfahrzentrale, a tiny, busy office that also arranges car-ride shares. Only EC bank cards and cash are accepted.

Bus Information BerlinLinien Bus
☎ *030/861–9331* ⊕ *www.berlinlinienbus. de.***Mitfahrzentrale** ☎ *01805/194444* ⊕ *www. mf24.de* ⊗ *Mon.–Fri. 9–6, Sat.–Sun. 10–2.*
ZOB-Reisebüro ⊠ *Zentrale Omnibusbahnhof, Masurenallee 4–6, at Messedamm, Masurenallee 4–6, at Messedamm, Charlottenburg* ☎ *030/301–0380 for reservations* ⊕ *www. zob-reisebuero.de* ⊗ *Weekdays 6 am–9 pm, weekends 6 am–8 pm.*

∎ CAR TRAVEL

Rush hour is relatively mild in Berlin, but the public transit system is so efficient here that it's best to leave your car at the hotel altogether (or refrain from renting one in the first place). All cars entering downtown Berlin inside the S-bahn ring need to have an environmental certificate. All major rental cars will have these—if in doubt, ask the rental-car agent, as without one you can be fined €40. Daily parking fees at hotels can run up to €18 per day. Vending machines in the city center dispense timed tickets to display on your dashboard. Thirty minutes cost €0.50.

That said, if you're going to drive in Germany, formalities for motorists are few: all you need is proof of insurance; an international car-registration document; and a U.S., Canadian, Australian, or New Zealand driver's license. If you or your car is from an EU country, Norway, or Switzerland, all you need is your domestic license and proof of insurance. *All* foreign cars must have a country sticker. There are no toll roads in Germany, except for a few Alpine mountain passes. Many large German cities require an environmental sticker on the front windshield. If your rental car doesn't have one, it's likely you'll be required to pay the fine.

CAR RENTAL

It is easy to rent a car in Germany, but not always cheap. You will need an International Driving Permit (IDP); it's available from the American Automobile Association and the National Automobile Club. These international permits are universally recognized, and having one in your wallet may save you problems with the local authorities. In Germany you usually must be 21 to rent a car. Nearly all agencies allow you to drive into Germany's neighboring countries. It's frequently possible to return the car in another West European country, but not in Poland or the Czech Republic, for example.

Rates with the major car-rental companies begin at about €55 per day and €300 per week for an economy car with a manual transmission and unlimited mileage. It is invariably cheaper to rent a car in advance from home than to do it on the fly in Germany. Most rentals are manual, so if you want an automatic, be sure to request one in advance. If you're traveling with children, don't forget to ask for a car seat when you reserve. Note that in some major cities, even automobile-producing Stuttgart, rental firms are prohibited from placing signs at major pickup and drop-off locations, such as the main train station. If dropping a car off in an unfamiliar city, you might have to guess your way to the station's underground parking garage; once there, look for a generic sign such as *Mietwagen* (rental cars). The German railway system, Deutsche Bahn, offers discounts on rental cars.

Depending on what you would like to see, you may or may not need a car for all or part of your stay. Most parts of Germany are connected by reliable rail service, so it might be a better plan to take a train to the region you plan to visit and rent a car only for side trips to out-of-the-way destinations.

GASOLINE

Gasoline costs are around €1.60 per liter—which is higher than in the United States. Some cars use diesel fuel, which is about €0.15 cheaper, so if you're renting a car, find out which fuel the car takes. German filling stations are highly competitive, and bargains are often available if you shop around, but *not* at autobahn filling stations. Self-service, or *SB-Tanken*, stations are cheapest. Pumps marked *Bleifrei* contain unleaded gas.

ROAD CONDITIONS

Roads are generally excellent. *Bundesstrassen* are two-lane state highways, abbreviated "B," as in B-38. Autobahns are high-speed thruways abbreviated with "A," as in A-7. If the autobahn should be blocked for any reason, you can take an exit and follow little signs bearing a "U" followed by a number. These are official detours.

ROAD MAPS

The best-known road maps of Germany are put out by the automobile club ADAC, by Shell, and by the Falk Verlag. They're available at gas stations and bookstores.

ROADSIDE EMERGENCIES

The German automobile clubs ADAC and AvD operate tow trucks on all autobahns. "Notruf" signs every 2 km (1 mile) on autobahns (and country roads) indicate emergency telephones. By picking up the phone, you'll be connected to an operator who can determine your exact location and get you the services you need. Help is free (with the exception of materials).

Emergency Services Roadside assistance
☎ *01802/222-222.*

RULES OF THE ROAD

In Germany, road signs give distances in kilometers. There *are* posted speed limits on much of the autobahns, and they advise drivers to keep below 130 kph (80 mph) or 110 kph (65 mph). A sign saying *Richtgeschwindigkeit* and the speed indicates this. Slower traffic should stay in the right lane of the autobahn, but speeds under 80 kph (50 mph) are not permitted. Speed limits on country roads vary from 70 kph to 100 kph (43 mph to 62 mph) and are usually 50 kph (30 mph) through small towns.

Don't enter a street with a signpost bearing a red circle with a white horizontal stripe—it's a one-way street. Blue "Einbahnstrasse" signs indicate you're headed the correct way down a one-way street. The blood-alcohol limit for driving in Germany is very low (.05%), and passengers, but not the driver, are allowed to consume alcoholic beverages in the car. Note that seat belts must be worn at all times by front- *and* back-seat passengers.

German drivers tend to drive fast and aggressively. There is no right turn at a red light in Germany. Though prohibited, tailgating is the national pastime on German roads. Do not react by braking for no reason: this is equally prohibited. You may not use a handheld mobile phone while driving.

■ CRUISE SHIP TRAVEL

The American-owned Viking River Cruises company tours the Rhine, Main, Elbe, and Danube rivers, with four- to eight-day itineraries that include walking tours at ports of call. The longer cruises (up to 18 days) on the Danube (Donau, in German), which go to the Black Sea and back, are in great demand, so reserve six months in advance. The company normally books American passengers on ships that cater exclusively to Americans. If you prefer to travel on a European ship, specify so when booking. Köln–Düsseldorfer Deutsche Rheinschiffart (KD Rhine Line) offers trips of one day or less on the Rhine and Mosel. Between Easter and October there's Rhine service between Köln and Mainz, and between May and October, Mosel service between Koblenz and Cochem. Check the website for special winter tours. You'll get a free trip on your birthday if you bring a document verifying your date of birth.

Cruise Lines KD Rhine Line ☎ *0221/208–8318* ⊕ *www.k-d.com.* **Viking River Cruises** ☎ *0800/258–4666, 800/1887–10033 in Germany, 800/319–6660 in U.K.* ⊕ *www. vikingrivercruises.com.*

▌ PUBLIC TRANSIT TRAVEL

The city has an efficient public-transportation system, a smoothly integrated network of subway (U-bahn) and suburban (S-bahn) train lines, buses, and trams (almost exclusively in eastern Berlin). Get a map from any information booth. **▌TIP→ Don't be afraid to try buses and trams—in addition to being well marked, they often cut the most direct path to your destination.**

From Sunday through Thursday, U-bahn trains stop around 12:45 am and S-bahn trains stop by 1:30 am. All-night bus and tram service operates seven nights a week (indicated by the letter *N* next to bus route numbers). On Friday and Saturday nights some S-bahn and all U-bahn lines except U4 run all night. Buses and trams marked with an *M* for Metro mostly serve destinations without an S-bahn or U-bahn link.

Most visitor destinations are in the broad reach of the fare zones A and B. The €2.60 ticket (fare zones A and B) and the €3.20 ticket (fare zones A, B, and C) allow you to make a one-way trip with an unlimited number of changes between trains, buses, and trams. There are reduced rates for children ages 6–13. Buy a Kurzstreckentarif ticket (€1.50) for short rides of up to six bus or tram stops or three U-bahn or S-bahn stops. The best deal if you plan to travel around the city extensively is the Tageskarte (day card for zones A and B), for €6.70, good on all transportation until 3 am (€7.20 for A, B, and C zones). A 7-Tage-Karte (seven-day ticket) costs €28.80 and allows unlimited travel for

fare zones A and B; €35.60 buys all three fare zones.

Tickets are available from vending machines at U-bahn and S-bahn stations. After you purchase a ticket, you are responsible for validating it when you board the train or bus. Both Einzelfahrt and Kurzstreckentarif tickets are good for 120 minutes after validation. If you're caught without a ticket or with an unvalidated one, the fine is €40.

▌TIP→ The BVG website *(www.bvg.de)* **makes planning any trip on public transportation easier. Enter your origin and destination point into their "Journey Planner" to see a list of your best routes, and a schedule of the next three departure times. If you're not sure which station is your closest, simply type in your current address and the system will tell you (along with the time it takes to walk there).**

Most major S-bahn and U-bahn stations have elevators, and most buses have hydraulic lifts. Check the public transportation maps or call the Berliner Verkehrsbetriebe. The Deutscher Service-Ring-Berlin e.V. runs a special bus service for travelers with physical disabilities, and is a good information source on all travel necessities, that is, wheelchair rental and other issues.

Public Transit Information Berliner Verkehrsbetriebe (*BVG*). ☎ *030/19449* ⊕ *www.bvg.de.* **S-Bahn Berlin GmbH** ☎ *030/2974–3333* ⊕ *www.s-bahn-berlin.de.* **VBB** ☎ *030/2541–4141 for info* ⊕ *www. vbbonline.de* ☾ *Weekdays 8–8, weekends 9–6.*

▌ TAXI TRAVEL

The base rate is €3.20, after which prices vary according to a complex tariff system. Figure on paying around €8 to €10 for a ride the length of the Ku'damm. **▌TIP→ If you've hailed a cab on the street and are taking a short ride of up to 2 km (1 mile), ask the driver as soon as you start off for a special fare (€4) called Kurzstreckentarif.** You can also get cabs at taxi stands or order one by calling; there's no additional fee if you call a cab by phone. U-bahn employees will call a taxi for passengers after 8 pm.

BikeTaxi, rickshawlike bicycle taxis, pedal along Kurfürstendamm, Friedrichstrasse, and Unter den Linden, and in Tiergarten. Just hail a cab on the street along the boulevards mentioned. The fare is €5 for up to 1 km (½ mile) and €3 for each additional kilometer, and €22.50 to €30 for longer tours. Velotaxis operate April–October, daily noon–7. ■ TIP→ **Despite these fixed prices, make sure to agree on the fare before starting the tour.**

Taxi Information Taxis ☎ *030/210–101, 030/443–322, 030/261–026.*

▌ TRAIN TRAVEL

All long-distance trains stop at Berlin's huge and modern central station, Hauptbahnhof, which lies at the northern edge of the government district in central Berlin. Regional trains also stop at the two former "main" stations of the past years: Bahnhof Zoo (in the West) and Ostbahnhof (in the East), as well as at the central eastern stations Friedrichstrasse and Alexanderplatz.

Deutsche Bahn (DB—German Rail) is a very efficient, semi-privatized railway. Its high-speed InterCity Express (ICE), InterCity (IC), and EuroCity (EC) trains make journeys between the centers of many cities—Munich–Frankfurt, for example—faster by rail than by air. All InterCity and InterCity Express trains have restaurant cars and trolley service. RE, RB, and IRE trains are regional trains. It's also possible to sleep on the train and save a day of your trip. CityNightLine (CNL) trains serving domestic destinations and neighboring countries have sleepers, couches, and recliners.

Once on your platform or *Bahnsteig*—the area between two tracks—you can check the notice boards that give details of the layout of trains (*Wagenstandanzeiger*) arriving on that track (*Gleis*). They show

the locations of first- and second-class cars and the restaurant car, as well as where they will stop along the platform. Large railroad stations have English-speaking staff handling information inquiries.

For fare and schedule information, the Deutsche Bahn information line connects you to a live operator; you may have to wait a few moments before someone can help you in English. The automated number is toll-free and gives schedule information. On the DB website, click on "English." A timetable mask will open up. To calculate the fare, enter your departure and arrival points, any town you wish to pass through, and whether you have a bike.

If you would like to work out an itinerary beforehand, Deutsche Bahn has an excellent website in English (⊕ *www.bahn. de*). It will even tell you which type of train you'll be riding on—which could be important if you suffer from motion sickness. The ICE, the French TGV, the Swiss ICN, and the Italian Cisalpino all use "tilt technology" for a less jerky ride. One side effect, however, is that some passengers might feel queasy, especially if the track is curvy. An over-the-counter drug for motion sickness should help.

BAGGAGE

Most major train stations have luggage lockers (in four sizes). By inserting exact change into a storage unit, you release the unit's key. Prices range from €1 for a small locker to €3 for a "jumbo" one. Smaller towns' train stations may not have any storage options.

Throughout Germany, Deutsche Bahn can deliver your baggage from a private residence or hotel to another or even to one of six airports: Berlin, Frankfurt, Leipzig-Halle, Munich, Hamburg, or Hannover. You must have a valid rail ticket. Buy a *Kuriergepäck* ticket at any DB ticket counter, at which time you must schedule a pickup three workdays before your flight. The service costs €13.80 for each of the first two suitcases and €15.80 for each suitcase thereafter.

DISCOUNTS

Deutsche Bahn offers many discount options with specific conditions, so do your homework on its website or ask about options at the counter before paying for a full-price ticket. For round-trip travel you can save 25% if you book at least three days in advance, 50% if you stay over a Saturday night and book at least three to seven days in advance. However, there's a limited number of seats sold at any of these discount prices, so book as early as possible, at least a week in advance, to get the savings. A discounted rate is called a *Sparpreis*. If you change your travel plans after booking, you will have to pay a fee. The surcharge for tickets bought on board is 10% of the ticket cost, or a minimum of €5. Most local, RE, and RB services do not allow for purchasing tickets on board. Not having a ticket is considered *Schwarzfahren* (riding black) and is usually subject to a €40 fine. Tickets booked at a counter always cost more than over the Internet or from an automated ticket machine.

The good news for families is that children under 15 travel free when accompanied by a parent or relative on normal, discounted, and some, but not all, special-fare tickets. However, you must indicate the number of children traveling with you when you purchase the ticket; to ride free, the child (or children) must be listed on the ticket. If you have a ticket with 25% or 50% off, a *Mitfahrer-Rabatt* allows a second person to travel with you for a 50% discount (minimum of €15 for a second-class ticket). The *Schönes Wochenend Ticket* (Happy Weekend Ticket) provides unlimited travel on regional trains on weekends for up to five persons for €37 (€35 if purchased online or at a vending machine). Groups of six or more should inquire about *Gruppen & Spar* (group) savings. Each German state, or *Land*, has its own *Länder-Ticket*, which lets up to five people travel from 9 am to 3 am for around €25.

If you plan to travel by train within a day after your flight arrives, purchase a heavily discounted "Rail and Fly" ticket for DB trains at the same time you book your flight. Trains connect with 14 German airports and two airports outside Germany, Basel and Amsterdam.

FARES

A first-class seat is approximately 55% more than a second-class seat. For this premium you get a bit more legroom and the convenience of having meals (not included) delivered directly to your seat. Most people find second class entirely adequate and first class not worth the cost. Many regional trains offer an upgrade to first class for as little as €4. This is especially helpful on weekends when local trains are stuffed with cyclists and day-tripping locals. ICs and the later-generation ICE trains are equipped with electrical outlets for laptops and other gadgets.

Tickets purchased through Deutsche Bahn's website can be retrieved from station vending machines. Always check that your ticket is valid for the type of train you are planning to take, not just for the destination served. If you have the wrong type of ticket, you will have to pay the difference on the train, in cash or by credit card. If you book an online ticket and print it yourself, you must present the credit card used to pay for the ticket to the conductor for the ticket to be valid.

The ReisePacket service is for travelers who are inexperienced, elderly, disabled, or just appreciative of extra help. It costs €11 and provides, among other things, help boarding, disembarking, and transferring on certain trains that serve major cities and vacation areas. It also includes a seat reservation and a voucher for an onboard snack. Purchase the service at least one day before travel.

PASSES

If Germany is your only destination in Europe, consider purchasing a German Rail Pass, which allows 4 to 10 days of unlimited first- or second-class travel within a one-month period on any DB train, up to and including the ICE. A Twin Pass saves two people traveling together 50% off one person's fare. A Youth Pass, sold to those 12–25, is much the same but for second-class travel only. You can also use these passes aboard KD Rhine Line (⇨ *Cruise Ship Travel*) along certain sections of the Rhine and Mosel rivers. Prices begin at $257 per person in second class. Twin Passes begin at $380 for two people in second class, and Youth Passes begin at $205. Additional days may be added to either pass, but only at the time of purchase and not once the pass has been issued. Extensions of the German Rail Pass to Brussels, Venice, Verona, Prague, and Innsbrück are also available.

Rail 'n' Drive combines train travel and car rental. For instance, two people pay $207 each for two rail-travel days and two car-rental days within a month. You can add up to three more rail days ($66 each), and each additional car-rental day is $63.

Germany is one of 21 countries in which you can use a Eurailpass, which provides unlimited first-class rail travel in all participating countries for the duration of the pass. Two adults traveling together can pay either €482 each for 15 consecutive days of travel or €622 each for 21 consecutive days of travel. The youth fare is €369 for 15 consecutive days and €435 for 10 days within two months. Eurailpasses are available from most travel agents and directly from ⊕ *www.eurail. com*.

Eurailpasses and some of the German Rail Passes should be purchased before you leave for Europe. You can purchase a Eurailpass and 5- or 10-day German Rail Passes at the Frankfurt airport and at some major German train stations, but the cost will be higher (a youth ticket for five days of travel is just under €149). When you buy your pass, consider purchasing rail pass insurance in case you lose it during your travels.

In order to comply with the strict rules about validating tickets before you begin travel, read the instructions carefully. Some tickets require that a train official validate your pass, while others require you to write in the first date of travel.

Many travelers assume that rail passes guarantee them seats on the trains they wish to ride. Not so. You need to book seats ahead even if you are using a rail pass; seat reservations are required on some European trains, particularly high-speed trains, and are a good idea in summer, on national holidays, and on popular routes. If you board the train without a reserved seat, you risk having to stand. You'll also need a reservation if you purchase sleeping accommodations. Seat reservations on InterCity trains cost €6, and a reservation is absolutely necessary for the ICE-Sprinter trains (€12 for second class). There are no reservations on regional trains.

Channel Tunnel Car Transport Eurotunnel ☎ *0870/535–3535 in U.K., 070/223–210 in Belgium, 0810/630–304 in France* ⊕ *www. eurotunnel.com.* **Rail Europe** ☎ *0870/241–5415* ⊕ *www.raileurope.co.uk.*

Channel Tunnel Passenger Service Eurostar ☎ *08432/186–186 in the U.K., 1233/617–575 outside the U.K.* ⊕ *www.eurostar.co.uk.* **Rail Europe** ☎ *888/382–7245 in U.S., 0870/584–8848 in U.K., inquiries and credit-card bookings* ⊕ *www.raileurope.com.*

Train Information Deutsche Bahn (*German Rail).* ☎ *0800/150–7090 for automated schedule information, 11861 for 24-hr hotline €0.39 per min, 491805/996–633 from outside Germany €0.12 per min* ⊕ *www.bahn.de.* **Eurail** ⊕ *www.eurail.com.* **Eurostar** ☎ *0870/518–6186* ⊕ *www.eurostar.com.*

ESSENTIALS

▌ COMMUNICATIONS

INTERNET

Nearly all hotels have in-room data ports, but you may have to purchase, or borrow from the front desk, a cable with an end that matches German phone jacks. If you're plugging into a phone line, you'll need a local access number for a connection. Wireless Internet (called WLAN in Germany) is more and more common in even the most average hotel. The service is not always free, however. Sometimes you must purchase blocks of time from the front desk or online using a credit card. The cost is fairly high, however, usually around €4 for 30 minutes.

There are alternatives. Some hotels have an Internet room for guests needing to check their email. Otherwise, Internet cafés are common, and many bars and restaurants let you surf the Web. Cybercafes. com lists more than 4,000 Internet cafés worldwide.

Cybercafes ⊕ *www.cybercafes.com.*

PHONES

The good news is that you can make a direct-dial telephone call from Germany to virtually any point on Earth. The bad news? You can't always do so cheaply. Calling from a hotel is almost always the most expensive option; hotels usually add huge surcharges to all calls, particularly international ones. In some countries you can phone from call centers or even the post office. Calling cards usually keep costs to a minimum, but only if you purchase them locally. Because most Germans own mobile phones, finding a telephone booth is becoming increasingly difficult. As expensive as mobile phone calls can be, they are still usually a much cheaper option than calling from your hotel.

The country code for Germany is 49. When dialing a German number from abroad, drop the initial "0" from the local area code.

Many companies have service lines beginning with 0180. The cost of these calls averages €0.12 per minute. Numbers that begin with 0190 can cost €1.85 per minute and more.

CALLING WITHIN GERMANY

The German telephone system is very efficient, so it's unlikely you'll have to use an operator unless you're seeking information. For information in English, dial ☎ *11837* for numbers within Germany and ☎ *11834* for numbers elsewhere. But first look for the number in the phone book or online (⊕ *www.teleauskunft. de*), because directory assistance is costly. Calls to 11837 and 11834 cost at least €0.50, more if the call lasts more than 30 seconds.

A local call from a telephone booth costs €0.10 per minute. Dial the "0" before the area code when making a long-distance call within Germany. When dialing within a local area code, drop the "0" and the area code.

Telephone booths are no longer a common feature on the streets, so be prepared to walk out of your way to find one. Phone booths have instructions in English as well as German. Most telephone booths in Germany are card-operated, so buy a phone card. Coin-operated phones, which take €0.10, €0.20, €0.50, €1, and €2 coins, don't make change.

CALLING OUTSIDE GERMANY

The country code for the United States is 1.

International calls can be made from any telephone booth in Germany. It costs only €0.13 per minute to call the United States, day or night, no matter how long the call lasts. Use a phone card. If you don't have a good deal with a calling card, there are many stores that offer international calls at rates well below what you will pay from a phone booth. At a hotel, rates will be at least double the regular charge.

Access Codes **AT&T Direct** ☎ *0800/225–5288.* **MCI WorldPhone** ☎ *0800/888–8000.* **Sprint International Access** ☎ *0800/888–0013.*

CALLING CARDS

Post offices, newsstands, and exchange places sell cards with €5, €10, or €20 worth of credit to use at public pay phones. An advantage of a card: it charges only what the call costs. A €5 card with a good rate for calls to the United States, United Kingdom, and Canada is Go Bananas!

MOBILE PHONES

You can buy an inexpensive unlocked mobile phone and a SIM card at almost every corner shop and even at the supermarket. Most shops require identification to purchase a SIM card, but you can avoid this by purchasing a card at any number of phone centers or call shops, usually located near train stations. This is the best option if you just want to make local calls. If you bring a phone from abroad, your provider may have to unlock it for you to use a different SIM card and a prepaid service plan in the destination. You'll then have a local number and can make local calls at local rates. If your trip is extensive, you could also simply buy a new cell phone in your destination, as the initial cost will be offset over time.

Many prepaid plans, like Blau World, offer calling plans to the United States and other countries, starting at €0.03 per minute. Many Germans use these SIM cards to call abroad, as the rates are much cheaper than from land lines.

If you have a multiband phone (some countries use different frequencies from what's used in the United States) and your service provider uses the world-standard GSM network (as do T-Mobile, AT&T, and Verizon), you can probably use your phone abroad. Roaming fees can be steep, however: 99¢ a minute is considered reasonable. And overseas you normally pay the toll charges for incoming calls. It's almost always cheaper to send a text message than to make a call, because text messages have a very low set fee (often less than 5¢).

Cellular Abroad rents and sells GMS phones and sells SIM cards that work in many countries. Mobal rents mobiles and sells GSM phones (starting at $49) that will operate in 140 countries. Planet Fone rents cell phones, but the per-minute rates are expensive.

■ TIP➜ **If you travel internationally frequently, save one of your old mobile phones or buy a cheap one on the Internet; ask your cell phone company to unlock it for you, and take it with you as a travel phone, buying a new SIM card with pay-as-you-go service in each destination.**

Contacts **Cellular Abroad** ☎ *800/287–5072* ⊕ *www.cellularabroad.com.* **Mobal** ☎ *888/888–9162* ⊕ *www.mobalrental.com.* **Planet Fone** ☎ *888/988–4777* ⊕ *www.planetfone.com.*

∎ CUSTOMS AND DUTIES

German Customs and Border Control is fairly simple and straightforward. The system works efficiently and professionally, and 99% of all travelers will have no real cause to interact with them.

You're always allowed to bring goods of a certain value back home without having to pay any duty or import tax. But there's a limit on the amount of tobacco and liquor you can bring back duty-free, and some countries have separate limits for perfumes; for exact figures, check with your customs department. The values of so-called duty-free goods are included in these amounts. When you shop abroad, save all your receipts, as customs inspectors may ask to see them as well as the items you purchased. If the total value of your goods is more than the duty-free limit, you'll have to pay a tax (most often a flat percentage) on the value of everything beyond that limit.

For anyone entering Germany from outside the EU, the following limitations apply: (1) 200 cigarettes or 100 cigarillos or 50 cigars or 250 grams of tobacco; (2) 2 liters of still table wine; (3) 1 liter of spirits over 22% volume or 2 liters of spirits under 22% volume (fortified and sparkling wines) or 2 more liters of table wine; (4) 50 grams of perfume and 250 milliliters of eau de toilette; (5) 500 grams of roasted coffee or 200 grams of instant coffee; (6) other goods to the value of €175.

If you have questions regarding customs or bringing a pet into the country, contact the Zoll-Infocenter.

Information in Germany Zoll-Infocenter
☎ *0351/4483-4510* ⊕ *www.zoll.de.*

U.S. Information U.S. Customs and Border Protection ⊕ *www.cbp.gov.*

▌ EATING OUT

Almost every street in Germany has its *Gaststätte,* a sort of combination restaurant and pub, and every village its *Gasthof,* or inn. The emphasis in either is on simple food at reasonable prices. A *Bierstube* (pub) or *Weinstube* (wine cellar) may also serve light snacks or meals.

Service can be slow, but you'll never be rushed out of your seat. Something else that may seem jarring at first: people can, and do, join other parties at a table in a casual restaurant if seating is tight. It's common courtesy to ask first, though.

Since Germans don't generally drink from the tap, water always costs extra and comes as still or sparkling mineral water.

BUDGET EATING TIPS

Imbiss (snack) stands can be found in almost every busy shopping street, in parking lots, train stations, and near markets. They serve *Würste* (sausages), grilled, roasted, or boiled, and rolls filled with cheese, cold meat, or fish. Many stands sell Turkish-style wraps called *Döner Kebab.* Prices range from €1.50 to €2.50 per portion. It's acceptable to bring sandwich fixings to a beer garden so long

as you order a beer there, just be sure not to sit at a table with a tablecloth.

Butcher shops, known as *Metzgereien,* often serve warm snacks or very good sandwiches. Try *Warmer Leberkäs mit Kartoffelsalat,* a typical Bavarian specialty, which is a sort of baked meat loaf with mustard and potato salad. In northern Germany try *Bouletten,* small meatballs, or *Currywurst,* sausages in a piquant curry sauce. Thuringia has a reputation for its bratwurst, which is usually broken in two and packed into a roll with mustard. Up north, the specialty snack is a herring sandwich with onions.

Restaurants in department stores are especially recommended for appetizing and inexpensive lunches. Kaufhof, Karstadt, Wertheim, and Horton are names to note. Germany's vast numbers of Turkish, Italian, Greek, Chinese, and Balkan restaurants are often inexpensive.

MEALS AND MEALTIMES

Most hotels serve a buffet-style breakfast (*Frühstück*) of rolls, cheese, cold cuts, eggs, cereals, yogurt, and spreads, which is included in the price of a room. Cafés, especially the more trendy ones, offer breakfast menus sometimes including pancakes, omelets, muesli, or even Thai rice soup. By American standards, a cup (*Tasse*) of coffee in Germany is very petite, and you don't get free refills. Order a *Pot* or *Kännchen* if you want a larger portion.

For lunch (*Mittagessen*), you can get sandwiches from most cafés and bakeries, and many fine restaurants have special lunch menus that make the gourmet experience much more affordable. Dinner (*Abendessen*) is usually accompanied by a potato or spätzle side dish. A salad sometimes comes with the main dish.

Gaststätten normally serve hot meals from 11:30 am to 9 pm; many places stop serving hot meals between 2 pm and 6 pm, although you can still order cold dishes. If you feel like a hot meal, look for a restaurant advertising *durchgehend geöffnet,* or look for a pizza parlor.

Once most restaurants have closed, your options are limited. Take-out pizza parlors and Turkish eateries often stay open later. Failing that, your best option is a train station or a gas station with a convenience store. Many bars serve snacks.

Unless otherwise noted, the restaurants listed in this guide are open daily for lunch and dinner.

PAYING

Credit cards are generally accepted only in moderate to expensive restaurants, so check before sitting down. You will need to ask for the bill (say "Die Rechnung, bitte") in order to get it from the waiter, the idea being that the table is yours for the evening. Round up the bill 5% to 10% and pay the waiter directly rather than leaving any money or tip on the table. The waiter will likely wait at the table for you to pay after he has brought the check. He will also wear a money pouch and make change out of it at the table. If you don't need change, say "Stimmt so" ("keep the change"), otherwise tell the waiter how much change you want back, adding in the tip. Meals are subject to 19% tax (abbreviated as "MwSt" on your bill).

For guidelines on tipping see Tipping, below.

RESERVATIONS AND DRESS

Regardless of where you are, it's a good idea to make a reservation if you can. In most fine dining establishments it's expected. We only mention them specifically when reservations are essential (there's no other way you'll ever get a table) or when they are not accepted. For popular restaurants, book as far ahead as you can (often 30 days), and reconfirm as soon as you arrive. (Parties of more than four should always call ahead to check the reservations policy.) We mention dress only when men are required to wear a jacket or a jacket and tie.

Note that even when Germans dress casually, their look is generally crisp and neat.

Jeans are acceptable for most social occasions, unless you're meeting the president.

SMOKING

For such an otherwise health-conscious nation, Germans smoke. A lot. New anti-smoking laws came into effect in 2008, effectively banning smoking in all restaurants and many pubs, but many Germans, particularly in Berlin and Hamburg, tend to ignore them. Many hotels have no-smoking rooms and even no-smoking floors. However, a smoker will find it intrusive if you request him or her to refrain.

WINES, BEER, AND SPIRITS

"Wines of Germany" promotes the wines of all 13 German wine regions and can supply you with information on wine festivals and visitor-friendly wineries. It also arranges six-day guided winery tours in spring and fall in conjunction with the German Wine Academy.

It's legal to drink beer from open containers in public (even in the passenger seat of a car), and having a beer at one's midday break is nothing to raise an eyebrow at. Bavaria is not the only place to try beer. While Munich's beers have achieved world fame—Löwenbräu and Paulaner, for example—beer connoisseurs will really want to travel to places farther north like Alpirsbach, Bamberg, Erfurt, Cologne, or Görlitz, where smaller breweries produce top-notch brews.

Wine Information German Wine Academy ☎ 06131/28290 ⊕ www.germanwines.de. **Wines of Germany** ☎ 212/994–7523 ⊕ www.germanwineusa.org.

▌ ELECTRICITY

The electrical current in Germany is 220 volts, 50 cycles alternating current (AC); wall outlets take Continental-type plugs, with two round prongs.

Consider making a small investment in a universal adapter, which has several types of plugs in one lightweight, compact unit. Most laptops and mobile phone chargers are dual voltage (i.e., they operate equally well on 110 and 220 volts) so require only an adapter. These days the same is true of small appliances such as hair dryers. Always check labels and manufacturer instructions to be sure. Don't use 110-volt outlets marked "for shavers only" for high-wattage appliances such as hair dryers.

Steve Kropla's Help for World Travelers has information on electrical and telephone plugs around the world. Walkabout Travel Gear has good coverage of electricity under "adapters."

Contacts Steve Kropla's Help for World Travelers ⊕ *www.kropla.com.* **Walkabout Travel Gear** ⊕ *www.walkabouttravelgear.com.*

▌ EMERGENCIES

Throughout Germany call ☏*110* for police, ☏*112* for an ambulance or the fire department.

Foreign Embassies U.S. Embassy ✉ *Pariser Platz 2, Berlin* ☏ *030/83050, 030/8305–1200 for American citizens (2 pm–4 pm only)* ⊕ *www.usembassy.de.*

▌ ETIQUETTE

CUSTOMS OF THE COUNTRY

Being on time for appointments, even casual social ones, is very important. There is no "fashionably late" in Germany. Germans are more formal in addressing each other than Americans. Always address acquaintances as Herr (Mr.) or Frau (Mrs.) plus their last name; do not call them by their first name unless invited to do so. The German language has an informal and formal pronoun for "you": formal is *Sie,* and informal is *du.* Even if adults are on a first-name basis with one another, they may still keep to the *Sie* form.

Germans are less formal when it comes to nudity: a sign that reads "freikörper" or "fkk" indicates a park or beach that allows nude sunbathing. At a sauna or steam bath, you will often be asked to remove all clothing.

GREETINGS

The standard *Guten Tag* is the way to greet people throughout the country. When you depart, say *Auf Wiedersehen. Hallo* is also used frequently, as is Hi among the younger crowd. A less formal leave-taking is *Tschüss* or ciao. You will also hear regional differences in greetings.

LANGUAGE

English is spoken in most hotels, restaurants, airports, museums, and other places of interest. However, English is not widely spoken in rural areas or by people over 40; this is especially true of the eastern part of Germany. Learning the basics before going is always a good idea, especially *bitte* (please) and *danke* (thank you). Apologizing for your poor German before asking a question in English will make locals feel respected and begins all communication on the right foot.

A phrase book and language-tape set can help get you started.

▌TIP➡ **Under no circumstances use profanity or pejoratives. Germans take these very seriously, and a slip of the tongue can result in expensive criminal and civil penalties. Calling a police officer a "Nazi" or using vulgar finger gestures can cost you up to €10,000 and two years in jail.**

▌ HEALTH

OVER-THE-COUNTER REMEDIES

All over-the-counter medicines, even aspirin, are only available at an Apotheke (pharmacy): the German term *Drogerie* or Pharmacie is a shop for sundry items.

Apotheken are open during normal business hours, with those in train stations or airports open later and on weekends. Apotheken are plentiful, and there is invariably one within a few blocks. Every district has an emergency pharmacy that is open after hours. These are listed as *Apotheken Notdienst* or *Apotheken-Bereitschaftsdienst* on the window of every other pharmacy in town, often with directions for how to get there. Pharmacies will have a bell you must ring to enter. Most pharmacists in larger cities speak enough English to help. Some drugs have different names: acetominophen—or Tylenol—is called *paracetomol.*

▌ HOURS OF OPERATION

Business hours are inconsistent throughout the country and vary from state to state and even from city to city. Banks are generally open weekdays from 8:30 or 9 am to 3 or 4 pm (5 or 6 pm on Thursday), sometimes with a lunch break of about an hour at smaller branches. Some banks close by 2:30 on Friday afternoon. Banks at airports and main train stations open as early as 6:30 am and close as late as 10:30 pm.

Most museums are open from Tuesday to Sunday 10–6. Some close for an hour or more at lunch. Many stay open until 8 pm or later one day a week, usually Thursday. In smaller towns or in rural areas, museums may be open only on weekends or just a few hours a day.

All stores are closed Sunday, with the exception of those in or near train stations. Larger stores are generally open from 9:30 or 10 am to 8 or 9 pm on weekdays and close between 6 and 8 pm on Saturday. Smaller shops and some department stores in smaller towns close at 6 or 6:30 on weekdays and as early as 4 on Saturday. German shop owners take their closing times seriously. If you come in five minutes before closing, you may not be treated like royalty. Apologizing profusely and making a speedy purchase will help.

Along the autobahn and major highways, as well as in larger cities, gas stations and their small convenience shops are often open late, if not around the clock.

HOLIDAYS

The following national holidays are observed in Germany: January 1; January 6 (Epiphany—Bavaria, Saxony-Anhalt, and Baden-Württemberg only); Good Friday; Easter Monday; May 1 (Workers' Day); Ascension; Pentecost Monday; Corpus Christi (southern Germany only); Assumption Day (Bavaria and Saarland only); October 3 (German Unity Day); November 1 (All Saints' Day—Baden-Württemberg, Bavaria, North Rhine-Westphalia, Rhineland-Pfalz, and Saarland); December 24–26 (Christmas).

Pre-Lenten celebrations in Cologne and the Rhineland are known as Karneval, and for several days before Ash Wednesday work grinds to a halt as people celebrate with parades, banquets, and general debauchery. Farther south, in the state of Baden-Württenburg, the festivities are called Fasching, and tend to be more traditional. In either area, expect businesses to be closed both before and after "Fat Tuesday."

▌ MAIL

A post office in Germany (*Postamt*) is recognizable by the postal symbol, a black bugle on a yellow background. In some villages you will find one in the local supermarket. Stamps (*Briefmarken*) can also be bought at some news agencies and souvenir shops. Post offices are generally open weekdays 8–6, Saturday 8–noon.

Airmail letters to the United States, Canada, Australia, and New Zealand cost €1.70; postcards, €1. All letters to the United Kingdom and within Europe cost €0.55; postcards, €0.45. These rates apply to standard-size envelopes. Letters take approximately 3–4 days to reach the United Kingdom, 5–7 days to the United States, and 7–10 days to Australia and New Zealand.

You can arrange to have mail (letters only) sent to you in care of any German post office; have the envelope marked "Postlagernd." This service is free, and the mail will be held for seven days. Or you can have mail sent to any American Express office in Germany. There's no charge to cardholders, holders of American Express traveler's checks, or anyone who has booked a vacation with American Express.

SHIPPING PACKAGES

Most major stores that cater to tourists will also ship your purchases home. You should check your insurance for coverage of possible damage.

The Deutsche Post has an express international service that will deliver your letter or package the next day to countries within the EU, within one to two days to the United States, and slightly longer to Australia. A letter or package to the United States weighing less than 200 grams costs €48.57. You can drop off your mail at any post office, or it can be picked up for an extra fee. Deutsche Post works in cooperation with DHL. International carriers tend to be slightly cheaper (€35–€45 for the same letter) and provide more services.

Express Services Deutsche Post
☎ 08105/345–2255 ⊕ www.deutschepost.de.
DHL ☎ 0800/225–5345 ⊕ www.dhl.de. **FedEx**
☎ 0800/123–0800 ⊕ www.fedex.com. **UPS**
☎ 0800/882–6630 ⊕ www.ups.com.

▮ MONEY

Credit cards are welcomed by most large businesses, so you probably won't have to use cash for payment in high-end hotels and restaurants. Many businesses on the other end of the spectrum don't accept them, however. It's a good idea to check in advance if you're staying in a budget lodging or eating in a simple country inn.

Prices throughout this guide are given for adults. Substantially reduced fees are almost always available for children, students, and senior citizens.

▮ TIP→ Banks almost never have every foreign currency on hand, and it may take as long as a week to order. If you're planning to exchange funds before leaving home, don't wait until the last minute.

ATMS AND BANKS

Twenty-four-hour ATMs (*Geldautomaten*) can be accessed with Plus or Cirrus credit and banking cards. Your own bank will probably charge a fee for using ATMs abroad, and some German banks exact €3–€5 fees for use of their ATMs. Nevertheless, you'll usually get a better rate of exchange via an ATM than you will at a currency-exchange office or even when changing money in a bank. And extracting funds as you need them is a safer option than carrying around a large amount of cash. Since some ATM keypads show no letters, know the numeric equivalent of your password. Always use ATMs inside the bank.

▮ TIP→ PINs with more than four digits are not recognized at ATMs in many countries. If yours has five or more, remember to change it before you leave.

CREDIT CARDS

All major U.S. credit cards are accepted in Germany. The most frequently used are MasterCard and Visa. American Express is used less frequently, and Diners Club even less. Since the credit-card companies demand fairly substantial fees, some businesses will not accept credit cards for small purchases. Cheaper restaurants and lodgings often do not accept credit cards.

It's a good idea to inform your credit-card company before you travel, especially if you're going abroad and don't travel internationally very often. Otherwise, the credit-card company might put a hold on your card owing to unusual activity—not a good thing halfway through your trip. Record all your credit-card numbers—as well as the phone numbers to call if your cards are lost or stolen—in a safe place, so you're prepared should something go wrong.

If you plan to use your credit card for cash advances, you'll need to apply for a PIN at least two weeks before your trip. Although it's usually cheaper (and safer) to use a credit card abroad for large purchases (so you can cancel payments or be reimbursed if there's a problem), note that some credit-card companies *and* the banks that issue them add substantial percentages to all foreign transactions, whether they're in a foreign currency or not. Check on these fees before leaving home, so there won't be any surprises when you get the bill.

■ TIP→ **Before you charge something, ask the merchant whether he or she plans to do a dynamic currency conversion (DCC). In such a transaction the credit-card processor (shop, restaurant, or hotel, not Visa or MasterCard) converts the currency and charges you in dollars. In most cases you'll pay the merchant a 3% fee for this service in addition to any credit-card company and issuing-bank foreign-transaction surcharges.**

Dynamic currency conversion programs are becoming increasingly widespread. Merchants who participate in them are supposed to ask whether you want to be charged in dollars or the local currency, but they don't always do so. And even if they do offer you a choice, they may well avoid mentioning the additional surcharges. The good news is that you *do* have a choice. And if this practice really gets your goat, you can avoid it entirely thanks to American Express; with its cards, DCC simply isn't an option.

Reporting Lost Cards American Express ☎ 800/333–2639 in U.S., 715/343–7977 collect from abroad ⊕ www.americanexpress. com. **Diners Club** ☎ 800/234–6377 in U.S., 303/799–1504 collect from abroad ⊕ www. dinersclub.com. **MasterCard** ☎ 800/622–7747 in U.S., 636/722–7111 collect from abroad ⊕ www.mastercard.com. **Visa** ☎ 800/847–2911 in U.S., 410/581–9994 collect from abroad ⊕ www.visa.com.

CURRENCY AND EXCHANGE

Germany shares a common currency, the euro (€), with 16 other countries: Austria, Belgium, Cyprus, Estonia, Finland, France, Greece, Ireland, Italy, Luxembourg, Malta, the Netherlands, Portugal, Slovakia, Slovenia, and Spain. The euro is divided into 100 cents. There are bills

of 5, 10, 20, 50, 100, and 500 euros and coins of €1 and €2, and 1, 2, 5, 10, 20, and 50 cents. Many businesses and restaurants do not accept €200 and €500 notes. It is virtually impossible to pay for anything in U.S. dollars, but you should have no problem exchanging currency. The large number of banks and exchange services means that you can shop around for the best rate, if you're so inclined. But the cheapest and easiest way to go is using your ATM card.

At this writing time, the exchange rate was €0.75 for a U.S. dollar. But the exchange rate changes daily.

■ TIP→ **Even if a currency-exchange booth has a sign promising no commission, rest assured that there's some kind of huge, hidden fee. (Oh . . . that's right. The sign didn't say no *fee*.) And as for rates, you're almost always better off getting foreign currency at an ATM or exchanging money at a bank.**

EXCHANGE RATES

There are a number of handy websites that can help you find out how much your money is worth. Google does currency conversion; just type in the amount and how you want it converted (e.g., "100 dollars in euros"), and voilà. Onada allows you to print out a handy table with the current day's conversion rates. XE also does currency conversion.

Conversion Sites Google ⊕ www.google. com. **Oanda** ⊕ www.oanda.com. **XE** ⊕ www. xe.com.

▌ PACKING

For visits to Berlin, pack as you would for an American city: dressy outfits for formal restaurants and nightclubs, casual clothes elsewhere. Jeans are as popular in Germany as anywhere else, and are perfectly acceptable for sightseeing and informal dining. In the evening, men will probably feel more comfortable wearing a jacket in more expensive restaurants, although it's almost never required. Many German women wear stylish outfits to restaurants and the theater.

Berlin is windy, which can be quite pleasant in summer but a complete bear in winter. To discourage purse snatchers and pickpockets, carry a handbag with long straps that you can sling across your body bandolier style and with a zippered compartment for money and other valuables.

For stays in budget hotels, pack your own soap. Many provide no soap at all or only a small bar.

PASSPORTS AND VISAS

Visitors from the United States and Canada, including children, are required to have a passport to enter the EU for a period of up to 90 days. There are no official passport controls at any of Germany's land borders, although customs checks are becoming more frequent. Most travelers will only show their documents on entering and leaving the EU. Your passport should be valid for up to six months after your trip ends or this will raise questions at the border. EU citizens can enter Germany with a national identity card or passport. Traveling with children can be problematic. Single parents traveling with their own children rarely face any hassle, but overzealous border guards have been known to ask children about their relationship with the other parent. If you are a parent or grandparent traveling with a child, it helps to have a signed and notarized power of attorney in order to dispel any questions.

RESTROOMS

Public restrooms are found in large cities, although you are not guaranteed to find one in an emergency. If you are in need, there are several options. You can enter the next café or restaurant and ask very politely to use the facilities. You can find a department store and look for the "WC" sign. Museums are also a good place to find facilities.

Train stations are increasingly turning to McClean, a privately run enterprise that demands €0.60 to €1.10 for admission to its restrooms. These facilities, staffed by attendants who clean almost constantly, sparkle. You won't find them in smaller stations, however. Their restrooms are usually adequate.

On the highways, the vast majority of gas stations have public restrooms, though you may have to ask for a key—we won't vouch for their cleanliness. You might want to wait until you see a sign for a restaurant.

Restrooms almost always cost money. It's customary to pay €0.20–€0.70 to the bathroom attendant.

To read up on restrooms in advance of your trip, the Bathroom Diaries is flush with unsanitized info on restrooms the world over—each one located, reviewed, and rated.

Find a Loo The Bathroom Diaries ⊕ *www. thebathroomdiaries.com.*

SAFETY

Germany has one of the lowest crime rates in Europe. There are some areas, such as the neighborhoods around train stations and the streets surrounding red-light districts, where you should keep an eye out for potential dangers. The best advice is to take the usual precautions. Secure your valuables in the hotel safe. Don't wear flashy jewelry, and keep expensive electronics out of sight when you are not using them. Carry shoulder bags or purses so that they can't be easily snatched, and never leave them hanging on the back of a chair at a café or restaurant. Avoid walking alone at night, even in relatively safe neighborhoods. Due to increasing incidents of violence in Berlin, Hamburg, and Munich, use caution late at night in the subway.

When withdrawing cash, don't use an ATM in a deserted area or one that is outside. It is best to avoid freestanding ATMs in subway stations and other locations away from a bank. Make sure that no one is looking over your shoulder when you enter your PIN. And never use a machine that appears to have been tampered with.

■ TIP→ **Distribute your cash, credit cards, IDs, and other valuables between a deep front pocket, an inside jacket or vest pocket, and a hidden money pouch. Don't reach for the money pouch once you're in public.**

Contacts Transportation Security Administration (*TSA*). ⊕ *www.tsa.gov*.

▌ TAXES

Most prices you see on items already include Germany's 19% value-added tax (V.A.T.). Some goods, such as food, books, and antiquities, carry a 7% V.A.T. as a percentage of the purchase price. An item must cost at least €25 to qualify for a V.A.T. refund.

When making a purchase, ask for a V.A.T. refund form and find out whether the merchant gives refunds—not all stores do, nor are they required to. Have the form stamped like any customs form by customs officials when you leave the country or, if you're visiting several European Union countries, when you leave the EU. After you're through passport control, take the form to a refund-service counter for an on-the-spot refund (which is usually the quickest and easiest option), or mail it to the address on the form (or the envelope with it) after you arrive home. You receive the total refund stated on the form, but the processing time can be long, especially if you request a credit-card adjustment.

Global Refund is a Europe-wide service with 225,000 affiliated stores and more than 700 refund counters at major airports and border crossings. Its refund form, called a Tax Free Check, is the most common across the European continent. The service issues refunds in the form of cash, check, or credit-card adjustment.

V.A.T. Refunds Global Refund ☎ *800/566–9828* ⊕ *www.globalblue.com*.

▌ TIME

All of Germany is on Central European Time, which is six hours ahead of Eastern Standard Time and nine hours ahead of Pacific Standard Time. Daylight Saving Time begins on the last Sunday in March and ends on the last Sunday in October. Timeanddate.com can help you figure out the correct time anywhere.

Germans use the 24-hour clock, or military time (1 pm is indicated as 13:00), and write the date before the month, so October 3 will appear as 03.10.

Time Zones Timeanddate.com ⊕ *www. timeanddate.com/worldclock.*

▌ TIPPING

Tipping is done at your own discretion. Theater ushers do not necessarily expect a tip, while waiters, tour guides, bartenders, and taxi drivers do. Rounding off bills to the next highest sum is customary for bills under €10. Above that sum you should add a little more.

Service charges are included in all restaurant checks (listed as *Bedienung*), as is tax (listed as MwSt). Nonetheless, it is customary to round up the bill to the nearest euro or to leave about 5%–10%. Give it to the waitstaff as you pay the bill; don't leave it on the table, as that's considered rude.

TIPPING GUIDELINES FOR GERMANY

Bartender	Round up the bill for small purchases. For rounds of drinks, around 10% is appropriate.
Bellhop	€1 per item.
Hotel Concierge	€3–€5 if the concierge performs a special service for you.
Hotel Doorman	€1–€2 if he helps you get a cab.
Hotel Maid	€1 per day.
Hotel Room-Service Waiter	€1 per delivery.
Taxi Driver	Round up the fare if the ride is short. For longer trips, about €1 is appropriate.
Tour Guide	€5–€10 per person, or a bit more if the tour was especially good.
Valet Parking Attendant	€1–€2, but only when you retrieve your car.
Waiter	Round off the bill, giving 5% to 10% for very good service.

▌VISITOR INFORMATION

The main information office of Berlin Tourismus Marketing is in the Neues Kranzler Eck, a short walk from Zoo Station. There are branches in the south wing of the Brandenburg Gate, at Hauptbahnhof (Level 0), and in a pavilion opposite the Reichstag that are open daily 10–6. The tourist-information centers have longer hours April–October. The tourist office publishes the Berlin Kalender (€1.60) six times a year and Berlin Buchbar (free) two times a year. Both are written in German and English. The office and Berlin's larger transportation offices (BVG) sell the Berlin Welcome-Card (€18.50 to €36.50), which pays for between three and five days of transportation depending on which one you get, along with 25%–50% discounts at museums and theaters (it does not include the state museums). Some Staatliche (state) museums are closed Monday. A free audio guide is included at all state museums. The MD Infoline provides comprehensive information about all of Berlin's museums, exhibits, and themed tours.

Visitor Information German National Tourist Office ☎ 212/661–7200 ⊕ www.germany. travel. **Visit Berlin** (Berlin Tourist Info). ⊠ Kurfürstendamm 22, in the Neues Kranzler Eck, Charlottenburg ☎ 030/250–025 ⊕ www. visitberlin.de ⊙ Mon.–Sat. 9:30–8, Sun. 10–6. **Museumsinformation Berlin** ☎ 030/2474–9888 ⊙ Weekdays 9–4, weekends 9–1. **Staatliche Museen zu Berlin** ☎ 030/2664–24242 operator ⊕ www.smb.museum ⊙ Weekdays, 9–4. **Tourist-Information Center in Prenzlauer Berg** ⊠ Kuturbrauerei closest entrance Schönhauser Allee 36, Schönhauser Allee 36, in the Kulturbrauerei, entrances on Knaackstr. or Sredzkistr., Prenzlauer Berg ☎ 030/4435–2170 ⊕ www.tic-berlin.de ⊙ Daily, 11-7.

INDEX

PHOTO CREDITS

Fodor's BERLIN

Publisher: Amanda D'Acierno, *Senior Vice President*

Editorial: Arabella Bowen, *Editor in Chief*; Linda Cabasin, *Editorial Director*

Design: Fabrizio La Rocca, *Vice President, Creative Director*; Tina Malaney, *Associate Art Director*; Chie Ushio, *Senior Designer*; Ann McBride, *Production Designer*

Photography: Melanie Marin, *Associate Director of Photography*; Jessica Parkhill and Jennifer Romains, *Researchers*

Maps: Rebecca Baer, *Senior Map Editor*; Mark Stroud and David Lindroth, *Cartographers*

Production: Linda Schmidt, *Managing Editor*; Evangelos Vasilakis, *Associate Managing Editor*; Angela L. McLean, *Senior Production Manager*

Sales: Jacqueline Lebow, *Sales Director*

Marketing & Publicity: Heather Dalton, *Marketing Director*; Katherine Punia, *Senior Publicist*

Business & Operations: Susan Livingston, *Vice President, Strategic Business Planning*; Sue Daulton, *Vice President, Operations*

Fodors.com: Megan Bell, *Executive Director, Revenue & Business Development*; Yasmin Marinaro, *Senior Director, Marketing & Partnerships*

Copyright © 2014 by Fodor's Travel, a division of Random House LLC

Writers: Kimberly Bradley, Chaney Kwak, Sally McGrane, Giulia Pines, Katherine Sacks

Editors: Caroline Trefler (lead editor); Joanna G. Cantor

Production Editor: Jennifer DePrima

2nd Edition

ISBN 978-0-8041-4204-5

ISSN 1065-4593

All details in this book are based on information supplied to us at press time. Always confirm information when it matters, especially if you're making a detour to visit a specific place. Fodor's expressly disclaims any liability, loss, or risk, personal or otherwise, that is incurred as a consequence of the use of any of the contents of this book.

SPECIAL SALES

This book is available at special discounts for bulk purchases for sales promotions or premiums. For more information, e-mail specialmarkets@randomhouse.com

PRINTED IN THE UNITED STATES OF AMERICA

10 9 8 7 6 5 4 3 2

ABOUT OUR WRITERS

A California-born midwestern New Yorker, writer and editor Kimberly Bradley has lived in Berlin since 2003, covering art, design, architecture and travel for publications including the *New York Times*, *Monocle*, and *ArtReview*. She also frequently contributes to monographs and art catalogs as an editor or writer, and teaches contemporary art at NYU Berlin. She's sad to see the art world's epicenter shift out of her neighborhood, Mitte, where she lives with her partner, an artist, and their daughter. She contributed to the Berlin Exploring chapter.

While pursuing a graduate degree at Berlin's Freie University, Chaney Kwak discovered his knack for writing about German culture and destinations. His writing appears in the *Best American Short Plays*, the *New York Times*, the *Washington Post*, *Süddeutsche Zeitung*, *Travel + Leisure*, *Condé Nast Daily Traveler*, the *Wall Street Journal*, *Hemispheres*, *Journey*, and other publications. He updated the Experience chapter of this edition.

Originally from San Francisco, Sally McGrane moved to Berlin ten years ago. As a journalist she has written for the *New York Times*, TheNewYorker.com, *TIME*, *Wired*, *Dwell*, and others. She contributed to the Berlin Exploring chapter.

Giulia Pines spent her first 23 years in New York, and is now proud to call Berlin home. She is a writer, photographer, and avid traveler who has contributed to numerous online and print publications both in Germany and internationally, including *ETime Out, NPR, Hemispheres, ExBerliner, Electronic Beats, Slow Travel Berlin,* and *Berlin.Unlike.* She updated the Berlin Exploring, Where to Eat, Nightlife and the Arts sections for this edition.

Katherine Sacks is a food and travel journalist living in Berlin. She developed a taste for the flavors of German *brezel* and *zitroneneis* (pretzels and lemon ice) while living on U.S. Army bases in Manheim, Mainz, and Wiesbaden during childhood. Her writing has been published in *Deutsche Welle, Kinfolk* magazine, and *Food & Wine,* among others. She updated the Where to Stay, Shopping, and Potsdam chapters of this edition.